Ethics, Politics, and Difference in Julia Kristeva's Writing

Edited by KELLY OLIVER

Ethics, Politics, AND Difference
IN Julia Kristeva's Writing

Edited by KELLY OLIVER

ROUTLEDGE   NEW YORK   LONDON

Published in 1993 by

Routledge
29 West 35 Street
New York, NY 10001

Published in Great Britain by

Routledge
11 New Fetter Lane
London EC4P 4EE

Library of Congress Cataloging-in-Publication Data

Ethics, politics, and difference in Julia Kristeva's writings: a collection of essays /
    edited by Kelly Oliver.
            p.   cm.
    Includes bibliographical references and index.
    ISBN 0-415-90703-9. — ISBN 0-415-90704-7 (pbk.)
    1. Kristeva, Julia, 1941–   —Ethics. 2. Kristeva, Julia, 1941– Political and
        social views. 3. Ethics, Modern—20th century. 4. Political science—
        Philosophy. 5. Feminist ethics. 6. Feminist theory. 7. Psychoanalysis and
        feminism.   I. Oliver, Kelly, 1959– .
    B2430.K754E84   1993
    170—dc20   92-47482
                                                                           CIP

British Library Cataloging-in-Publication also available.

Contents

Introduction:
Julia Kristeva's Outlaw Ethics

Kelly Oliver

Discourse That Breaks Down Identity

In an interview with *psych & po*, Kristeva says that she concentrates on discourses that break down identity because she is a woman.[1] Because she is a woman and concentrates on discourses that break down identity, Kristeva claims that her "work obeys ethical exigencies."[2] She suggests that women are more aware of ethics because of their marginal relation to the Symbolic; and her texts in particular carry an ethical imperative to break down identity through practice.[3] Her concern is to link the ethical with negativity so that it won't degenerate into either conformity or perversion. Without negativity, ethics is mere conformity. And without ethics, negativity is mere perversion.[4] At the limit, without negativity, ethics is tyranny; and without ethics, negativity is delirium. By linking ethics and negativity, Kristeva tries to steer between tyranny and delirium.

Before we can discuss ethics or formulate our possible obligations to others we need to renegotiate how we conceive of the relation between subject and other; we need to conceive of the relation between subject and other as a relation of difference. Some traditional ethical theories postulate an autonomous agent whose obligations to the other come from his realization that the other must be the same as himself. The autonomous subject of these traditional ethical theories does not have a relation to any other; rather this subject always and only has a relationship to the self-same. Until we can reconceive of a true relation between subject and other, we cannot conceive of ethics. We cannot conceive of obligations to others.

Using models from poetic language, maternity, and psychoanalysis, Kristeva's writing can provide the beginnings of this project. The essays in this collection evaluate and extend Kristeva's contribution to a reconception of the ethico-political subject. Kristeva attempts to break down the identity of

1

the autonomous subject in order to link negativity with ethics by reconceiving of a relation between subject and other. She uses the models of poetic language, maternity, and psychoanalysis to construct a new model of otherness within the subject. In each of these three models, Kristeva imagines an otherness at the very core of the subject. Each of these models suggests a "subject-in-process/on-trial." Kristeva proposes that these models of alterity can inform a new way to conceive of the structure of the relation to others and thereby inform a new way to conceive of ethics.

Poetry

Kristeva suggests that "the ethics of a linguistic discourse may be gauged in proportion to the poetry that it presupposes."[5] In addition, the ethics of a social discourse may be gauged by how much poetry it allows. She argues that all of the great tyrannies and repressive systems have legislated and censored poetry. From Plato's imaginary Republic to Stalin's brutal dictatorship, censorship has been the sign of repression, tyranny, and death. Poetry signals tolerance in a society. The openness to poetry is the openness to difference.

In the case of poetic language, symbolic identity is full of difference and yet maintains its integrity as language. Here the heterogeneity in language is at its most apparent. Poetic language is language which is also not language, language which is other to itself. Meaningful but nonsignifying aspects of language—rhythm, tone, music—are just as important in poetry as the signifying elements of language. In poetry it is obvious that words are both meaningful for what they signify and meaningful for how they sound and how they affect the listener. Poetry points to this heterogeneity of language. Kristeva argues that it shows how signification comes to be out of nonsignifying, semiotic, bodily drives.[6]

She argues that instinctual rhythm passes through symbolic theses, and "meaning is constituted but is then immediately exceeded by what seems outside of meaning: materiality."[7] The pleasure found in drive-discharge through language is in excess of meaning and representation. The materiality of language itself can discharge drives through the symbolic but always necessarily in excess of the symbolic. It is not that language represents the drive, which is impossible. Rather, language, specifically poetic and avant garde language, can reactivate drives. And it is precisely because this drive-discharge is not representation that poetic language "pulverizes" signification.

Poetry is a type of borderline case that calls into question all that is central to representation. In addition to the discharge of drive, poetry "pre-alters" representation. Poetry pre-alters representation by showing the **process of representation itself.** Within poetry, representation cannot appear as a self-sustaining unity or a necessary relationship between signifier and signified. Rather, poetry functions to show how signifiers and signifieds are produced. For example, the signified cannot be stable if poetry shows that the signified is merely the effect of signifiers which are themselves overdetermined and therefore never stable. Moreover, poetry shows this signified-effect as merely one stage in the whole ongoing process of signification. The absolute signified cannot be the end point of signification precisely because it would put an end to signification. There would be no need to say any more; we keep talking because of the overdetermination of the signifier.

Poetic language is explicitly involved in the destructuring and structuring of language at the "outer boundaries" of the Symbolic.[8] Because the authority of the Symbolic requires unity and autonomy, the semiotic disposition in poetry destabilizes the Symbolic even while recreating, and in order to recreate a new Symbolic. For Kristeva this is the nature of all *signifiance*. Poetry reveals the nature of all *signifiance* through its **practice.**

Kristeva defines a practice as the acceptance of the symbolic law together with the transgression of the law for the purpose of renovating it.[9] And it is because poetic language is text as practice that it constructs a "new symbolic device—a new reality corresponding to a new heterogeneous object."[10] This new heterogeneous reality is the reality of a new heterogeneous subject, what Kristeva calls the "subject-in-process/on-trial." By pointing to signification in process, poetry also points to a subject-in-process. The revolution in poetic language is also a revolution in the subject; for Kristeva claims that any theory of language is also a theory of the subject.

Poetic language puts the subject on trial through a double operation. Insofar as poetic language shatters the unity of the thetic, it also shatters the unity of the subject position.[11] Without a unified thetic, there is no unified position. The unified subject becomes merely one stage in the process of signification. In addition, Kristeva suggests that there is a transference that can take place between the reader and the text.[12] Through this transference the subject identifies with the text. The revolutionary poetic text, however, is never a unified text. It is always in process and points to the process of *signifiance* itself. The subject, then, through this transference, takes the place of the process. Through this transference, the subject is put in-process/on-trial.

Kristeva maintains that poetry's subject-in-process necessitates a new ethics that operates as "the negativizing of narcissism within practice."[13] Within ethical practice, negativity works to "make visible the process underlying" signification.[14] By making the process visible, negativity calls into question any stable identity. By calling into question stable identity, negativity is the catalyst for a narcissistic crisis in identity. Kristeva (re)turns this crisis to the very structure of narcissism. Drives are part of the narcissistic structure. They are part of identity. So identity is always heterogeneous.

This means that the new ethics is also heterogeneous. It can never be fully articulated or represented within symbols because it is driven by an element that is heterogeneous to the symbolic. For Kristeva, "[t]he ethical cannot be stated, instead it is practiced to the point of loss, and the text is one of the most accomplished examples of such a practice."[15]

In her contribution to this collection, "'Transgression in Theory: Genius and the Subject of La révolution du langage poétique," Susan Guerlac analyzes Kristeva's notion of poetry as practice. She argues that Kristeva revolutionizes Derrida's notion of différance by attaching its operations to a transgressive revolutionary subject. She proposes that Kristeva's transgressive subject is a combination of a revolutionary and a theoretical subject who makes revolutionary poetic practice possible. In her essay "Trans-Position of Difference: Kristeva and Post-Structuralism," Tilottama Rajan also suggests that Kristeva politicizes Derrida's notion of différance by employing the metaphor of the body. And at the center of Kristeva's texts is the maternal body.

Maternity

As Ewa Ziarek points out, maternity and not poetry is the most powerful model of alterity-within because it exists at the heart of the social and the species.[16] The maternal body is the very embodiment of alterity-within. It cannot be neatly divided into subject and object. "It is an identity," says Kristeva, "that splits, turns in on itself and changes without becoming other."[17]

Pregnancy is "the splitting of the subject," the subject in-process/on-trial.[18] Pregnancy is a case where identity contains alterity as a heterogeneous other without completely losing its integrity. The maternal body problematizes the very notions of identity and difference.[19]

Pregnancy, says Kristeva, is an "institutionalized psychosis": Am I me or it?[20] The other cannot be separated from the self. The other is within the self. It is not in its place—the place of the Other. Rather, it is in the place of the subject. This inability to separate self from other is a symptom of psychosis. But pregnancy, says Kristeva, is the only place where this psychosis is socially acceptable.

How can we account for this other which resides in the maternal body without destroying the identity of the mother? And if our mothers have no identity, are we born out of a void? The mother's identity is questionable and, as such, it points to the questionable identity of the subject itself. After all, is not the mother a subject too? Kristeva argues that to suppose that the mother is the master of her gestation preserves her identity. In this case, she is the master of a process which is prior to the social contract of the group, a process that is presymbolic and therefore without identity. She risks losing her identity again at the same time as she wards off its loss.

It seems, then, that we recognize that there is a presymbolic process out of which we are produced. But Kristeva argues that we deny this. We assure ourselves that "mamma is there" and that her presence in, and identity through, the process guarantees that everything is representable.[21] Of course this is to cover over "mamma's" questionable identity in this process. "In a double-barreled move," claims Kristeva, "psychotic tendencies are acknowledged, but at the same time they are settled, quieted, and bestowed upon the mother in order to maintain the ultimate guarantee: symbolic coherence."[22]

Kristeva says that maternity is a bridge between nature and culture, the drives and the Symbolic. The mother's body is the "pivot of sociality," "at once the guarantee and a threat to its stability."[23] The mother's body guarantees the continuation of the species and yet her questionable identity threatens the Symbolic unity. Kristeva defines the maternal as "the ambivalent principle that is bound to the species, on the one hand, and on the other stems from an identity catastrophe that causes the Name to topple over into the unnameable that one imagines as femininity, nonlanguage, or body."[24]

This is because the mother cannot be on the side of the drives or we are born out of something nonsocial and nonsymbolic. Yet, she cannot straddle the drives and the Symbolic for the same reason. And she cannot be completely within the Symbolic or we lose the child. The Symbolic can deal with the mother only as myth and fantasy (the Virgin mother, the denigrated woman) which cover over this psychotic process and undecidable identity. Maternity is impossible for the Symbolic.

In *Tales of Love* Kristeva uses maternity as a model for an outlaw ethics, what she calls "herethics." Herethics is founded on the ambiguity in pregnancy and birth between subject and object positions. It is an ethics which challenges rather than presupposes an autonomous ethical agent. Herethics sets up one's obligations to the other as obligations to the self and obligations to the species. This ethics binds the subject to the other through love and not Law. The model of ethical love is the mother's love for the child, which is a love for herself and a love for her own mother.[25] To imagine this herethics, Kristeva suggests that it is necessary to listen to the mother and her music. She claims that Motherhood needs the support of a mother's mother (even in the person of a father or imaginary father).[26] The mother's oscillating union/disunion with her child recalls her own union with her mother. When we listen to Kristeva, the mother, we see that her mother is present in her own motherhood:

> ... Recovered childhood, dreamed peace restored, in sparks, flash of cells, instant of laughter, smiles in the blackness of dreams, at night, opaque joy that roots me in her bed, my mother's, and projects him, a son, a butterfly soaking up dew from her hand, there, nearby, in the night. Alone: she, I, and he.[27]

The love that founds herethics is a daughter's love through identification with her mother. A mother's love is her reunion with her own mother, not only as a third party, but also as herself. The child's transferential identification with the imaginary father, then, is an identification with its mother's reunion with her mother.[28] It is this union which satisfies, makes one complete.

What does a mother want, especially in childbirth? She wants her mother. "The Paradox: Mother or Primary Narcissism," the subtitle of "Stabat Mater," points to the mother as the site of the primary identification which Kristeva calls the "imaginary father." If the mother loves an Other it is her own mother. And she loves her mother not only as an Other, but also as herself, now the mother. This love which is narcissism, within patriarchal analysis "the inability to love," is the basis of Kristeva's herethics. The mother's love is also the willingness to give herself up, to embrace the strangeness within herself in order to love herself.[29] It is treating the self as an other.

Several of the authors in this collection address Kristeva's notion of an alternative ethics modeled on maternity. In her essay "Kristeva and Levinas: Mourning, Ethics and the Feminine," Ewa Ziarek uses Kristeva's theory of maternal alterity together with Levinas's theory of unmediated alterity in order to formulate the beginnings of a feminist ethics that can articulate feminine specificity without essentialism. She reads Kristeva's diagnosis of feminine sexuality, which is fundamentally melancholic because there is no mourning, as the refusal to think of alterity in terms of losses and compensations, in favor of confronting alterity in its excess. Ziarek suggests that, taken together, Kristeva and Levinas's ethics can provide a transition from an ethics of individuation to an ethics of otherness.

In "Identification with the Divided Mother: Kristeva's Ambivalence," Allison Weir argues that what we learn from Kristeva's theory of maternity is that in order to undermine patriarchal concepts of woman and the feminine, we need to give up the traditional psychoanalytic notion of a phallic mother who is the source of all gratification. Rather than pit the mother against the father and make the mother the source of gratification and the father the source of law, she maintains that Kristeva provides a theory of a divided mother that allows the possibility for the mother to both participate in the symbolic and yet remain heterogeneous to it. Weir suggests that Kristeva's theory of the divided mother initiates a reformulation of identity which could found a reformulation of ethics.

Mary Bittner Wiseman also focuses on maternity. In her article "Renaissance Paintings and Psychoanalysis: Julia Kristeva and the Function of the Mother," she argues that Kristeva challenges the traditional psychoanalytic discourse of maternity. Whereas Freud assumed that the mother is feminine, Wiseman points out that for Kristeva the mother is not feminine. She explains that in Kristeva's theory the mother is neither subject nor object but a function. The implications of conceiving of the mother as a function in relation to the child are significant for theories of the feminine and Oedipal separation from the mother. If the mother is not feminine, "alone of her sex" as Kristeva says, then the child does not have to separate from feminine sexuality in order to separate from the mother; this is especially important for envisioning feminine sexuality as anything other than melancholic. Wiseman formulates Kristeva's shift from the traditional Oedipal story, with its emphasis on the father, to a mother-centered story that focuses on the Madonna by analyzing three Renaissance paintings of the Madonna.

Judith Butler, in "The Body Politic of Julia Kristeva," is not as hopeful for the usefulness of Kristeva's theories of feminine sexuality or maternity. She argues that for Kristeva feminine sexuality is hopelessly melancholic and lesbian sexuality is psychotic. Rather than see Kristeva's theory of maternity as the foundation for a new conception of identity, Butler sees it as merely perpetuating a conception of identity that recuperates all difference and thereby debilitates all possibility for change or revolution. In addition Butler claims that Kristeva's theory makes maternity compulsory for women. Butler would not think that Kristeva's herethics or psychoanalytic theory provides a fruitful place to start to formulate an ethics of difference.

Psychoanalysis

Like herethics, psychoanalysis posits a subject-in-process/on-trial that is based on a relation of alterity within. The notion of the unconscious makes any stable or unified subject, truth, meaning, impossible. Even the individual is full of difference, other to itself. Kristeva says that psychoanalysis analyzes a series of splittings—birth, weaning, separation—as indispensable to an individual's identity.[30] Psychoanalysis is a science of subjects-in-process/on-trial. It records the evolutions and devolutions of these strangers. Like subjects undergoing psychoanalysis, maternal bodies, and avant-garde poets, for Kristeva we are all subjects-in-process, *étrangers à nous-mêmes*.

The logic of the psyche, which sets up the relation between conscious and unconscious, is analogous to the logic of the social, which sets up the relation between self and others. Analyzing the logic of the psyche can help us to understand the logic of the social relation. Renegotiating the psychic dynamic may suggest ways in which to renegotiate the social dynamics. By taking the psyche as a model for the social relation we can recreate ethics. The ethics of psychoanalysis is founded on the structure of the relation between the conscious and unconscious. This ethics asks "what happens when we take the split subject of psychoanalysis as the subject of ethics?"

Kristeva maintains that psychoanalysis sets up an ethics which respects this irreconcilable strangeness.[31] Psychoanalysis accepts, even invites, difference, nonmeaning, otherness. It can provide a new way of identifying the other, the stranger, not in order to reify and exclude it, but in order to welcome it. This was Freud's project.[32] Freud tried to show that alterity is within us and created psychoanalysis as an invitation to live with it.

If psychoanalysis can provide a way to acknowledge the processes through which we become invested in fixed representations, then we may be more tolerant of the excluded elements which are both essential to, and results of, these processes. Real political dissidence is not waging one fundamental ideal against another. It is neither taking up a position nor absorbing conflict. Rather, for Kristeva, it is analyzing conflict in an "attempt to bring about multiple sublations of the unnameable, the unrepresentable, the void."[33] Multiple sublations are fantasies which open up further analysis rather than closing it off. They are not stable identities or alternative positions. Kristeva emphasizes the need to steer between stable identities/positions, which become forms of religion on the one hand, and the complete dissolution of identities on the other. She wants an outlaw ethics that steers between both tyranny and delirium.

The ethics of psychoanalysis is a precarious ethics. Operating at the borders of meaning, psychoanalysis is constantly threatened by totalitarianism on the one side and delirium on the other. Kristeva says that "[s]ituating our discourse near such boundaries might enable us to endow it with a current ethical impact."[34] Between the two extremes lies what she calls "the modern version of liberty" which she says is played out in the analytic session.[35] The analytic session provides a space for liberty because the analyst's ethics is not normative but "directed." It is directed to a space where the analysand can embrace the Other in herself—that alien Other which is both her unconscious and her cultural heritage—in order to live with her crisis in value.[36] For Kristeva it is this crisis in value which is the empty signature of our culture. And the direction of analysis is not to deny the crisis, but to elaborate the crisis.

Jean Graybeal describes Kristeva's call for elaboration as the Delphic injunction to "know thyself." In her essay "Kristeva's Delphic Proposal: Practice Encompasses the Ethical," Graybeal indicates how Kristeva's work is driven by the dual imperatives to avoid oppression on the one hand and madness on the other. She suggests that Kristeva prescribes a playful practice with which to know oneself by putting oneself in the place of the other. This practice is an ongoing process which requires investigating the unconscious, the body, and the process of the production of practice and knowledge itself. Through psychoanalytic practice, in a broad sense, the subject-in-process can maintain the precarious balance between tyranny and madness.

Although poetry, religion, and psychoanalysis all deal with the "subject's battle with symbolic collapse" by releasing the drives into the Symbolic without threatening its collapse, psychoanalysis is an "elaboration" of the psychic causes of suffering. Poetry and religion, on the other hand, are "closer to catharsis."[37] Kristeva stresses that this is not to say that psychoanalysts should not make use of cathartic solutions to their patients' suffering. On the contrary, she insists that analysts need to pay greater attention to "these sublimatory solutions to our crises," and incorporate them into their practices, in order to be "lucid counterdepressants rather than neutralizing antidepressants."[38] While antidepressants (including drugs) treat only the symptoms without working through the causes, counterdepressants work through symptoms in order to treat the cause, and realign the psychic structure (so to speak).

Whereas poetry "displaces" and "dissolves" semiotic forces, analysis names them.[39] Like poetic discourse, analytic discourse is involved in the creation of metaphors which, through the processes of imagination, transfer semiotic forces into language. In addition to this metaphorical process, analytic discourse involves interpretation. It is this combination of semiotic discharge and interpretation that gives analytic discourse its force. Because analytic discourse both discharges and **interprets** semiotic forces, it can work not only as a safety valve for repressed drives but also as a tool for altering the place of those drives within the psychic structure. While in her earlier writings Kristeva proposed that merely **showing** the repressed processes could change the very structure of those processes, in her later writings she emphasizes the necessity of interpreting the repressed processes.

Unlike poetic discourse, analytic interpretation produces what Kristeva calls a "knowledge effect."[40] This knowledge effect helps to fasten the analysand to the Symbolic, but in order to allow her to play with it. The knowledge effect gives her the confidence to use her imagination. The knowledge effect created by analytic discourse, however, is much different from the knowledge effect created by philosophical or traditional scientific discourses. Kristeva argues that analytic knowledge effects are always only provisional. And their provisional status points to a process in which they are merely moments. She says that in analytic interpretation we say "for the **moment**, this means such-and-such." Unlike philosophical or scientific interpretation, analytic interpretation does not purport to be absolute."[41] Analytic interpretation is free "from the authoritarian domination of a *Res externa*, necessarily divine or deifable."[42] The object of analytic interpretation is not real. Rather, it is imaginary. Therefore, the status of "correct" interpretation or analytic "truth" is much closer to narrative fiction than philosophical or scientific truth.[43]

This is not to say that analysis is not concerned with truth. Kristeva maintains that all of her work is concerned with truth. In the last section of *In the Beginning Was Love*, "Is Psychoanalysis a Form of Nihilism?" Kristeva tries to ward off claims that psychoanalysis is a form of nihilism. In fact, she claims that "psychoanalysis is the modest if tenacious antidote to nihilism in its most courageously and insolently scientific and vitalist forms."[44]

Psychoanalysis does not grant control, or the role of creator, to anyone including the analyst. The analyst, insofar as she is subject to the unconscious, is also an analysand. Moreover, for Kristeva psychoanalysis does not objectify either analysand or analyst. Rather, since the analytic situation is a dialogue spoken through language, it is a process and not an object. It is a process that operates between two subjects and does not allow one unified subject to exist in isolation.[45] Kristeva suggests that because of this necessary relationship between two subjects-in-process, and the fact that a subject's desire is known only through an other, psychoanalysis may be the basis for a morality in this nihilistic age:

. . . [Psychoanalysis'] vital efficacy is inseparable from its ethical dimension, which is commensurate with love: the speaking being opens up to and reposes in the other.

... No restrictive, prohibitive, or punitive legislation can possibly restrain my desire for objects, values, life, or death. Only the meaning that my desire may have for an other and hence for me can control its expansion, hence serve as the unique, if tenuous, basis of a morality.[46]

While it is true that human beings are subject to unconscious drives, these drives operate within the social environment of language. Since human beings are linguistic beings, they desire. And within Lacanian theory, desire always comes through an other. So for human beings, it is only through a relationship with an other that meaning exists. This is to say that meaning, in its heterogeneity, is both in and beyond the subject who is always a work-in-progress. In analysis it is not the case that meaning does not exit. Neither is it the case that meaning is the construction of some individual. Rather, meaning is an ongoing process that moves between two subjects engaged through language.

Kristeva suggests that the analyst's interpretative position "builds a strong ethics" because she is called upon to suspend her desire at the same time that she experiences it for the sake of the other. She has an ethical obligation to her patient. Yet, as she insists, this ethics is neither normative nor guaranteed by transcendence. Still, it is "directed" to helping others and promoting life.[47]

But the ethics that Kristeva imagines as operative in psychoanalysis is not a normative ethics.[48] It does not rely on laws and/or punishments. The analyst does not threaten the analysand or deny the reality of her experience. Rather, the analyst legitimates the analysand's experience and "allows the patient to seek out other means, symbolic or imaginary, of working out her suffering."[49]

In part it is psychoanalysis's elaboration of the crisis that makes it an ethical practice.[50] In part it is the direction or goal of the psychoanalytic elaboration which makes it an ethical practice. The analyst's goal is to increase the analysand's "capacity for working-through and sublimation, for understanding and play."[51] But there are no guarantees.

In the precarious exchange between analyst and analysand "the modern version of liberty is being played out, threatened as much by a single, total and totalitarian Meaning as it is by delirium."[52] In the analytic relationship, linked through language, we are creating meanings in a process bordered by totalitarianism on one side and delirium on the other. For Kristeva it is only through "love" that we can avoid both extremes.

Politics of Psychoanalysis

After over a decade of denouncing politics, in *Strangers to Ourselves*, Kristeva provides the foundation for a politics which she argues grows out of the ethics of psychoanalysis:

> The ethic of psychoanalysis implies a politic: it would involve a cosmopolitanism of a new sort that, cutting across governments, economies, and markets, might work for a mankind whose solidarity is founded on the consciousness of its unconscious—desiring, destructive, fearful, empty, impossible.[53]

Alice Jardine traces Kristeva's changing relationship to politics in her contribution to this collection "Opaque Texts, Transparent Contexts: The Political Difference of Julia Kristeva". Psychoanalysis calls on us to work toward this humanity whose solidarity is rounded on a consciousness of its unconscious.[54] Kristeva instructs us to recognize the difference in ourselves as the condition of our being with others.[55] It is the unconscious which allows us to be with others. For the first time in history, says Kristeva, in the absence of any community bond other than economic, without either a community embracing our particularities or the power to transcend them, we must live with differences in moral codes.[56] She concludes *Etrangers* with the image of a "paradoxical community" which is "made up of foreigners who are reconciled with themselves to the extent that they recognize themselves as foreigners."[57]

While Kristeva maintains that politics must be informed by psychoanalysis which recognizes unconscious structures, at the same time she emphasizes the importance of a politics of individuals. That is to say, she is not content to analyze signifying systems, including political institutions, merely in terms of their structures. In addition, she is not willing to reduce politics to party or class struggles. She rejects political interpretations which merely absorb individuals into groups:

> My reproach to some political discourses with which I am disillusioned is that they don't consider the individual as a value. . . . That's why I say that, of course, political struggles for people that are exploited will continue, but they will continue maybe better if the main concern remains the individuality and particularity of the person.[58]

In her analysis of political identity and difference, Kristeva does recognize that struggles in the name of group identities will and must continue in order to overcome oppression. She acknowledges, for example, that feminist movements have made great advances by using the group identity "woman."[59] Still, this tactic has its dangers. Kristeva warns that it must be practiced with care, or politics of liberation become mere politics of exclusion and counter-power. Political interpretations which claim group identities can lead to "dogmatism," "violence," and the annihilation of personal differences.[60] In spite of her concern with personal differences, Kristeva's theories have been called essentialist by some of her critics. In her contribution to this collection, "Kristeva's Politics of Change: Tracking Essentialism with the Help of a Sex/Gender Map," Tina Chanter traces the history of the essentialism debate in order to diagnose why and how Kristeva's theory came to be seen as essentialist in the Anglo-American context. She suggests that American feminists have been afraid of the female body, and Kristeva's return to sex, which unsettles the sex/gender distinction, also unsettles some feminists.

Kristeva's latest theoretical text as of this writing, *Strangers to Ourselves,* is all about how we can live with differences. As early as "Women's Time," however, Kristeva set out the premise of her theory. There, analyzing feminism, she argues that we must address difference within personal identity itself. She suggests that this is the central step toward a "demassification of the problematic of *difference,*" which can acknowledge difference without attempting to totalize it, annihilate it, or reconcile it.[61] In this way, the violence directed toward the other can be disintegrated "in its very nucleus."[62] The subject can understand the other, sympathize with the other, and moreover, take the place of the other, because the subject is other.[63]

As Kristeva is quick to point out, this does not mean that subject and other share their strangeness, their otherness.[64] That is to say, they are not the **same** in their strangeness. Rather, the subject can relate to an other as other because she is an other to herself.

Just as Kristeva brought the speaking body back into language by putting language into the body, she brings the subject into the place of the other by putting the other into the subject. Just as the pattern and logic of language is already found within the body, the pattern and logic of alterity is already found within the subject. And this is why the subject is never a stable identity, but always a subject-in-process/on-trial. Kristeva's strategy is to make the social relation interior to the psyche:

> This process could be summarized as an *interiorization of the founding separation of the sociosymbolic contract,* as an introduction of its cutting edge into the very interior of every identity whether subjective, sexual, ideological, or so forth. This in such a way that the habitual and increas-

ingly explicit attempt to fabricate a scapegoat victim as foundress of a society or a countersociety may be replaced by the analysis of the potentialities of *victim/executioner* which characterize each identity, each subject, each sex.[65]

This paragraph from "Women's Time" becomes the central argument of *Etrangers à nous-mêmes*. Kristeva argues that what we exclude as a society or a nation—in order to be a society or a nation—is interior to our very identity. It is our own unconscious which is projected onto those whom we exclude from our society/nation.[66] In this way we protect our own proper and stable identity both as individual subjects and as nation-states. Kristeva argues that when we flee or combat strangers or foreigners, we are struggling with our own unconscious.[67] The stranger or foreigner is within us.

As Kristeva has argued throughout her writings, identity is formed on the basis of exclusion. For example, in *Revolution in Poetic Language* she discusses the exclusions necessary for subjects to enter language. In *Powers of Horror* she discusses the exclusions necessary for religious and moral codes to bond societies. In *Tales of Love* she discusses the exclusions necessary for narcissistic identity. In *Black Sun* she discusses the exclusions necessary for subjects' "at-homeness" in language. Finally, in *Etrangers à nous-mêmes* and *Lettre ouvert à Harlem Désir* she discusses the exclusions necessary for nation-states to exist.

In *Etrangers a nous-mêmes* Kristeva suggests that the exclusions which are necessary in order for the nation-state to exist can be analyzed as analogues to the exclusions that are necessary for narcissistic identity. Like psychic identity, group identity forms itself by excluding the other.[68] For Kristeva, in the case of psychic identity, it is necessary for individuals to distinguish themselves from others through this type of exclusion in order to communicate.[69] Just as the individual must learn to deal with the return of the repressed or excluded other, so too the nation-state and its citizens must learn to deal with those elements that are excluded and foreign. Kristeva maintains that this problem is condensed in the person of the stranger or foreigner, the main character of her *Etrangers a nous-mêmes*.[70]

Several of the authors in this collection take up Kristeva's relation to, and theory of, the foreigner. In *"Des Chinoises:* Orientalism, Psychoanalysis, and Feminine Writing," Lisa Lowe argues that in *About Chinese Women,* in particular, Kristeva cites China and Chinese women only in terms of Western debates and, as such, completely recuperates them into Western discourse. She maintains that Kristeva romanticizes China, Chinese women, and the Chinese language, especially when she figures the maternal as oriental. Lowe concludes that *"Des Chinoises* curiously reproduces the postures of desire of two narratives it ostensibly seeks to subvert: the narratives of orientalism and romantic courtship, whose objects are the 'oriental' and the 'woman'."

Norma Claire Moruzzi is also critical of Kristeva's notion of the foreigner in *Strangers to Ourselves.* In "National Abjects: Julia Kristeva on the Process of Political Self-Identification," she points to the absence of discussions of race and racism in Kristeva's discussions of nationalism and the foreigner. She maintains that Kristeva overlooks important informal internal dynamics of exclusion and assimilation that underlie the formal structures of exclusion that Kristeva analyzes. Moruzzi suggests that part of the problem with Kristeva's analysis is that she returns to an Enlightenment conception of the subject which makes any real notion of heterogeneity impossible. In the end, however, Moruzzi is optimistic about Kristeva's "polyglot cosmopolitanism."

Although she is also critical of Kristeva's analysis of exclusion, especially her proposals for change, Noëlle McAfee uses Kristeva's theories of the foreigner and abjection together with Heidegger's notion of the nothing in order to construct the foundation for an ethics of difference. McAfee uses Heidegger in order to analyze the ontological underpinnings of Kristeva's "ethics of respect." She concludes that "the foreigner presents an opportunity and not an abyss."

These authors address the Kristevan question "How do we confront that which we have excluded in order to be, whether it is the return of the repressed or the return of strangers?" For Kristeva, fundamentally, the problem is how to confront alterity. She suggests that in order to understand how and why we confront strangers in the ways in which we do, we must understand the stranger within ourselves. This analysis can help us to find a way to "live with the others, to live *as others,* without ostracism but also without leveling" difference.[71] It is a question of cohabitation, says Kristeva, not of absorption.[72] Just as we must learn to live with the other within us, so too we must learn to live with the others around us. Always the analyst, Kristeva creates fantasies to help bridge the space between pain, frustration, violence, and anger, and conscious rational thought She writes texts which engage in the practice of breaking down identity as an ethical imperative.

Outlaw Ethics

In *Revolution in Poetic Language* and *Polylogue* Kristeva suggests that the subject-in-process necessitates a new concept of ethics. First she argues that "the subject of a new political practice can only be the subject of a new discursive practice."[73] Then she claims that "an other sociality is required by a subject-in-process/on-trial which averts with the very same gesture the madness and the subordination cleaving him to the law."[74]

For Kristeva, to recognize the subject-in-process is to recognize the death drive and eros. It is to recognize drive force which transgresses the Law. Kristeva says that the subject-in-process speaks to the ethical concern "because it assumes that we recognize, on the one hand, the unity of the subject who submits to a law—the law of communication, among others; yet who, on the other hand, does not entirely submit, cannot entirely submit, does not want to submit entirely."[75] To recognize the subject-in-process expands our conception of the social. Human life becomes an open system.[76]

Kristeva proposes an ethics that is not a question of morals or submission to the law.[77] Rather, it is a question of the boundaries of the law—what is on the other side of the law. Her reformulation of ethics results in an ethics that is not based on restriction and repression. When sexuality is reconceived as grounded in pleasure and violence, *jouissance*, rather than the repression of *jouissance*, then the ethical imperative is reconceived as the necessity to articulate that *jouissance:*

> Ethics used to be a coercive, customary manner of ensuring the cohesiveness of a particular group through the repetition of a code—a more or less accepted apologue. Now, however, the issue of ethics crops up wherever a code (mores, social contract) must be shattered in order to give way to the free play of negativity, need, desire, pleasure, and jouissance, before being put together again, although temporarily and with full 'knowledge' of what is involved.[78]

It is the case that post-structuralism and deconstruction, with their code shattering, have given new life to the discussion of ethics. In this context, ethics has a new urgency. Marilyn Edelstein carefully delineates Kristeva's position in these debates in her essay "Toward a Feminist Postmodern *Poléthique:* Kristeva on Ethics and Politics." Edelstein suggests that Kristeva's work provides a meeting place for feminism and postmodernism. She maintains that Kristeva's postmodern reformulation of ethics is useful for feminism. Tilottama Rajan also positions Kristeva within the post-structuralist discourse in her essay "TransPosition of Difference: Kristeva and Post-Structuralism."

Kristeva identifies the beginning of the reformulation of ethics with Marx, Nietzsche, and Freud. She points out that the urgency of this new ethics, "between law and transgression," comes from its borders: Fascism and Stalinism.[79] The urgency comes from the fact that Hitler can (can't) read Nietzsche and Stalin can (can't) read Marx. What is an ethics between law and transgression? How can we talk about ethics in this context? How can we afford not to?

For Kristeva, ethics operates as an open system. It moves between law and transgression, always in process, on trial, under revision. In this way, even the structure of ethics is open to change. The Law is always interactive, never absolute. In order for people to live together ethically, we must acknowledge transgression. Kristeva suggests that we must encode transgression so that it can be understood by the social. Transgression becomes law, which itself gives way to transgression. She likens this oscillation between Law and its transgression to the Freudian oscillation between the eros and the death drive.[80] By acknowledging the death drive, we broaden our conception of the social. This is Kristeva's project. With her new discourses of ethics, Kristeva attempts to broaden our conception of the social. Hers is an ethical project.

Kristeva's models for ethics—poetry, maternity, and psychoanalysis—are all alternatives to juridical models of ethics, which presuppose autonomous subjects who relate to each other through the force of law. The models that Kristeva proposes operate outside/before the law in the sense that the law or obligation is already internal to the subject. The law is turned inside out. In other words, there is no need for an external law which insures the social relation, The social relation is inherent in the subject.

This theory does away with the solipsism which threatened Descartes and Husserl. It does not have to explain how an autonomous subject would know anything about, let alone care about or feel obligated to, any other. In addition, it does not require a sympathy for others which is founded on their similarity, even identity, to the subject. The subject does not have to imagine that the other is the same as himself. He does not have to impose a Kantian imperative or golden rule in order to insure that he will be treated justly or kindly by others. Rather than love the other as himself, the ethical subject-in-process will love the other in herself. She will love what is different. She will love alterity because it is within but not because it is homogeneous.

Some critics, among them Andrea Nye, Nancy Fraser, and Eleanor Kuykendall, have argued that Kristeva's ethics does not allow for any effective ethical agent. Nye maintains that Kristeva's theory does not allow for any relation between adults and lacks any account of interpersonal relationships.[81] Fraser argues that "neither half of Kristeva's split subject can be a feminist political agent. Nor, I submit, can the two halves joined together."[82] And Kuykendall argues that Kristeva's ethics does not allow for a "female agency."[83] Her claim is that, for Kristeva, the feminine falls outside of ethics.[84]

To say that the feminine falls outside of ethics is not to say that women are not the subjects of ethics. The feminine is not synonymous with women. And if Kristeva suggests that the feminine falls outside of ethics, she does so in order to bring it back to ethics. What has been repressed in Western culture, including the feminine, must return so that we can talk about a nontotalizing, nonrestrictive ethics. Kristeva maintains that in order to have an ethics of life, women must be involved.[85] But, she does say that in order for women to be the subjects of ethics, we must go beyond feminism.[86] She is referring to a feminism that merely replaces one restrictive law with another; she is referring to a feminism that is as intolerant of others as patriarchy is of it. She suggests that women can "conceive and construct a new comprehensive legitimacy for their *jouissance(s)*, an ethics guaranteed not by constraint but by a logic, that is always a poly-logic, of love."[87] In order for women, and everyone on the margins of the social, to be the subjects of ethics, we must reconceive of ethics.

In "Julia Kristeva—Take Two," Jacqueline Rose addresses some of the criticism that has been levied against the usefulness of Kristeva's theories for developing a feminist ethics. Rose sees the very dilemmas or paradoxes in Kristeva's work that arm her critics as the central dilemmas of contemporary feminism. As Rose says, Kristeva is concerned to expose "an image of femininity which escapes the straitjacket of symbolic forms" without becoming essentialist. Rose claims that at the heart of Kristeva's writing and contemporary feminist theory is the concern "to challenge the very form of available self-definition without losing the possibility of speech."

What her critics do not acknowledge when they argue that Kristeva excludes women from traditional ethics is that she is challenging traditional notions of ethics. Some traditional ethics presuppose a unified subject who affirms only the self-same. And the logic of these traditional ethics always leads to exclusion and repression which, in turn, taken to the extreme, can lead to oppression and murder. Within traditional ethics which presuppose an autonomous unified subject, ethical imperatives are externally imposed. An obligation to an other cannot come from this isolated unified subject because the very existence of the other is always presented as an afterthought and/or a fight to the death. Within Kristeva's model, on the other hand, the other is always within and originary to the subject who is always in process. There is already a relationship between the subject and the other. Sociality itself is rounded on this **ongoing** relationship. The subject-in-process is not bound to its other through external restrictions.

Here Kristeva not only presents an ethics modeled on psychoanalysis, but she also presents an alternative view of psychoanalysis. It is not a tyrannical superego or paternal Law which restricts the relation between the subject and the return of the repressed. For her, a breakdown in sociality is not a breakdown in the superego or the paternal Law.[88] Rather it is a break down of love. It is love which binds the subject to its other. The relation between the subject-in-process and its other, part of that process, is not a Hegelian struggle for recognition. Rather it is an embrace of what has been lost through the traditional logic of identity.

Kristeva's is an outlaw ethics. For her, ethics is not a matter of enforcing the Law. It is a matter of embracing the return of the repressed other, the foreigner, the outcast, the unconscious, *jouissance* in all of its manifestations. She suggests that if we can bring about multiple sublations of this other which has been excluded then we won't need to kill it; if, through this outlaw ethics-in-process, we acknowledge the death drive, then there might be fewer deaths.

The essays in this collection attempt to delineate both those aspects of Kristeva's theories that hinder the possibility for an ethics of difference and those aspects of her work that provide the starting points for an ethics of difference. This collection pushes Kristeva's theories to their limits in order to expand her notions of maternity, feminine sexuality, revolution, alterity, ethics, and politics.[89]

Notes

1. Julia Kristeva, "Oscillations Between Power and Denial," and "Woman Can Never Be Defined," in *New French Feminisms,* ed. Elaine Marks and Isabelle Courtivron (New York: Schocken Books, 1981), p. 138.

2. Ibid., p. 138.

3. Ibid., p. 138.

4. Julia Kristeva, *La Révolution du langage poétique* (Paris: Editions du Seuil, 1974). *Revolution in Poetic Language,* trans. Margaret Waller (New York: Columbia University Press, 1984), p. 233.

5. Julia Kristeva, "The Ethics of Linguistics," trans. Thomas Gora, Alice Jardine, and Leon Roudiez, in *Desire in Language,* ed. Leon Roudiez (New York: Columbia University Press, 1980), p. 25.

6. Kristeva makes a distinction between two heterogeneous elements of signification: the semiotic and the symbolic. The semiotic is the drives as they are expressed in language. Kristeva identifies the semiotic with the rhythms and tones in language. The symbolic is that which enables a judgment or position. Kristeva associates the symbolic with the grammar and logic of language. It is important to distinguish Kristeva's specific use of "symbolic" in this context from Lacan's use of the Symbolic. For Kris-

teva, the Symbolic is the realm of signification and it is heterogeneous. The Symbolic is made up of both semiotic and symbolic elements. I will indicate the distinction by capitalizing Symbolic when it refers to signifying practices in general and by using lower case when it refers to the symbolic element within signifying practices.

7. Julia Kristeva, *Revolution in Poetic Language,* p. 100.

8. Ibid., p. 17.

9. Julia Kristeva, "The System and the Speaking Subject," in *The Kristeva Reader,* ed. Toril Moi (New York: Columbia University Press, 1986), p. 29; *Revolution in Poetic Language,* pp. 195–234.

10. Julia Kristeva, *Revolution in Poetic Language,* p. 181.

11. Kristeva defines the thetic in *Revolution in Poetic Language* as the point at which taking a position or making a judgment becomes possible for the child.

12. Julia Kristeva, *Revolution in Poetic Language,* p. 210.

13. Ibid., 233.

14. Ibid.

15. Ibid., p. 234.

16. Ewa Ziarek, "At the Limits of Discourse: Heterogeneity, Alterity, and the Maternal Body in Kristeva's Thought," *Hypatia, a journal for feminist philosophy* 7:1, 1992.

17. Julia Kristeva, "A New Type of Intellectual: The Dissident," in *The Kristeva Reader,* p. 297.

18. Julia Kristeva, "Le temps des femmes," *34/44 Cahiers de recherche de sciences des textes et documents 5.* "Women's Time," trans. A Jardine and H. Blake, *Feminist Theory: A Critique of Ideology,* ed. N.O. Keohane, M.Z. Rosaldo, and B.C. Gelpi (Brighton: Harvester Press, 1982), p. 49.

19. Ewa Ziarek, "At the Limits of Discourse," 1990.

20. Edith Kurweil, "An Interview with Julia Kristeva," *Partisan Review* 53 (2): p 297.

21. Julia Kristeva, "Interview with Julia Kristeva," in *Women Analyze Women,* ed. Elaine Baruch and Lucienne Serrano (New York: New York University Press, 1980), p. 238.

22. Ibid., 238.

23. Edith Kurweil, "An Interview with Julia Kristeva," p. 297.

24. Julia Kristeva, "Interview," in *Women Analyze Women,* p. 235.

25. For a more detailed account of Kristeva's suggestion that a mother loves her own mother through her child, see my "Julia Kristeva's Imaginary Father and the Crisis in the Paternal Function," *diacritics,* July 1991.

26. Julia Kristeva, *Histoires d'amour* (Paris: Editions Denoël, 1983). *Tales of Love,* trans. Leon Roudiez (New York: Columbia University Press, 1987), p. 227.

27. Ibid., 247.

28. For a detailed account of my argument that Kristeva's imaginary father can be read as screen for the mother, see "Julia Kristeva's Imaginary Father and the Crisis in the Paternal Funciton," *diacritics,* July 1991.

29. Julia Kristeva, *Tales of Love,* pp. 262–3.

30. Julia Kristeva, *Au commencement était l'amour,* trans. Arthur Goldhammer as *In the Beginning Was Love: Psychoanalysis and Faith* (New York: Columbia University Press, 1988), p. 132.

31. Julia Kristeva, *Etrangers à nous-mêmes* (Paris: Fayard, 1989). *Strangers to Ourselves,* trans. Leon Roudiez (New York: Columbia University Press, 1990), p. 182.

32. Ibid., 192.

33. Julia Kristeva, "A New Type of Intellectual," p. 300.

34. Julia Kristeva, "The Ethics of Linguistics," p. 25.

35. Julia Kristeva, "Psychoanalysis and the Polis," in *The Kristeva Reader,* p. 319.

36. Julia Kristeva, *In the Beginning Was Love,* p. 55.

37. Julia Kristeva, *Soleil Noir: Depression et Mélancolie* (Paris: Gallimard, 1987), p. 24.

38. Ibid., p. 25.

39. Julia Kristeva, "Psychoanalysis and the Polis," p. 318.

40. Julia Kristeva, *Tales of Love,* p. 276.

41. Ibid.

42. Ibid., pp. 276–7.

43. Julia Kristeva, *In the Beginning Was Love,* p. 19.

44. Ibid., 63.

45. Ibid., 60.

46. Ibid., 60–61, 63.

47. Julia Kristeva, "Psychoanalysis and the Polis," p. 319.

48. Ibid.

49. Julia Kristeva, *Soleil Noir,* p. 86.

50. Julia Kristeva, "Psychoanalysis and the Polis," p. 319.

51. Julia Kristeva, *In the Beginning Was Love,* p. 57.

52. Julia Kristeva, "Psychoanalysis and the Polis," p. 319.

53. Julia Kristeva, *Strangers to Ourselves,* p. 195.

54. Ibid.

55. Ibid., p. 192.

56. Ibid., p. 195.

57. Ibid.

58. Julia Kristeva, "Julia Kristeva in Conversation with Rosalind Coward," *Desire* (ICA Documents, 1984), p. 27.

59. Julia Kristeva, in *New French Feminisms,* p. 138.

60. Julia Kristeva, in *Desire,* p. 27.

61. Julia Kristeva, "Women's Time," p. 52.

62. Ibid.

63. Julia Kristeva, *Strangers to Ourselves,* p. 13.

64. Ibid., p. 24.

65. Julia Kristeva, "Women's Time," p. 52.

66. Julia Kristeva, *Strangers to Ourselves,* pp. 183–84.

67. Ibid., p. 191.

68. Ibid., p. 41.

69. Ibid.

70. Ibid., p. 151.

71. Ibid., p. 2.

72. Ibid., p. 3.

73. Julia Kristeva, *Polylogue* (Paris: Editions du Seuil, 1977), p. 20.

74. Ibid., p. 21.

75. I. Lipkowitz and A. Loselle, "An Interview with Julia Kristeva," *Critical Texts* 3:3, 1986: p. 8.

76. Ibid.

77. Ibid.

78. Julia Kristeva, "The Ethics of Linguistics," p. 23.

79. Ibid.

80. I. Lipkowitz and A. Loselle, "An Interview with Julia Kristeva," p. 8.

81. Julia Kristeva, *In the Beginning Was Love,* pp. 681–2.

82. Julia Kristeva, *Lettre ouvert à Harlem Désir* (Paris: Editions Rivages, 1990), p. 98.

83. Julia Kristeva, *Strangers to Ourselves,* p. 181.

84. Ibid., 189.

85. Julia Kristeva, "Stabat Mater," in *Tales of Love,* trans. Leon Roudiez (New York: Columbia University Press, 1987), p. 262.

86. For an extended analysis of Kristeva's relation to feminism see my *Reading Kristeva. Unraveling the Double-bind* (Bloomington, Ind.: Indiana University Press, 1993). Much of my analysis here is taken from the conclusion of *Reading Kristeva.*

87. Julia Kristeva, "A partir de Polylogue," *Revue des sciences humaines* 168, 1977: pp. 495–501. "Talking about Polylogue," trans. Sean Hand, in *French Feminist Thought: A Reader,* ed. Toril Moi (New York: Basil Blackwell Publisher, 1987), pp. 115-16.

88. Julia Kristeva, *Tales of Love,* p. 378.

89. I would like to thank Greg Reihman for preparing the index for this volume.

1

Opaque Texts and Transparent Contexts: The Political Difference of Julia Kristeva
(abridged version)
Alice Jardine

I think that one of the most difficult things to remember, here in the United States, is that the various people we designate by the phrase "contemporary French thought" not only represent a particular set of *epistemological* questions (questions upon which most of those people can agree)—but that they also represent a set of highly politicized conceptual systems offered as working responses to those questions—and that *there* ends the agreement among them. Anecdotes about how none of these people can talk to each other in Paris may be amusing to *us* here, but the disagreements which led to those estrangements are more deeply rooted in fundamental political issues than they are in squabbles among personalities. The clearest example of what I mean by this is perhaps the way in which the French intellectuals most well known here have taken, at one point or another, a rigorously anti-Marxist, or at the very least para-post-Marxist stance—to the extent that Marxism has remained bound to traditional conceptualizations of dialectics, the human subject, the function, even existence of something called literature, etc. Foucault's archeologies, Lacan's unconscious, Althusser's ideology, Deleuze and Guattari's machines, Lyotard's figurations, Derrida's deconstructions, Irigaray's and Cixous's feminine, etc.—*are* their individual logics as responses to that Marxist thought. They are highly politicized elements of interpretive systems brought to bear not only upon narrow textual questions, but upon some of the most difficult larger epistemological questions facing the West today. Through those responses, each of these writers has created his or her own *ethos*, that conceptual place where they are most at home. And those places are very different.

Let us briefly recall some of the unchanging coordinates of Kristeva's *ethos*—by now, probably overfamiliar to some of you, but nevertheless important to situate continually with regard to the most pressing questions of our current historical moment. *My* situating of what is ultimately a complex and constantly evolving conceptual apparatus is necessarily biased. Kristeva's thought is peculiar: it is transparent enough that it tends to be reduced very quickly to a set of bipolar opposites by her critics (and thereby criticized as being everything from ultraanarchistic to ultraconservative); but at the same time, it is opaque enough to be uncritically idealized by her most fervent admirers. I will try to avoid both extremes.

There are, in a sense, three Kristevas—and for the sake of brevity, I will refer to them as the Kristevas of the 1960s, 70s and 80s. (I am sure there are more Kristevas to come.)

The Kristeva of the 1960s was the Kristeva of *Tel Quel* and semanalysis. Semanalysis was the term first proposed in *Semeiotike: Recherches pour une sémanalyse,* published in 1969 to describe what she called then a new materialist theory of signification whose own internal logic would remain isomorphic to its privileged object: poetic language. While rarely used in her subsequent work, the term designates both the terrain and process through which Kristeva has contributed to a reformulation of the speaking subject and its text over a period of now almost two decades.

The new science of semanalysis, announced in the blissful aftermath of 1968, was, first of all, an effort to take account of and valorize those radical signifying practices excluded from or assigned to the margins of official mass culture in the West. It was addressed to what she and others would later call "limit-texts," with special emphasis on those texts written since the late nineteenth century and in dialogue with twentieth-century crises in Western thought. It was to analyze the epistemological and ideological ruptures signaled or already realized by these limit-texts as well as to set the ground for a new, general theory of writing and subjectivity. It was in this early work that Kristeva emphasized—as did other members of *Tel Quel*—the most radical moments of Marx's theory of production, Freud's analysis of dreams, Saussure's work on anagrams, and Althusser's on ideology, in order, as she put it, to reconceptualize the figurability of history and the history of figurability.

By the early 1970s, Kristeva had thoroughly formalized the most important components of semanalysis, and they became part of a system: a non-Cartesian theory of the subject, not dependent on the ideology of language only as a transparent communication system, but as reverberated through the Freudian and Lacanian unconscious. Her vocabulary was refined and signed: the semiotic and symbolic, the phenotext and genotext, etc.—and all was elaborately developed in the style of the first half of *La Révolution du langage poétique.* It was, in fact, with the Kristeva of *La Révolution* that the Krinteva of the 70s took form. There, Mallarmé and Lautréamont served as examples of how semanalyzing poetic language could help us to shed our stubborn Cartesian and Humanist skins—and begin to look beyond the so-called "message" or "ethic" of a text to its form, its networks of phantasies; to a sentence's rhythm, articulation, and its style—how it could help us to understand how those elements *are* the message, bound up in a conceptuality that we cannot hope to change only at the level of the utterance. For her, it is the economy *of* language and sexuality—not the history of ideas *on* language and sexuality—that articulates social relationships in the West.

It was in 1974, the year of *La Révolution,* that there appeared, in all of its explicitness, on Kristeva's intellectual horizon, the two limits which continue to mean the most to her: the two political extremes of our century and its responses to the crises of monological Western thought: Fascism and Stalinism, and thus inevitably anti-Semitism. According to Kristeva, those two limits—besides being historical, political phenomena, rooted in concrete historical and economic contexts as well as personalities—are also rooted in the psychic mechanisms of the human subject and are laid bare in the psychic traces of the radically poetic text. For her, Fascism is the return of the repressed (of what she calls the feminine-connoted semiotic) into rigid religious or political structures. Instead of being socialized, the semiotic is unchained. From this point of view, Stalinism is but the default of Fascism: the barbarous other side of the human face.

I might just remind you here that Kristeva is Bulgarian and that through the biographemic texture of her writing can be traced a certain *fear,* a fear not unlike that which many of us are experiencing today with regard to the larger political climate in which we are living; a climate which we often qualify in shorthand as a backlash, but which is much more than that. It is a climate of sustained, popularly supported—and, indeed, massively desired—paranoia, particularly with regard to the relationship between production and reproduction, the *regulation* of the mother's body once again serving as ground for a monolithic, nationalistic ideology. Here, Kristeva's insistent return to the 1930s—what *were* those intellectuals and writers doing?—can provide food for thought. For me, her work intervenes at the tense intersection between this actively informed *fear* and our naively passive *belief* that Fascism or Stalinism cannot possibly return.

Kristeva's one basic question became increasingly more insistent and explicit. How can we give a sign, a discourse, to that which is and has been repressed throughout Western history? How can we find a subject for what has been repressed while avoiding these two extremes: psychic explosion and psychic censorship? What can be new modalities for reshaping the monological and monotheistic laws at the foundations of our Western culture without inviting the return of the repressed in its potentially monstrous and apocalyptic reality?

It was in *La Révolution* that Kristeva first talked about ethics: an increasingly important element in her work of the 1970s, for her, ethics can no longer be the observation of laws, moralistic or normative judgment, scientific or otherwise. But the question of ethics must not be scorned or rejected (as with Lacan, for example); left in perpetual suspension (as in Deleuze and Guattari); or deferred (sometimes rather guiltily, as in Derrida). Ethics can no longer be "a coercive, customary manner of ensuring the cohesiveness of a particular group through the repetition of a code," but, rather, must come up "wherever a code (mores, social contract) must be shattered in order to give way to the free play of negativity, need, desire, pleasure, and jouissance, before being put together again, although temporarily and with full knowledge of what is involved." And, in her words, "Fascism and Stalinism stand for the barriers that the new adjustment between a law and its transgression comes against."[1] For Kristeva, the only possible ethicity for the late twentieth century in the West is what she terms the negativization of narcissism within a practice. In other words, what is ethical is a practice which dissolves narcissistic fixations—dissolving them before they become rigidified as sociosymbolic structures. And that is the ethical—hence political—function of an artistic and theoretical practice which ruptures the representations of even the most liberal and progressive discourse.

It goes without saying that this includes the discourse of feminism. It was during the 1970s that Kristeva wrote the most explicitly about the feminine, and sketched the outlines of her own participation in gynesis—a participation which rings differently from its male versions.[2] That is, when taken up by female voices, gynesis becomes strangely subversive, promising, at the very least, new kinds of questions unburdened by the repetition of the dialectics of master/slave oppression. On the other hand, she does not include the category of "women as subjects" with the boundaries of gynesis. She began her concentration on the feminine by analyzing it only as a kind of "glue" that has held our patriarchal history and its conceptual systems together. She began to analyze the ways in which the feminine has been sublimated or fetishized in different cultures and at different points in history. She began emphasizing how this feminine is linked to the Mother within the classical Western Oedipal structure. But she refused to definitively untangle the woman subject from the feminine. Except for scattered comments on women's need for maternity (often rather shocking to the American feminist's ears), she broke with Irigaray and Cixous completely when it came to prescribing what women's relationship today should be to that feminine—or at least, has always approached that topic with extreme caution. She has consistently rejected the notion that women should either valorize or negate this feminine whose function in Western culture is still changing with the evolution of our modernity.

It became increasingly clear through the 1970s that Kristeva was not going to participate in hypothetical descriptions of the female subject's potential liberation from patriarchy. In fact, her writing took a decisive turn. By the mid-70s, it was obvious that it was the Male-Subject-Creative-of-Our-Dominant-*and*-Marginal-Culture that Kristeva was going to x-ray—building a sort of inventory of possible male libidinal economies. One may regret and criticize her lack of attention to women subjects and their texts—I certainly do—but there can be no doubt that this was a calculated political decision on her part.

What Kristeva did do was continue her search for a conceptuality which would provide space for her definition of ethics: an understanding of that which pulverizes the truths of our age before they become too rigid, but one that does not lose sight of those truths, thereby descending into an esoteric, mystical, or even—*à la limite*—psychotic discourse. For example, *La traversée des signes,* a collection of essays on Chinese, Indian, and other sign systems, was not just a result of Kristeva's involvement with *Tel Quel* and its 70-ish Maoism, as is often charged—but was, rather, fully consistent with her project of x-raying other forms of intelligibility, mapping their promises and limits for changing Western culture. *Polylogue*—a collection of essays all written in the 1970s—treats everything from Giovanni Bellini to film theory. But what unites the essays is Kristeva's backing away from *explicating* her theoretical apparatus toward looking at individual signifying practices by men in terms of two other limits: language *before* it signifies and communicates meaning; and language at the point where it is losing or has *lost* meaning: that is, at language acquisition and at psychosis. Her emphasis shifted even more radically toward an understanding of the place of the archaic mother and father, or more precisely, of the fantasies engendered by them. This intensification of focus on the two limits of language—its *before* and *after,* if you like—continued Kristeva's ethical project: not the condensation or solidification of meaning, but an understanding of meaning's doubleness, its unnameable, its unspeakable—its grounding in the unsignifiable.

The importance of one particular event in Kristeva's personal trajectory during the 1970s cannot be overestimated. She decided to become a psychoanalyst, and, in my opinion, what came out of Kristeva's practice as an analyst, and, in particular, out of her extreme attention to the mechanisms of transference, was a return, with renewed fascination, to her main, most consistent concern—political extremes—but this time, as someone more independent and sure of her critical voice.[3] She assumed fully her place as a cultural critic, someone attuned to the epistemological and psychic logics underwriting today's more overtly moral or political dilemmas. She struck out on a somewhat singular, at times lonely intellectual path in Paris—and, in fact, even in terms of the Paris/U.S. connection. Refusing both the positivism of American interpretive systems and what she sees as the interminability of new French philosophies, she turned to what, in clinical language, is termed "the borderline patient," and to the problems of interpretation intrinsic to this new kind of human subject—more specifically, the male writing subject of Western culture in the late twentieth century. Kristeva delved, head first, into our turn-of-the-century *mal du siècle*, looking for what is specific to it—and for what can be done about it, if anything.

The Kristeva of the 1980s began, in my opinion, with the publication of *Folle vérité* in 1979. She writes there of the *vréel*—the kind of new "truth" modern men seem to be desperately searching for and can't seem to find, a truth which has "massively left behind the secure terrain of logic and ontology."[4] She attacked the questions of how to render this *vréel vraisemblable* before it might explode in what we call "reality." The word *vréel* is composed, of course, of three words: the true (*vrai*), the real (in Lacan's sense), and the feminine pronoun *elle*. From an analysis of the resurgence of mysticism in our time to readings of sophistic thought, these essays bear witness to our time as one of obsession with the *vréel*—an obsession with the feminine psychic spaces repressed throughout 2,000 years of Western history. Their explosion today, into new languages—both liberating and destructive—is no accident according to Kristeva.

In her book *Pouvoirs de l'horreur*, Kristeva explored what she sees as the fundamental condition of late-twentieth-century man—and by man, she means *men*: Abjection. Much stronger in French, this word designates the psychic state of the borderline subject who is no longer a subject and is no longer sure of an object (or can't find one): the subject who is fascinated with the boundaries between subject and object, with the ambiguous, the mixed, *l'entre-deux*. As for exploring the intricacies of this new "male condition," I will leave you to the text. But I think it is important to point out briefly the place of this project within Kristeva's ethical trajectory. She ends the book in the following way, and we can see the same concerns that have haunted her work from the beginning surface once again:

> Rivetted to meaning like Raymond Roussel's parrot to his chain, psychoanalysts, because they interpret, are no doubt among the rare contemporary witnesses to the fact that we are all dancing on a volcano. If there is where they are to find their perverse pleasure, so be it: on the

condition that they help explode, by virtue of their qualifications as a man or woman *sans qualités,* the deepest logics of our anguishes and our hatreds. Can they x-ray that horror without capitalizing on the power it gives them? Exhibit the abject without confusing their own position with it?

Probably not. But at least they should know that, from this field of knowledge mined with forgetfulness and laughter, with the knowledge of the abject, he, she—they—are preparing themselves for the first really major demystification of Power (religious, moral, political, and verbal) that humanity has lived through, necessary produced from within the demise of Judeo-Christian monotheism, the religion of sacred horror. In the meantime, others will continue their long march toward idols and truths of all kinds, armed with the necessarily true faiths of wars to come, necessarily sacred wars. . . . [my translation][5]

The tone of this ending to Kristeva's book may appear apocalyptic—or even melodramatic to some—but that may be because those of us who rather stubbornly insist on continuing to function every day must put out of our minds the real or potential horrors of a contemporary world whose "deep logic" Kristeva seems to want to pursue on every page. (And as an aside and purely personal remark, I might just add that if feminists get upset because Kristeva does not center her work more around questions of female subjectivity, her male readers are getting even more upset, or perhaps hostile would be a better word, by her current rather relentless focus on the politics of male sexuality.)

Kristeva has most recently written on the most banal topic in the world: love, the inverse of abjection. But she has removed love from the television screen—as well as from the advertising pages of the NYRB—and put it back into our bedrooms and nurseries and, most importantly, back into history. She reminds us that there is a history of love, a history important to evoke in the context of radical shifts in the love stories being told today, stories in which what has been called love risks collapsing because of a lack of object in the language of the end of the twentieth century. Her unsentimental approach to this concept—in a contemporary world where, when not sentimentalized, love is thought of only in terms of desires that have lost, given up on, or banished their potential objects—promises some fairly interesting reading for the American pragmatic mind. So will, I'm sure, her current work on a third facet of our contemporary, dominant male libidinal economy: the dark lining of love, the condition of melancholy.

Finally, I would like to pause for just a minute over one of Kristeva's last articles published in English. Entitled "Psychoanalysis and the Polis,"

it appeared in a special issue of *Critical Inquiry* on "The Politics of Interpretation."[6] I mention this article for two reasons: first, because it seems
to me a perfect example of the Kristeva of the 1980s—a Kristeva whom,
I hear, a lot of Americans don't like because they find her, well, *too psychoanalytic*. But that is the second reason I call attention to it. The article appears at the center of this volume of *Critical Inquiry* as the only
female voice, and as the only voice from France, adopting the politics of
saying what is not being said, adopting the micropolitics of psychoanalysis.
She does this surrounded by eight Anglo-American males contemplating how
awful everything is and pronouncing on what I can only describe as the
ethics, indeed morality of our most popular modes of interpretation—
Marxist, deconstructionist, historical, and yes there is even a so-called
male feminist there. Into this ultramoral—and rather transparent—context,
Kristeva injected a very opaque text, preceded by a prefatory remark added
after the conference at which these papers were read. In that preface, she
reminds the reader of something that has been fundamental to French
thinking for the last twenty years but which here, in the United States, seems
just too difficult to confront: that "there are political implications inherent in the act of interpretation itself," whatever meaning that interpretation ultimately bestows. That to give an (empirically) political meaning to
something is

> perhaps only the ultimate consequence of the epistemological attitude
> which consists, simply, of the desire *to give meaning*. This attitude is not
> innocent but, rather, is rooted in the speaking subject's need to reassure
> himself of his image and his identity faced with an object. Political inter-
> pretation is thus the apogee of the obsessive quest for A Meaning."[7]

I would emphasize two things here: First of all, the words "reassure
himself of *his* image and *his* identity" are no accident. That it should be
uniquely a woman and feminist, Gayatri Spivak, who has taken the time
to reply (if angrily) to Kristeva's article on the *male* politics of interpretation—including Kristeva's insistence on the contextual maleness of *this*
inquiry—is fascinating to me.[8] In any case—and secondly—Kristeva's lone
voice and gesture at the center of this volume brings me to what I see as
Kristeva's political difference. For all of her work insists on two kinds of
reading and on her sense that the difference between these two kinds of reading is, above all, a political and ethical difference: a difference in attitude
toward interpretation. Kristeva knows and continues to remind us that
the text—any text—can always be read *both* ways, transparently and
opaquely, that what it signifies is always both possible and impossible,

both can and cannot exist, both does and does not exist, and that, indeed, a text *must* be read both ways—its difference respected—with neither reading being excluded, overlooked, or denied because of convention, law, or privilege.

In my opinion, this is not to advocate some kind of warmed-over critical pluralism, but is, rather, to adopt purposefully a kind of ethicity which, at least temporarily, might allow women to continue interpreting without being afraid of and without becoming victims of either modernity or feminism.

Notes

A longer version of this article was published in *The Poetics of Gender,* ed. Nancy K. Miller (New York: Columbia University Press, 1986).

1. Julia Kristeva, "The Ethics of Linguistics," in *Desire in Language,* ed. Leon S. Roudiez, trans. Thomas Gora, Alice Jardine, and Leon S. Roudiez (New York: Columbia University Press, 1980), p. 28.

2. See my *Gynesis: Configurations of Woman and Modernity* (Ithaca, N.Y.: Cornell University Press, 1985).

3. Jacqueline Rose has suggested to me that, on the contrary, experience as an analyst may have made things more difficult and contradictory for Kristeva. I suspect that both of our observations are relevant. Kristeva's move in the 1970s from collective to individual labor (from *Tel Quel* to private practice) gave *her* a stronger, more independent voice (as someone primarily committed to the insights of Freudian analysis); yet that change in voice has no doubt rendered the interpretation of her *oeuvre* (committed to much more than Freud) more difficult and contradictory perhaps, for us. See Jacqueline Rose's fine "Julia Kristeva—Take Two," chapter 3 of this volume.

4. Julia Kristeva, "Le vréel," in *Folle vérité* (Paris: Editions du Seuil, 1979), p. 11.

5. Julia Kristeva, *Pouvoirs de l'horreur* (Paris: Editions du Seuil, 1980). A translation has appeared in English since this article was published: *Powers of Horror,* trans. Leon S. Roudiez (New York: Columbia University Press, 1982), pp. 247–48.

6. Julia Kristeva, "Psychoanalysis and the Polis," *Critical Inquiry* 9(1), September 1982: pp. 77–92.

7. Ibid, p. 78.

8. Gayatri Chakravorty Spivak, "The Politics of Interpretations," *Critical Inquiry* 9 (1), September 1982: pp. 259–78.

2

Kristeva's Delphic Proposal: "Practice Encompasses the Ethical"

Jean Graybeal

It is impossible to read the work of Julia Kristeva without becoming aware of the ethical motivation and orientation of her writings. Kristeva's works are indirect and subtle reflections on the good life, on the constitution of human identity and subjectivity, and on the possibilities for human existence. The broad questions that underlie her more particular concerns in any moment are profoundly ethical ones; through her reflections on psychoanalysis, literature, and politics, she evokes in her readers such questions as these: "How may we avoid reifying or substantializing the process that is the subject? . . . for if we do not, we totalize and oppress." "How is it possible to balance the contrary forces between which we are suspended, in such a way as to maximize *jouissance,* to allow the productive creation of art, literature, and meaning? . . . For if we do not, we go mad." "How do we continue the necessary struggle toward equal rights and opportunities for women? . . . without claiming to say what 'women' are." All such questions are ethically motivated, driven by dual imperatives to avoid oppression and madness. Erich Fromm wrote that "ethics has to do with the nature of human character; it attempts to discover the optimal organization . . . of human energies and the conditions necessary to bring it about."[1] If we accept his definition, surely Kristeva is an ethical thinker *par excellence.*

Of course, to know how to live, to "discover the optimal organization of our energies," to know what to do and how to be, is an exceedingly puzzling mystery. Most of us, as we age more or less successfully, begin to learn what it is that we like to do, and what we do well, and what others prefer for us to do, and we come to a kind of tacit agreement with ourselves and our environment, a conclusion that now we do at last know how to live and what to do. We commonly leave behind the intensity with which we asked such questions when we were younger, the awful and harsh light that shone on our daily choices, the clear awareness that life is given, but meaning is not, and that the invention of our own lives was the one task that we really could not get anyone else to do for us. Looming behind that awareness was the knowledge also of death, and of the individual's trajectory toward that solitary end. The responsibility for our own lives, and our own deaths, issued some days in despair, some days in judgmental self-right-eousness, some days in anarchic rebellion. But we were aware of the questions, living in their light, groping in their darkness.

People who unexpectedly re-experience the full intensity of those big questions, which never really go away but only become submerged under the answers provided by daily life, frequently consult an *oracle*. They turn to a trusted friend or a counselor, someone who they hope can give them the answer they need to the conundrum they face. The most ancient of ora-cles, the oracle of Apollo at Delphi, had the injunction "Know thyself" inscribed on the wall near its entrance. I have come to see that advice, that most fundamental response to our questions about life, as the centerpiece of Kristeva's ethical reflections. Her whole work is devoted to an explo-ration of both the difficulty and the possibility of self-knowledge, and that central focus is mandated by the ethical consequences of self-knowledge or the lack thereof.

The poet H.D. claims that "Know thyself" was an *ironic* teaching of the Delphic oracle (probably because most people consult an oracle when they believe they need to learn something about others or the world, not about themselves); she interprets the saying to mean that "to know yourself in the full sense of the words was to know everybody."[2] And if you were to "know everybody," there would be no need to consult the oracle about your specific question at all. To read Kristeva is to learn about how it may be possible to know the self, and about what the consequences and con-comitants of self- and other-knowledge might be. Both the oracle at Del-phi and Kristeva address the questions of the desirable relation to others and the various ways to live and act in the world by referring to the oth-erness within, to the difficulty and the necessity of self-knowledge, and to the pathways that make it possible.

Nietzsche too reflected on the Delphic counsel to "Know thyself." He wondered whether to know the self might mean to become "objective":

> A matter that becomes clear ceases to concern us. What was on the mind of that god who counseled: "Know thyself!" Did he mean: "Cease to con-cern yourself! Become objective!" And Socrates? And "scientific men"?[3]

Although Nietzsche's intent with this question was most probably to ridicule the notion that ceasing to concern oneself and thereby becoming objective were even possible, much less desirable, I believe the suggestion that a type of objectivity might result from the injunction to "know thyself" does indeed have some validity. For the advice to know the self is indeed a very paradoxical instruction. Surely the attempt to know the self is the most subjective of activities, and Kristeva's work is deeply concerned with the nature and structures of the *sujet en procès*, the **subject**-in-process/on-trial. But, as Kierkegaard has also taught us, the peculiar nature of the self requires that self-knowledge be attained through indirect means, and it is precisely through that process of gaining self-knowledge that a kind of objectivity may also be attained, an objectivity which makes it possible to know both the difference within the self, and the connections between self and other. If to know the self is both to "know everybody" and in some sense to "become objective," it seems to me that the one who knows him/herself would indeed be very wise, and would at least be on his or her way toward a very advanced state of awareness, a state ideal for ethical reflection and living.

It is all very well to instruct the inquirer, "Know thyself," as both the Delphic and Kristevan oracles do. But what kind of knowledge of the self is possible, given Kristeva's perspectives on its nature? For the self she posits is an unstable, dynamic, ever-changing process; the most basic mistake in thinking about it would be to stabilize or substantialize it as any kind of an entity rather than a process. The self is constantly engaged in self-production as well as self-dissolution, in both building up and breaking down its ever-evolving identity and in constructing and eroding its own meaning. It is a "strange land of border and othernesses ceaselessly constructed and deconstructed."[4] Of course, various means of avoiding or bringing unreal closure to the very unsettling process that is the subject are always available, and such tactics constitute some of the disorders both of personality and of social meaning systems that Kristeva analyzes.

In order to know the self in both its negativity and its positivity, in its processes, in its self-constitution as well as its dissolution, some means is necessary whereby we might gain access to and awareness of those processes. Kristeva asserts that they are accessible in the experience of *practice*. The creation of and engagement with aesthetic productions is for her the premier arena of self-awareness, as well as of self-creation. She goes so far as to assert, ". . . you do not take place as such, but as a stance essential to a practice."[5] To be engaged in the production of music, of sculpture, of a poem, is, according to her, the most reliable path to self-knowledge available to us.

Kristeva refers to practice when she is discussing the subject's suspension between the symbolic and semiotic dispositions in language, and in this dialectic she counterposes practice to mastery. She sees the subject as implicated in a complex relationship to meaning, a relationship that demands both "our ability to insure our mastery of [meaning] (through technique or knowledge) as well as our passage through it (through play or practice)."[6] Passage *through* meaning, the effect of play or practice, helps to ensure that a sense of meaning as univocal, final, determined, or universal does not have a chance to become established. This would seem to imply that too intense a focus on technique and knowledge is detrimental to ethical awareness. I shall explore below what some of the ramifications of that suggestion might be.

John Lechte has noted that "... Kristeva views art less as an object, and more as a process, or practice, which 'creates' the subject."[7] He quotes Kristeva thus: "I would even say that signs are what produce a body, that—and the artist knows it well—if he doesn't work, if he doesn't produce his music or his page or his sculpture, he would be, quite simply, ill or not alive."[8]

In *Revolution in Poetic Language,* Kristeva explicitly addresses the ethical function of art. She writes,

> Practice, . . . positing and dissolving meaning and the unity of the subject, . . . encompasses the ethical. The text . . . is a practice assuming all positivity in order to negativize it and thereby make visible the *process* underlying it. It can thus be considered, precisely, as that which carries out the ethical imperative."[9]

To "carry out the ethical imperative" is thus to make visible the processes underlying the production and dissolution of meaning and identity, the processes that constitute the subject itself. Practices and texts which bring these processes to light are those that lead to ethical awareness. Kristeva asserts that the text must not itself carry a moral or spell out a specific ethical message:

> The univocal enunciation of such a message would itself represent a suppression of the ethical function as we understand it. . . . The text fulfills its ethical function only when it pluralizes, pulverizes, 'musicates' these truths, which is to say, on the condition that it develop them to the point of laughter."[10]

The kinds of texts or practices to which Kristeva looks for ethical enlightenment are therefore precisely those which raise the questions of identity, meaning, and truth, rather than provide their answers.

A similarity to Kristeva's view is apparent in Nietzsche's thinking about the effect of discipline. He wrote,

> What is essential 'in heaven and on earth' seems to be . . . that there
> should be *obedience* over a long period of time and in a *single* direction:
> given that, something always develops, and has developed, for whose sake
> it is worth while to live on earth: for example, virtue, art, music, dance,
> reason, spirituality—something transfiguring, subtle, mad, and divine.[11]

The obedience and singleness required for the practice of aesthetic creation are here seen by Nietzsche as giving rise not only to art, music, and
dance but to virtue, reason, and spirituality. Both Nietzsche and Kristeva
could be said to have an aesthetic ethic.

There may be another parallel to Kristeva's perspective about the path
to ethical awareness in traditional Buddhist teachings. The interwoven
nature of Buddhist ethical and aesthetic ideas and the reliance on self-
knowledge for their attainment is well expressed by Rita Nakashima Brock.
She notes that while Western Christianity has tended to split the therapeutic,
the aesthetic, and the ethical into different fields of concern, Buddhism
has always seen them as deeply interrelated. She writes, "Buddhists have
tended to focus on intense inner self-awareness as the key to ethical behavior and to set compassion and wisdom in the larger aesthetic context of harmony and beauty, the beauty of the cosmos."[12] The Buddhist ethical ideals
of compassion and wisdom arise from meditation and other practices giving access to self-knowledge; they function as an expression both of the
emptiness of the self and of the essential interrelatedness of all that exists.
That perspective seems to me to have much in common with the ethical
awareness sought by Kristeva, an awareness that we ourselves are the others, the foreigners, the different.

Just how is it that practice helps to create the ethical subject, the subject capable of self-knowledge, and what sorts of practice might work in
this way? Practice, as it is defined and advocated by Kristeva, clearly
involves allowing or facilitating access to the unconscious, without knowledge of which any self-knowledge remains very partial. To write, to impro-
vise music, or to dance is to become aware, however dimly, of the contents
and processes of the unconscious, and to access the unconscious is to begin
to recognize or re-experience one's connection, similarity, or relatedness to
everyone else. Such a recognition also helps to reveal and unmask the
workings of projection, which is surely one of the most obvious sources of
unethical action.

In addition to facilitating access to the unconscious, Kristevan practice
creates the subject by drawing on the body, its energies, rhythms, and
hitherto inarticulate experience. The body finds expression through the
semiotic dimension of language, the rhythmic aspects of music, dance, and

painting, the symptoms and symbolic ailments that arise for analysis. Practice facilitates an overcoming of the body-mind split, the dangerous illusion that we are moral selves encased or housed in potentially immoral bodies.

Finally, a practice leading to self-knowledge must teach the practitioner about his/her limits, about what one is and is not capable of at a particular time. As anyone knows who has ever engaged in any kind of creative practice, such activity continually and dependably works to undermine notions of grandeur, feelings of egotism, and fantasies of control. Although mastery does grow, as technique and knowledge expand, to continue to *practice* is to allow the dimension of "passage through meaning," represented by both practice and play, to counterbalance the fantasy of mastery. As we have seen above, Kristeva calls both mastery of and passage through meaning necessary to our unstable and unsettling relationship to ourselves and our identity.

Of course, psychoanalysis is also a practice in this sense: "Psychoanalysis is ... experienced as a journey into the strangeness of the other and of oneself, toward an ethics of the irreconcilable."[13] It is a practice in which both analyst and client embark together on an attempt to know the self, and to come to terms with the unconscious, the body, and limitations. As Kristeva writes about it, analysis has far more in common with aesthetic practices of all sorts than with a scientific investigation.

Like most good ethical theorists, Kristeva has an ideal or a goal in mind, a picture of the kind of subject she hopes will evolve, when she proposes that we undertake this arduous and risky path of self knowledge. She aims for the self capable of love because it is an *open* system, and capable of creative work. These criteria, the abilities to love and to work, are classic Freudian measures of health. Kristeva might add to these the capacity for *jouissance,* the ability to *know* oneself as a subject-in-process/on-trial, never finally stable or unified, always balancing between finally irreconcilable forces, and capable of taking a kind of unstable pleasure in that fact.

Kristeva's interest in individual self-knowledge does not end with the individual, of course. A large part of the ethical motivation of her perspective has to do with the hope of creating a society that is capable of difference, one that not only tolerates diversity but welcomes it and sees it as constitutive of its own identity. She writes:

> [T]oday ... we confront an economic and political integration on the scale of the planet: shall we be, intimately and subjectively, able to live with the others, to live *as others,* without ostracism but also without leveling?[14]

There is a connection between these two concerns, between Kristeva's views about the individual's sense of him/herself and the social questions of otherness. She believes that when the person "ceases to consider himself as unitary and glorious but discovers his incoherences and abysses,"[15] he or she begins to look at all otherness differently. We might be able to accept and welcome those others, simply because we recognize that we ourselves are other to ourselves.

It seems to me that here Kristeva is banking on the possibility of reinducing in people that peculiar experience that for some comes during adolescence, and for many during young adulthood, and perhaps for some never at all: the experience of truly recognizing, of deeply accepting in a very personal way, that not only one's *own* life or self is complex, weighty, and real, but that other beings too have that same experience of their own existence; that they also know the universe as constituted by their own involvement in it; and that their experience, their reality is indeed as valuable and worthy of respect as one's own. Such a realization is a moment both of looking at one's self objectively, seeing oneself as other, knowing that oneself is constituted just in the same way as others are constituted, and of knowing the other as a self. Kristeva puts it this way: "It is not simply—humanistically—a matter of our being able to accept the other, but of *being in his place,* and this means to imagine and make oneself other for oneself."[16] To be capable of being in the place of the other is to recognize one's own otherness, one's own objectivity. If the paths of artistic practice and of psychotherapy can indeed induce such an awareness, such intense and revealing self-knowledge, then perhaps Kristeva's ultimate optimism is justified; perhaps a world that can both accept and welcome otherness is a real possibility.

Kristeva's perspectives on the ethical function of art or practice have some important practical consequences. First, if we accept her notion that anything univocally stated is inherently anti-ethical, because univocality involves suppression rather than expression of the ethical function, then monolithic statements of any sort are to be avoided, including those which claim to state moral truths. Ethics and the study and cultivation of ethical living would need to proceed more experimentally, exploring tentatively and questioningly, artistically, rather than didactically or assertively.

This first consequence leads to a second, suggesting a method or process by which ethical education or training in ethical development might proceed. If it is indeed through practice that knowledge of the self and therefore ethical awareness have the opportunity to develop, then the exploration of and commitment to various forms of aesthetic practice are at least one of the paths we should follow in attempting to encourage in people an awareness of the self-creation of their subjectivity. Rather than providing more hours of "values clarification" or "moral awareness training" in the schools, as so many propose today, what would be called for is practice in the creation of art, whether music, literature, dance, or visual or performing art. The opportunities that such practice provides in terms of encounter with the unconscious, experience of the body, and awareness of one's limits and possibilities, would be invaluable in creating a populace more ethically self-conscious and engaged.

Similarly, rather than more emphasis on the basics, which have come to be defined as the elements of technique and knowledge, a balance between mastery of and passage through meaning must be sought. Meaning that can be mastered is an illusion, says Kristeva. Technique and knowledge give the fantasy of control, of the unitary self, and if not balanced by the countervailing forces of play and practice, lead to the rejection and suppression of otherness, both within and without.

Kristeva's Delphic proposal ultimately involves taking the postmodern threat to the unitary, self-contained subject as our greatest opportunity. If, in the face of uncertainty about how to live and about how to live together, we were seriously to consider the wisdom of our own "Delphic" oracle—mysterious and ambiguous though it may be—we might rely as much on play and practice as ways of coming to know ourselves as we do on technique and knowledge. In doing so, we would lend an ear to the wisdom that says that we are not only or simply ourselves, that the otherness that we so much fear and that causes us so much distress as we try to regularize and control it, is really within. Kristeva says,

> The ethics of psychoanalysis implies a politics: it would involve a cosmopolitanism of a new sort that, cutting across governments, economies, and markets, might work for a mankind whose solidarity is founded on the consciousness of its unconscious—desiring, destructive, fearful, empty, impossible.[17]

To know ourselves in these ways might indeed be the beginning of wisdom.

Notes

1. Don S. Browning, *Generative Man: Psychoanalytic Perspectives* (Philadelphia: Westminster Press, 1973), p.124.

2. H.D., *Tribute to Freud* (New York: New Directions Books, 1974), pp. 72–73.

3. Friedrich Nietzsche, *Beyond Good and Evil*, trans. Walter Kaufmann (New York: Vintage Books, 1966), §80, p. 81.

4. Julia Kristeva, *Strangers to Ourselves;* trans. Leon S. Roudiez (New York: Columbia University Press, 1991), p.192.

5. Julia Kristeva, "The Novel as Polylogue," in *Desire in Language: A Semiotic Approach to Literature and Art,* ed. Leon Roudiez (New York: Columbia University Press, 1990), p. 165.

6. Julia Kristeva, *Desire in Language.*, preface, p. x.

7. John Lechte, "Art, Love, and Melancholy in the Work of Julia Kristeva," in *Abjection, Melancholia, and Love,: The Work of Julia Kristeva,* ed. John Fletcher and Andrew Benjamin (New York: Routledge, 1990), p. 24.

8. Perry Meisel, "Interview with Julia Kristeva," trans. Margaret Waller, in *Partisan Review* 51, Winter 1984: pp. 131–2. Quoted in Lechte, "Art, Love, and Melancholy," p. 25.

9. Julia Kristeva, *Revolution in Poetic Language* (New York: Columbia University Press, 1984), p. 233.

10. Ibid.

11. Friedrich Nietzsche, *Beyond Good and Evil,* §188, p. 101

12. Rita Nakashima Brock, "On Mirrors, Mists, and Murmurs," in *Weaving the Visions: New Patterns in Feminist Spirituality*, ed. Judith Plaskow and Carol P. Christ (New York: Harper Collins, 1989), p. 239.

13. Julia Kristeva, *Strangers to Ourselves,* p. 182.

14. Ibid, pp. 1–2.

15. Ibid, pp. 2–3.

16. Ibid, p. 13.

17. Ibid, p. 192.

3

Julia Kristeva—Take Two
Jacqueline Rose

In an article published in 1975, Julia Kristeva wrote, "The symbolic order is assured as soon as there are images which secure unfailing belief, for belief is in itself the image: both arise out of the same procedures and through the same terms: *memory, sight and love. . . .*" [emphasis added][1] The article appeared in a special issue of *Communications* on *Psychoanalysis and the Cinema* which marked a type of turning-point within semiotics when psychoanalysis was brought to bear on the cultural analysis of the sign. Cinema was central to that shift because it so clearly rested on the twin axes of identification and fantasy—mechanisms built into the very structure of the apparatus and then merely given their most appropriate and predictable content, bodied forth as it were, in Hollywood's endless sagas of love. Writing on identification, Freud had put love and hypnosis together because of the idealization, subjection, compliance, and sapping of initiative that they are capable of inducing in the subject.[2] In view of which, Julia Kristeva's latest book—*Histoires d'amour* (*Histories of Love* or *Love Stories*)—which takes a cinematic image, that of *ET*, as the truth of a culture suffering a dearth of love and idealization, appears as something of an ironic twist.[3] What has happened? How can we best understand this move? Where has Julia Kristeva been and gone?

This question can only be posed, I believe, historically and psychoanalytically, which means tracing out a conceptual movement and context which, for Kristeva at least, has constantly been informed by psychoanalysis—a movement which then turns back on itself insofar as psychoanalysis provides many of the terms through which it can itself be understood. Kristeva is also a self-diagnostician, and the psychic drive or investment of much of her writing can often be lifted straight out of her texts. "I desire the Law," she writes in a key chapter of this latest book,[4] voicing a panic which—psychoanalysis itself might have anticipated—was bound to be the ultimate effect of that earlier onslaught on the securing identity of the image, which Kristeva and the *Tel Quel* group had

41

castigated throughout the 1970s as little more than bourgeois deceit.

Julia Kristeva's work belongs to that semiotic tradition most closely identified with the work of Roland Barthes, in which the analysis of the structure of language rapidly became a critique of the stabilizing illusion of the sign, and of those forms of writing, in particular the nineteenth-century novel, which were seen to embody and guarantee that illusion for a bourgeois society binding its subjects into the spurious unity of a culture inaccessible to change. The unity of the culture and the psychic unity of subjects went together, with the second as precondition of the first, complementary facades which bound over the psychic and social divisions beneath. Kristeva now argues that this dual emphasis set her apart from the pitfalls of structuralism and of what became for many the predominant strand of "poststructuralism" alike: "For some the important task was to 'deconstruct' phenomenology and structuralism as a minor form of metaphysics unaware of being so. For others, amongst whom I count myself, it was indispensable to give the structure its 'dynamic' by taking into consideration, on the one hand the speaking subject and his or her unconscious experience, and, on the other, the pressures of other social structures."[5]

The point was made by Kristeva in 1974: "Crude grammatology abdicates the subject . . . uninterested in symbolic and social structures, it has nothing to say in the face of their destruction or renewal."[6]

It is worth noting already therefore that the appeal to the unconscious was part of a move to bring back history and social structures into that form of "structuralism and after" which, in direct proportion to its repudiation of metaphysics, was seen by Kristeva as increasingly locked within its terms.

From that original diagnosis, Julia Kristeva then set herself a wager—which she herself has defined as exorbitant[7]—to confront language at the point where it undoes itself, pushing against that illusion of safety through which alone it can function, uncovering the psychic forces which sustain that illusion but which equally put it at risk. From among the *Tel Quel* group with whom she was associated from the late 1960s, Kristeva could be seen as the only writer who took to its limits the engagement between psychoanalysis and semiotics (already in 1969 she was calling her work a "*sémanalyse*"),[8] an engagement which had in many ways seemed to stall at the concepts of "identification," "interpellation" and "the subject's position in language" which had been brought in, via Lacanian psychoanalysis, to buttress Althusser's theory of ideology and the state.

In a move whose force and difficulty can perhaps only be fully understood now, Kristeva chose to drive that engagement with language and the sign into the most violent depths of their own process, where the dangers for psychic coherence, and indeed for the social (Kristeva's previous book

Pouvoirs de l'horreur, could be seen as her book about fascism)[9] made that earlier concept of subjectivity and its illusions look as comforting and facile as the literary forms which had been the object of its critique.

"Site of maximum abjection," the only place where the "savagery" of the speaking being can be heard,[10] psychoanalysis became for Kristeva the means of taking that shift to subjectivity and the unconscious at its word (body and letter) through a clinical engagement with the acquisition, dissolution and pathology of language, all of which had lain beneath the earlier analysis of literary form and style. The more explicitly psychoanalytic project followed directly therefore from the investigation of avant-garde writing. It reflected the need to confront speech in the throes of a pathology otherwise in danger of being restricted to its aesthetic mode. There is also an important historical link between psychoanalysis and the literary avant garde in France through the surrealists. Against a medical institution largely unsympathetic to psychoanalysis which addressed madness "from the place of reason" with a prophylactic aim, the surrealists had tried in the 1920s and 30s to speak of madness "from the place of madness itself."[11]

I. "Only the superego must see the light of day[12]

That such a wager (such a speech) should finally be impossible is in fact given in advance by Kristeva's early writing. Kristeva's work has become best known for the concept of the "semiotic" which she defines as the traces of the subject's difficult passage into the proper order of language (the symbolic or "thetic" instance). It inherits Freud's concept of the primary processes as well as that of the drive—aspects of subjectivity which are only every partially bound into the norms of psychic and sexual life. It then inflects these concepts through Lacan's account of subjectivity which gives language, or representation, central importance as the means through which these norms are vehiculed into place. Disorders of psychic identity and linguistic disorders are tied into each other, a link which is permitted by the psychoanalytic emphasis on the centrality—and fragility—of speech. But if Kristeva concentrates on the signs of that fragility (troubles of phonological, syntactic and enunciating laws), she can only do so in terms of the order of language against which they break. The semiotic can never wholly displace the symbolic since it relies on that very order to give to it its albeit resistant, shape.

In Kristeva's analysis of Mallarmé's poetry, for example, she describes the sound patterns of the language in terms of the basic mechanisms of the drive (explosion, implosion), drawing on Roman Jakobson's famous article "Why Mama and Papa?" which traced the consonant opposition to the primary vocal gestures and needs of the infant.[13] But even if these oppositions can evoke once again these earliest affective processes, they can only do so now by underscoring the phonological patterns which form the ground rules of ordinary speech. They are also immediately caught up in—and cannot operate without—the semantic content which is made explicit by the text, as well as being held in check by a syntax, disrupted but still recognizable, which Mallarmé himself referred to as his "sole guarantee."[14] Kristeva talks of Mallarmé's use of syntax as at once a "super-competence" and a "risk" for the subject.[15] In the section of *La révolution du langage poétique* on "the semiotic apparatus of the text," she concentrates on the shifters (the movement of the first person pronoun across the text), allusions to other texts (the place of the text in a history of writing) and syntax (transformations and their rules) as much as on the phonological patterns of the language which are all to easily assimilated to the idea of a body at play. On this Kristeva is explicit: the body can only ever by *signified*, it is never *produced*. *Après-coup*, rather than regression, this is neither a pure body in process nor a total disintegration of speech.

Furthermore, the extent to which the semiotic is confined to the expression and celebration of its heterogeneity and disruptive charge alone is the index not only of its psychic, but also of its *political* limitations. This is a point which has been overlooked in most commentaries on Kristeva's writing.[16] In *La révolution du langage poétique,* Lautréamont and Mallarmé are chosen by Kristeva because of the sexual and linguistic scandal which they represented for bourgeois moral and literary forms—an excess confined to marginal expression by a repressive culture and state (we can recognize in this analysis the project of the later Russian Formalists—"A Slap in the Face of Public Taste"—to which Kristeva adds a psycho-sexual emphasis).[17] But insofar as these writers fail to move back in the opposite direction and to take up the recognizable social institutions and meanings from which they have been banned, so they fall prey to aestheticism, mysticism, and anarchy. In a later article on dissidence Kristeva will talk of the "*verve anarchist*" of the Paris Commune against "power, institutions and beliefs,"[18] but there has never been a promotion of anarchy as such. For Kristeva, to abdicate symbolic norms—to enact that abdication—opens the way to psychosis: "The way to psychosis—foreclusion of the thetic instance—remains open . . . and this situation translates the ideological limitations of the avant-garde."[19]

For Kristeva, as far back as 1974 therefore, the "logical, thetic, binding, instance" (also called meaning or "*sens*") was the "*sine qua non* of practice."[20] Mallarmé's refusal of politics, Lautréamont's silence on sexual and familiar ideologies, were the direct consequence of a failure to reengage that instance, even though it is the crisis to which they so relentlessly subject it which constitutes the value of their work. The question therefore becomes not how to disrupt language by leaving its recognizable forms completely *behind,* but how to articulate the psychic processes which language normally glosses over *on this side of* meaning or sense. The avant-garde text, like the speech of the psychotic and the neurotic symptom, speaks a truth in a form which is too easily banished.

Despite the apparent dualism of that semiotic/symbolic division, there is therefore no strict demarcation between them. There cannot be if the semiotic is to find articulation and if the symbolic is to feel its effects. The symbolic is not, as has been argued, a rigid, monolithic structure,[21] but unstable and shifting. Kristeva's recognition of this is simply the other side of her acknowledgment that the semiotic has to work through the very order of language it defies. Their relationship is one of a "dynamic." "Complete repression (were such a thing possible) would entail consequences preventing the symbolic function,"[22] It is in fact a tenet of Freudian psychoanalysis that repression can never be absolute. If it were, the very concept of repression could never be thought.

It is worth stressing these points simply because they show how closely Kristeva's concept of social transformation, as early as 1974, already approximated to the idea of the analytic *cure.* Kristeva has often been criticized for inadequately posing her appeal to semiotic heterogeneity in terms of social practice, although this was in fact her own criticism of the avant-garde text. But that criticism, advanced by Kristeva herself, relied in turn on the notion that resistance must finally be articulated in a voice which can be heard, and this necessarily involves, as it does in the analytic setting, a partial reintegration of speech. Paradoxically, the very aspect of the theory which stopped Kristeva's writing from spinning off into the gratuitous celebration of noise is the aspect now criticized for its psychically normative implications; as if "being an analyst" (the opening words of Kristeva's own statement on the back of this latest book), and working toward an at least partial symbolization of the repressed meant, by definition, abdicating any commitment to social change. In the 1970s, Kristeva herself criticized psychoanalysis on exactly these grounds,[23] but a closer look shows that some form of integration was always seen by her as the precondition of any effectivity in the social; it is the concept of what that effectivity should aim for which has altered. This fact suggests to me at least that Kristeva's discarding of Marxism can hardly be laid at the door of her increasing involvement with psychoanalysis. From the very beginning, the psychoanalytic insight and the concept of practice *together* acted as a check on that original critique of the subject as a purely ideological lure. Psychosis—we can be thankful—was never offered as a revolutionary ideal.

The problems raised by Kristeva's challenge to language and identity can perhaps be recognized as another version of a more familiar political question: how to effect a political transformation when the terms of that transformation are given by the very order which a revolutionary practice seeks to change. The presence of "revolution" in the title of that early book was never, it should be stressed, part of a suggestion that psychic or aesthetic disruption could substitute for other forms of politics. But it did aim at this larger issue of the conditions, and limits, of revolutionary change. In 1974, Kristeva located this logical "impasse," or bind, in the Marxist theory of a class whose abolition, along with that of class itself, will emerge out of the same historical conditions which produced it. The proletariat has a privileged consciousness of a social totality tending towards its own elimination, which also means eliminating the very class and consciousness which had grasped its totality as such.[24] It is a concept of self-negation which, in a less quoted but central chapter of *la révolution du langage poétique*, Kristeva then carries over into her discussion of the subject's relation to language and psychic life. In his paper on "Negation," Freud had made the negative instance the precondition of logical thought—the subject expels part of itself in order that it may come to be.[25] This description of loss as the founding moment of subjectivity then forms the basis, via Lacan, of Kristeva's concept of psychic life. But equally important, it already bears the weight of that other question—whose difficulty has become more and more pressing—of a transformation which will finally mean relinquishing the very forms of self-recognition through which it was first desired. The classic opposition between revolution and reform takes on another meaning when what is involved is the subject's very ability to hold itself together in speech.

The problem was perhaps bound to emerge as soon as the question of identity (psychic and sexual) was introduced into the analysis of how a specific social order is upheld. The turn to subjectivity and sexuality had originally been part of a rejection of those forms of economism or traditional Marxist analysis which excluded these questions from politics or else seemed to relegate them to second place. This was central to *Tel Quel's* commitment to Maoist China and the concept of a cultural revolution in the 70s. But insofar as the conception of sexuality was a psychoanalytic one, so it rapidly touched on aspects of subjectivity which cannot be managed even by more progressive institutional and familial forms. Although *Tel Quel* prefaced their Summer 1974 issue with a quotation from Reich on the socially liberating power of sexuality, it was clear from the outset that, unlike

Reich, their idea of sexuality was not that of a quantity to be released but of processes which unsettle the most fundamental self-definition of the subject. No priority, therefore, to "psychic liberation,"[26] first because the psychic was always the *non-sufficient* condition of genuine social transformation, second because it was precisely not "liberation" that was at stake. For that very reason, the psychoanalytic move immediately found itself hedged in on both sides: by an appeal back and away from questions of sexuality to the politics of a purely class opposition which it had been the crucial intention to shift,[27] or else by a call from off the very edge of language. It could be argued—and was argued by Kristeva—that by ignoring language, or not seeing language as an issue, the first of these positions firmly entrenches itself within its laws. Kristeva herself has said over and again that her own aim is to avoid both of these alternatives: no absolutism of the thetic which then gets erected as a theological law, but no denial of the thetic which brings with it the fantasy of "an irrationalism in pieces."[28]

In assessing the changes in Kristeva's work, we need therefore to distinguish a number of different levels.

Firstly, what appears to me as an increasing recognition on Kristeva's part that there can be no direct politicization of the unconscious since this is to confuse political and psychic resistance or, more simply, struggle and symptomatic distress.

Secondly, a discarding on Kristeva's part of revolutionary politics (Marxist and then Maoist), and, since 1977, of any political discourse which totalizes the social, in favor of a highly individualistic conception of dissidence and worth.[29] Kristeva has set the latter against all politics—including feminism—but this does not necessarily follow; the critique of totalities, for example, could be related to recent feminist criticism of the monolithic language and organization of the Left.[30] To this extent, Kristeva's image of feminism as a political movement in these moments is drawn from only one half of the description which she herself gives of it in "Women's Time."[31]

Thirdly, a continuing focus on questions of psycho-sexual identity whose basic insight has not changed: that identity is necessary but only ever partial and therefore carries with it a dual risk—the wreck of all identity, a self-blinding allegiance to psychic norms. To hold onto both sides of this dynamic is, Kristeva argues, almost impossible, although one is in fact always implicated in both. Certainly Kristeva sees psychoanalysis as one of the few places in our culture where this dynamic is fully allowed to speak, at the same time as her work also veers from one side to the other of the divide.

Clearly these are related, but we collapse the levels into each other at a price. To say that the unconscious cannot be politicized does not necessarily entail setting up psychoanalysis as an alternative to all politics. To argue that questions of sexuality are not—in a one-to-one relation—managed or exhausted by traditional political discourse or transformation does not mean that we have to discard these questions from political understanding and debate. The fact that Kristeva now seems to withdraw the analytic insight from the directly political arena does not mean that it was always and necessarily asocial from the start. Nor can psychoanalysis be seen in a simple way, as the sole cause and determining factor in the political shift. Kristeva's abandonment of that earlier concept of revolution can also be related to changes—some of which have been welcomed by feminism—in the field of politics itself. It would be possible to argue, for example, that some form of political pluralism, case for local initiatives, and multiple political strategies, follows more logically from the rejection of revolutionary Marxism which, for *Tel Quel* and their subsequent journal *Infini,* has been accompanied by an unmistakable shift to the right. It was, after all, feminism which first argued that subjectivity (the "personal") was a political stake. Kristeva's move can in fact be turned back on itself, since she herself has never discarded the attempt to understand the different and changing forms of social articulation through which identities are moved in—and out of—place.

II "A freudful mistake"[32]

I do not think we should be surprised, therefore, nor too comfortably critical or dismissive, when Kristeva proceeds to fall, at various points throughout her work, into one or other side of the psychic dynamic which she herself describes. The latest book, with its appeal to the "father of individual pre-history," can certainly be seen, as I have already suggested, as a race back into the arms of the law. But Kristeva's own work, and response to Kristeva, have equally been marked by the opposite impulse, notably around the concept of the semiotic which has acquired something of an existence of its own, outside the realm of meaning without which, strictly, it does not make sense. The attraction of the theory was always that it pointed to aspects of language which escaped the straitjacket of symbolic norms. But this has also made the theory vulnerable to some very archaic notions of the content of the repressed. Variously, and at times conjointly, Kristeva has attributed to the semiotic: femininity, color, music, body, and affect—concepts whose oppressive lyricism has at times been welcomed by feminism but which feminism has also been the quickest to reject. It is also through these concepts that Kristeva takes her leave of Lacan. The concept of "affect," for example, comes through André

Green, a member of the *Association Psychanalytique de France* founded when its members split with Lacan in 1964 (Kristeva trained as an analyst with this school). Published in 1973, one year before *La révolution du langage poétique*, Green's book *Le discours vivant* developed the concept of affect in Freud as part of a critique of Lacan's central premise that psychic life is ruled by the exigencies of representation and the linguistic sign.[33] In an article published in the journal of the *Association* in 1979, Kristeva reiterated Greens' critique of Lacan—that Lacan's concept of language assimilates into itself and absorbs "what the dualism of Freudian thought holds to be strangely irreducible: drive, affect"—although she immediately qualifies: "Is there any need to recall that the position which takes the semiotic as heterogeneous does not arise from a concern to integrate some alleged concreteness, brute corporality, or energy-in-itself into a language suspected of being too abstract. . . . This semiotic is without primacy and has no place as origin."[34]

There is no doubt, however, that the push here is against language itself, even though Kristeva herself is again the best analyst of the dangers this might imply. In an interview in 1977 on the United States, Kristeva praised the "non-verbal" aspects of modern American culture which draw more "radically and profoundly than in Europe" on the realms of "gesture, colour and sound," but then she asked whether than same nonverbalization might not also be the sign of a resistance, the almost psychotic hyperactivity of a violent and overproductive culture incessantly on the go.[35] Even if we do not accept the representation of American culture, Kristeva's own check on the celebration of a place beyond language is worthy of note.

It is, however, almost impossible not to assign the status of origin to the semiotic once it is defined as beyond language in this way. Elsewhere Kristeva defines heterogeneity as the "archaisms of the semiotic body," "logically and chronologically prior to the institution of the symbolic," "genetically detected in the first echolalias of infants." And it is this concept of priority which lies behind Kristeva's psychoanalytic interest in the acquisition of language and in object relations theory which concentrates on the interaction between the mother and child. But the emphasis on this relationship immediately produces a split between the order of the mother and of the father, giving to the first the privilege of the semiotic and separating it out from the culture in which it is inscribed. Juliet Mitchell has discussed how in the 1920s and 30s attention was focused on this relationship because it was felt to hold the key to the pre-Oedipal sexuality of the female child. She also argues that the effect of this was to close off the question of sexual difference—of the symbolically produced and only ever partial division between men and women, masculinity and femininity, a division which this theory takes for granted and thus helps to reproduce.[36] Lacan's emphasis on the symbolic was first of all developed against this tendency. It represented an attempt to return to the larger questions of cultural determination figured in Freud's myth of the beginnings of culture in *Totem and Taboo*.[37] In Kristeva's case, the attention to the mother does not ignore these wider issues but becomes part of a more general question about the place of the mother-child relation in the constitution of cultural taboos (see below). But as soon as Kristeva gives to this relation the status of origin—psychic or cultural, or both—it is handed over to the realm of the senses, outside of all history and form. Kristeva uses this quotation from Freud to support the identification of the semiotic with an essentially maternal domain: "It [an advance in intellectuality] consists, for instance, in deciding that paternity is more important than maternity, although it cannot, like the latter, be established by the evidence of the senses."[38]

For Kristeva, this relinquishing of the maternal is loss, as much as advance, and it is never complete, but this does not alter the fully ideological division between maternal and paternal, senses and ideation, which it serves to reinforce.

But the problematic nature of this tendency in Kristeva's thought is perhaps best illustrated by the very term of the semiotic itself, which Kristeva calls *chora* or receptacle after Plato's cosmology (*The Timaeus*), where it stands for the mediating instance in which the copies of the eternal model receive their shape. Plato himself describes the *chora* as maternal, and from the beginning Kristeva based the link to Freud on: "this rhythmic space without thesis or position, the process where *signifiance* comes to be, Plato indicates as much when he designates this receptacle nursing, maternal."[39] But if Plato did so, it was because the mother was seen as playing no part in the act of procreation, a receptacle or empty vessel *merely* for the gestation of the unborn child.[40]

III "I hate Maria and when I see her portrait I go down on my knees"[41]

It seems to me now that the concept of the semiotic, especially in those formulations which identify it with the mother and place it beyond language, is the least useful aspect of Kristeva's work, even though it is the concept for which she is best known. For what happens to this maternally connoted and primitive semiotic is that it is first defined as the hidden underside of culture (we can recognize the proximity of this to the classical demonic image of femininity) and then idealized as something whose value and exuberance the culture cannot manage and has therefore had to repress (a simple reverse of that first image which makes femininity the ideal excluded instance of all culture).

Kristeva herself charts these dramatic reversals from idealization of the woman to degradation and back again throughout her discussion of the writings of Mallarmé and Céline. But she does so by analyzing them as *fantasies* whose violent oscillations, especially in the case of Céline, bring greater and greater violence in their train. Furthermore, as Kristeva has constantly insisted, idealization of the semiotic in itself involves a denial or coverup of the psychic pain and violence which in fact characterizes the early interaction between the mother and child. This is why Kristeva is able at one and the same time to lay out the horrors of the fantasmatic structure which underpins the writings of an author like Céline, while at the same time praising that writing for exposing a psychic drama which—with massive social repercussions—is constantly denied, projected onto the other, and then played out by the culture at large.[42] Céline's writing is a *symptom*. It reveals *horror* as a matter of *power*—the power of fascination when we are confronted with the traces of our own psychic violence, the horror when that same violence calls on social institutions for legitimation, and receives it.

In *Pouvoirs de l'horreur,* Kristeva takes up the question with which she ended *La révolution du langage poétique*: "How can negativity, or the reject be articulated in the social?"[43] returning to a mostly forgotten emphasis of that earlier book—the negativity or reject, horror or abjection as she now calls it, which characterizes the semiotic realm. She then charts the way that different religious cultures have drawn up the boundaries (soiling, abomination, sin) of what they can—bodily—contain. It is another version of the problem which has run right through her writing—of what can be articulated on this side of culture without breaking its limits—only the account of what needs to be spoken has got considerably worse.

Kristeva could also be seen here as feeding back the issue of pre-Oedipal sexuality into the theorization of cultural origins which Freud—following his changed account of femininity—had himself failed to do. She makes the point that discussions of the incest taboo have concentrated on the place of the father together with the forms of disorder (obsessional neurosis and paranoia) associated with his prohibitory role, leaving the mother precisely as the idealized relic of what comes to be forbidden, a kind of lost territory which says nothing of the psychic ambivalence of that early relation, nor of the disorders (psychosis and phobia) with which it can be clinically linked. Kristeva's increasing interest in those analysts who concentrate on the most difficult aspects of that early relation (Rosenfeld, Bion) stems from this critique. If this is object-relations theory, therefore, it is with a difference, since there is no concept of "adequacy" at stake. Rather it seems that, in response to an idealization latent in her own formulations, Kristeva was replying that the semiotic is no "fun."

For what does it mean, we can ask, to place the mother at the source and fading-point of all subjectivity and language—a point which, as Kristeva herself has argued, threatens the subject with collapse? Surely this is already the effect of an idealization which barely conceals the reproach, felt threat, and feared loss of identity fermenting underneath?

As soon as Kristeva asks this question, then the whole of her work seems to turn on itself, implicating her own concepts in the fantasies, ambivalence and projections which she describes. Kristeva had criticized Mallarmé for the way that he targets, or fixates onto the woman the disruptions of language played out in his writing, making the woman the bearer of their eternal secret, mystifying them and thus depriving them of what might otherwise be their more unsettling social effects.[44] And in *Pouvoirs de l'horreur,* she describes the way in which Céline fantasizes his own mortality as feminine and projects it onto the woman who then appears as a persecutor, for the life she not only gives, but denies. Much of this book is about the way in which the limits of language and its dissolution are constantly thought in terms of sexual difference, the way that cultures define and secure their parameters by relegating the woman to their outer edge.

Yet, in a twist which gives back to these same fantasies the weight of a primordial truth, Kristeva asks whether they may not find their basis in a femininity whose overpowerful and physical reality effectively places cultures at risk. Is the repudiation of this power of the mother ("maleficent in its power to give mortal life") indeed the precondition of symbolic identity on which all cultures rest? Is this same power *"historic or fantasmatic,"* *"attributed"* to the woman, or is the early relation to the mother its *"unconscious base?"*[45] Kristeva says that her question is not about primacy or cause and effect, although at one point she does describe the taboo on the mother as the "primary mytheme" of all culture,[46] which seems to give the psychic a primacy and brings her uncomfortably close to the form of argument advanced against Malinowski in the 1920s and 30s by Ernest Jones. In fact Kristeva oscillates, but in the process she has turned a much older debate about the relationship between psychic and social determination in the production of social forms into a query about the origins and persistence (not least of all in her own writing) of some of the most disturbing images of femininity in our culture.

Kristeva's work splits on a paradox, or rather a dilemma: the hideous moment when a theory arms itself with a concept of femininity as different, a something other to the culture as it is known, only to find itself face to face with, or even entrenched within, the most grotesque and fully cultural stereotypes of femininity itself. Unlike some of her most virulent detractors,[47] however, Kristeva at least knows that these images are not so easily dispatched. It is not by settling the question of their origins that we can necessarily dismantle their force.

IV Feminism and its fantasies

Kristeva's relationship to these highly charged and ambivalent images, and the way that she works at the limits of psychic identity, explains, I think, the strength but also the tension of her writing for feminism. Kristeva has never fully identified with feminism and it has never been the place from which she has chosen to speak, although she does describe her place as a woman as central to her overall project: "It was necessary perhaps to be a woman to attempt to take up that exorbitant wager of carrying the rational project to the outer borders of the signifying ventures of men."[48]

Kristeva has, however, been attractive to feminism because of the way that she exposes the complacent identities of psycho-sexual life. But as soon as we try to draw out of that exposure an image of femininity which escapes the straitjacket of symbolic forms, we fall straight into that essentialism and primacy of the semiotic which is one of the most problematic aspects of her work. And as soon as we try to make of it the basis for a political identity, we turn the concept inside out, since it was as a critique of identity itself that it was originally advanced. No politics without identity, but no identity which takes itself at its word. The tension is captured in the title of one of Kristeva's best known articles—"D'une identité, l'autre"—which has been translated as "From One Identity to Another," but which is also aimed at the opposite: "identity and its other"—that is, the other of identity itself.[49] This is why Kristeva has increasingly distanced herself from a feminism which she has described as "too existentialist"[50] (this relates specifically to psychoanalysis and echoes Juliet Mitchell's 1974 critique of feminist rejections of Freud[51]), and which she sees—wrongly as far as I am concerned—as a monolithic entity which, in its claim for identity and power (identity as power), repeats and reinforces the rigidity of the culture which produced it.[52]

At its most simple, therefore, the question becomes "What could it mean to construct a political identity out of processes heralded as the flight of identity itself?" Especially given that recognition of the aberrant nature of those processes was, in a sense, the price we paid for moving out of a psychic functionalism that had underlain the earlier accounts of the subject's ideological place.

At the same time, Kristeva gives to women the privilege of the central dilemma caught by her writing: how to challenge the very form of available self-definition without losing the possibility of speech. Against the offered and familiar alternatives of bureaucracy and madness, it is women, for Kristeva, who know the necessity of, and demand, a place on the historical stage, while also calling the bluff of a psychic and sexual order of things which they pass through and across: "*traverser*," a word central to Kristeva's writing, implies that you go *through* certainly, but also *out*.[53]

Of these two directions—toward identity and its other side—Kristeva calls the second "negativity," which recalls the negativity of the semiotic and underlines the psychic difficulty at stake. It can be summarized as a refusal: "Ce n'est jamais ça"—"No, it's not that" or "That won't do" which, taken together with the translation "Woman Can Never Be Defined," make the woman the subject as well as the object of the statement.[54] The other side of this negativity Kristeva calls the ethics of femininity, or women's commitment to an ethics which saves them, as she puts it, from a "Nietzschean rage."[55] Criticized recently for linking this to women's experience of motherhood,[56] Kristeva is nonetheless echoing a longstanding feminist demand that this aspect of femininity should be allowed a voice in constructing the priorities of the political domain. And while this may seem to come close to a history of oppressive discourses which have given to women as mothers the privilege of the ethical (and not a great deal else), for Kristeva *ethics* has nothing whatsoever to do with *duty* or the idea that women should people the race. No ethics *without* maternity, but not mothering as ethical *duty* or *role*: "The ethical which aims for a negativity is opposed to ethics understood as the observation of laws.[57] Ethics plus (as) negativity describes a subjective position which avoids conformity (the first without the second) and esoterism or marginality (the second without the first), capturing alternatives which have historically presented themselves to feminism: between an equality which risks absorption into the law, and an absolute difference which can only defy it.

But perhaps even more difficult in relation to feminism, and less commented on, is this issue of the negative aspects that Kristeva identifies in the semiotic which feminism has at times been tempted to claim as its own special realm. Difficult precisely because Kristeva has not stopped at the positive aspects of this process but has gone over to the other side, dredging up archaic images of the mother which, for all their status as fantasy (because of their status as fantasy), are not without their effects. If we stop at the critique of identity—the celebration of a heterogeneity which it is too easy politically to rebuff—we avoid this more troubling area which consists of the psychic ambivalence of the drives. But if we follow this through, then we find ourselves having to relinquish an idealized vision of the lost maternal continent which we have often and so fiercely wished to protect: "Death explodes inside the peace we thought to have absorbed (nirvana, intoxication, silence)."[58] But once that has been said, it becomes impossible to avoid talking about fantasy, not just by men of women, but also among women, and even within feminism itself: "to extol a centripetal, becalmed and softened feminine sexuality, only to exhume most recently, under the cover of idylls amongst women, the sado-masochistic ravages beneath."[59]

A question, or image, of feminine paranoia? In what appears to me as one of the most powerful moments of self-diagnosis in her text, Kristeva certainly says so[60] (the structure of paranoia was already there in the article I started with on the hallucinatory power of film). But since Freud at least, we have ceased to use diagnosis as a cause for dismissal, still less as a category of abuse. Rather it is the moment when Kristeva recasts *for* women the problem of identity to which she has constantly returned. For what could be a simple love between women, since identity is always in opposition *to*? And yet what could be a place without identity, other than a falling into the realm of the unnameable, body without language, a realm to which women have often and so oppressively been confined? Even between women (that mother-daughter relationship of which politically we have asked so much), the act of differentiation-recognition of the other leads—if not to violence—then at least, and of necessity, to psychic pain.

V "The King Is With the Body"[61]

This latest book (*Histoires d'amour*) is therefore no idyll since "hatred . . . underpins, carries, determines" the identity it now pleads for and the love whose history it describes.[62] "Narcissus in troubled water"—one of the chapter headings of the previous book—is there to caution us against a return to identity, narcissism, and idealization which, at first glance, bears all the signs of a retreat. Kristeva now outlines the precondition for a psychic identity which neither the abjection of the mother nor the punishing imago of the Oedipal father can ground, repair, or sustain. She finds this precondition in a primary identification with a non-Oedipal "father of individual pre-history": "pre-history" because, it seems, Kristeva is still searching for an ideal and prior psychic instance now lost on the side of the mother (too abject for words), "non-Oedipal" because she still wants to save this idealization from the tyranny of the symbolic in which ideals are shaped.

Yet again, we can ask what separation (or splitting) this is. For although Freud does refer to the child's early identification with such a pre-Oedipal father, there is ambivalence (abjection?) in this identification *from the very first,* and in a key passage from *Group Psychology and the Analysis of the Ego* to which Kristeva refers, he describes this identification as a derivative of the oral drive which assimilates and annihilates its object.[63] Kristeva calls this identification the advent of the psychic and a deferring of the oral drive, but she has been asked whether this imaginary father and the phallic mother might not be one and the same thing.[64] In fact Kristeva's concept seems at times to come close to Maud Mannoni's attempt to ground psychic identity in the paternal genealogy of the child.[65] It is worth noting, however, that it is only those moments in Kristeva's own writing where she too rigidly demarcates identity and drive, symbolic and semiotic, conscious and unconscious, and distributes them between the realms of the father and the mother, that allows for this paternal return.

It is nonetheless a striking move from Kristeva's early assertion that paternal power will symbolically flourish wherever the question of sexuality is not specifically and critically posed.[66] It was an assertion that echoed the belief within feminism that the key to women's subordination lay in the symbolic enshrinement and perpetuation of patriarchal law. For even if we now recognize that women's subordination cannot be made so easily or so fast,[67] the analysis holds surely still as a castigation of the values in which a culture embodies its own worth. At the same time it must be said, however, that once the precise connections between symbol and concrete power have been questioned or opened up for debate, then we cannot say what political effects will follow from a recognition of the father and his place in the psychic life of the child.

Nor is it a simple idealization which is being promoted here, the idea of a paternally grounded identity which simply receives and comforts the subject. Kristeva criticizes interpretations of Judaic writing which uncover the latent violence of its rhetoric and celebrate part object without identity, or letter without the law, but she nonetheless knows that the risk awaiting those who obey the law of the father is the paranoia of the chosen.[68]

As I understand it, what is most clearly at stake is a psychic necessity: at its most simple, the confrontation of the therapist with the pain of a fragmentation without identity or place. For even the one who plays with language through writing has of course come through to the other side: "The writer: a phobic who succeeds at metaphor so as not to die of fear but to resuscitate through signs."[69]

I do not think that Kristeva should be criticized therefore for her commitment to the concept of psychic identity, nor for her increasingly analytically informed aim to understand the processes through which it is produced—a commitment that does not have to imply a collusion with the way identity is paraded in the culture at large. Since, far from this involving a denial of the other psychic forces which have been at the center of her writing, it could be seen as the only place from which they can be known. This recognition was there from the outset and, as I have tried to argue, it was this, paradoxically, which saved Kristeva's writing from the anarchy of its own terms. Nor do I think that Kristeva should be dismissed for her analysis of love as a strategy which allows individual subjects to negotiate the troubled psychic waters which she herself so graphically describes. To which we could add that this love does not have to be incompatible with politics. Did not Kristeva herself say that without love of women there was no point in going to China in 1974?[70]

In this latest book, Kristeva pleads for love in response to what she sees as a dearth of idealization in our culture (shades of Christopher Lasch?), a dearth which is precipitating an abolition of psychic space which gives nothing but abjection the reign. "I plead for the Imaginary as antidote to the crisis."[71] But then, as is so often the case, Kristeva provides the self-diagnosis: "doubtless a Cartesian deformation to dream of such a pre-Cartesian subject in love," the critique: "only for mirrors infatuated with stable images do crises exist," and the caution: "we lack today an amatory code, but it would be an imposture to propose new ones."[72]

Finally, one can also point to the overall consistency of Kristeva's project in which this latest book has its place. In 1983 Kristeva argued, against an easy misreading of the title of *Tel Quel*'s new journal *Infini*, that for her at least it does not represent the return of a "religious psychology or ideology" but rather the "never abandoned effort to take transcendence seriously and to track down its premises into the most hidden recesses of language. My prejudice is that of believing that God is analyzable. Infinitely.[73]

For me Kristeva's work remains important because of the way it is poised on that interface of politics/psychoanalysis/feminism. In response to the demand for an attention to sexuality, some forms of Marxism will argue for a return to the politics of class. In response to the questions of psychic identity raised by sexuality, feminism seems at moments to come close to dropping the psychoanalytic understanding of sexuality itself, or at least Julia Kristeva who, it should also be said, has too long served as an ideal. But sexuality—the crucial ways it determines and structures our lives—cannot be understood without acknowledging the importance of fantasy, and fantasy in turn reveals aspects of subjectivity which crush the splendor of our (conscious) dreams.

Kristeva's reversals from celebration of the semiotic to abjection and back to a (now paternal) ideal reveal the instability of fantasy itself. They also underscore the problem which arises when political discourse turned on the category of identity and its illusions and accused it of upholding or of being the precondition of all other social norms—recognizing in that moment that if sexuality was so intractable, it is because it strikes at the heart of identity itself. And having once gained that insight, we cannot just drop the question of identity and its impasses from the debate.

Kristeva was not the first to bring these issues onto the political stage. They are already there in the confrontation with violence, in the debates about the limits of censorship, about sado-masochism, pornography and the law. Kristeva writes across ("*traverser*") these problems and has pushed them to (her own) breaking point. Her work gives us the measure of the difficulties when politics tries to open itself up to the ravages of the unconscious mind.

Notes

This essay was first presented as a paper at the "Feminism/Theory/Politics" Conference held at the Pembroke Center for Teaching and Research on Women, Brown University, in March 1985; it will also be published in the papers of the Conference. It was written in part as a response to Ann Rosalind Jones, "The Politics of Interpretations." *Critical Inquiry* 9(1), (September 1982): pp. 259–78.

1. Julia Kristeva, "Ellipse sur la frayeur et la séduction spéculaire," *Communications,* special issue *Psychoanalyse et Cinéma,* 23, 1975, p. 77. (Trans. Dolores Burdick, "Ellipsis on Terror and The Specular Seduction," *Wide Angle* 3:2, 1979.)

2. Sigmund Freud, *Group Psychology and the Analysis of the Ego* (1921), SE 18, pp. 111–16; PF 12, pp. 141–47.

3. Julia Kristeva, *Histoires d'amour* (Paris: Collection "Infini," 1983).

4. Julia Kristeva, "Stabat Mater" in *Histoires d'amour,* p. 237; this chapter first appeared as "Héréthique d'amour," *Tel Quel* 77, Winter 1974. (Trans. in *The Kristeva Reader*).

5. Julia Kristeva, "Mémoires," *Infini* 1, 1983: p. 44.

6. Julia Kristeva, *La révolution du langage poétique,* p. 130.

7. Julia Kristeva, *Desire in Language,* ed. Leon S. Roudiez, tr. Thomas Gora, Alice Jardine and L. Roudiez (Oxford, 1984), preface, p. x.

8. Julia Kristeva, *Semeiotikè: Recherches pour une sémanalyse.* (Paris, 1969).

9. Julia Kristeva, *Pouvoirs de l'horreur: essai sur l'abjection,* (Paris, 1980). *Powers of Horror,* trans. Leon Roudiez (New York: Columbia University Press, 1982).

10. Julia Kristeva, "Mémoires," pp. 45, 53.

11. Elisabeth Roudinesco, "Histoire de la psychanalyse en France," *Infini* 2, 1983: p. 66.

12. Julia Kristeva, *La révolution du langage poétique*, p. 477.

13. Roman Jakobson, :Why Mama and Papa?" *Studies on Child Language and Aphasia*, (1959), (Hague, 1971).

14. Cit. in *La révolution du langage poétique*, p. 29.

15. Ibid., p. 270.

16. See, for example, Terry Eagleton, *Literary Theory*, pp. 190–91.

17. First manifesto of the Cubo-futurists issued in 1912 and signed by Mayakovsky, Burlyuk, Khlebnikov and Kruchyonykh.

18. Julia Kristeva, "Un nouveau type d'intellectuel: le dissident," *Tel Quel* 74, Winter 1977: p. 4. (Trans. "A New Type of Intellectual: The Dissident" in *the Kristeva Reader*).

19. Julia Kristeva, *La révolution du langage poétique*, p. 169.

20. Ibid., p. 616.

21. Ann Rosalind Jones, "The Politics of Interpretations." *Critical Inquiry* 9(1), September 1982: p. 68.

22. Julia Kristeva, *La révolution du langage poétique*, p. 48.

23. Ibid., p. 493 and Julia Kristeva, "Sujet dans le langage et pratique politique," *Tel Quel* 58, Summer 1974: p. 27.

24. Julia Kristeva, *La révolution du langage poétique*, pp. 386–87.

25. Sigmund Freud, "Negation" (1925), SE 19; PF 11.

26. Ann Rosalind Jones, "The Politics of Interpretations," p. 61.

27. One of the clearest examples of this tendency is the article by Peter Dews, "The *Nouvelle Philosophie* and Foucault," *Economy and Society* 8: 2, May 1979.

28. Julia Kristeva, *La révolution du langage poétique*, p. 80.

29. Julia Kristeva, "La littérature dissidente comme refutation du discours de gauche," *Tel Quel* 76, Summer 1978 and "*Histoires d'amour*—Love Stories," in *Desire*, ed. Lisa Appignansi (London: Institute of Contemporary Arts Documents, 1983).

30. Sheila Rowbotham *et al.*, *Beyond the Fragments*.

31. Julia Kristeva, "Le temps des femmes," *34/44: Cahiers de recherche de science de textes et documents* 5, Winter 1979. (Trans. Alice Jardine and Harry Blake, "Women's Time," in N.O. Keohane *et al.*, *Feminist Theory: A Critique of Ideology*, (Chicago, 1981), (Brighton, 1982); also in *The Kristeva Reader*).

32. Joyce, cit. in *La révolution du langage poétique*, p. 504.

33. André Green, *Le discours vivant*, op. cit.

34. Julia Kristeva, "Il n'y a pas de maître à langage," *Nouvelle Revue de Psychanalyse. Regards sur la psychanalyse en France*, 20, Autumn 1979: pp. 130–31.

35. Julia Kristeva, with Philippe Sollers and Marcelin Pleynet, "Pourquoi les Etats Unis?" *Tel Quel* 71–73, Autumn 1979: p. 4, 19 (tr. "The US Now: A Conversation," *October* 6, Fall 1978; also in *The Kristeva Reader*).

36. Juliet Mitchell, "Introduction I," *Feminine Sexuality*, pp. 19–20.

37. Sigmund Freud, *Totem and Taboo* (1913), SE 13; PF 12.

38. Sigmund Freud, *Moses and Monotheism* (1938–39), SE 23, p. 118; PF 13, p. 365, cit. in *La révolution du langage poétique*, p. 445n.

39. Ibid., pp. 24–25, p. 579n.

40. Francis MacDonald Cornford, *Plato's Cosmology, The Timaeus,* trans. and with a running commentary (London and New York, 1937), p. 187.

41. Stephane Mallarmé, Lettre à Cazalis, *Correspondance,* 1, p. 77, cit. in *La révolution du langage poétique*, p. 453.

42. Julia Kristeva, *Powers of Horror.*

43. Julia Kristeva, *La révolution du langage poétique*, p. 545.

44. Ibid., pp. 468, 474.

45. Julia Kristeva, *Powers of Horror*, pp. 158, 91, 100, 106 (translations modified).

46. Ibid., p. 106.

47. Jennifer Stone, "The Horrors of Power: A Critique of Julia Kristeva," *The Politics of Theory,* Proceedings of the Essex Conference in the Sociology of Literature, July 1982, Colchester 1983; Peter Gidal, "On Julia Kristeva," *Undercut* (Journal of the London Filmmakers Cooperative) 12, 1984.

48. Julia Kristeva, *Desire in Language,* preface, p. x.

49. Julia Kristeva, "D'une identité, l'autre," *Tel Quel* 62, Summer 1975 (trans. "From One Identity to Another," *Desire in Language*).

50. Julia Kristeva, *Histoires d'amour,* p. 242.

51. Juliet Mitchell, *Psychoanalysis and Feminism,* op. cit.

52. Julia Kristeva, "Sujet dans le langage et pratique politique," p. 26; "La femme, ce n'est jamais ça." *Tel Quel* 59, Autumn 1974: p. 24. (Trans. Marilyn August, "Woman Can Never Be Defined," *New French Feminisms,* ed. Elaine Marks and Isabelle de Courtivron, (Brighton 1981), p. 141.) *Powers of Horror,* p. 208.

53. Julia Kristeva, "Polylogue," *Tel Quel* 57, Spring 1974. Trans. in *Desire in language,* p. 164, as "experience."

54. Julia Kristeva, "Woman Can Never Be Defined."

55. Ibid., p. 138 (tr. modified).

56. Ann Rosalind Jones, "The Politics of Interpretations," p. 62.

57. Julia Kristeva, *La révolution du langage poétique*, p. 102.

58. Julia Kristeva, *Histoires d'amour,* p. 81.

59. Ibid., p. 349.

60. Ibid., pp. 242–44.

61. Shakespeare, *Hamlet,* IV, ii, 26.

62. Julia Kristeva, *Histoires d'amour,* p. 121.

63. Sigmund Freud, *The Ego and the Id,* pp. 31–2; pp. 370–1; *Group Psychology and the Analysis of the Ego,* p. 195; pp. 134–5; *Histoires d'amour,* pp. 31–2.

64. Louise Burchill. "The Last Word of This Adventure: Interview with Julia Kristeva," *On the Beach* 1984: p. 26.

65. Maud Mannoni, *L'Enfant,* sa "maladie" et les autres, op. cit.

66. Julia Kristeva, *La révolution du langage poétique,* p. 452.

67. Rosalind Coward, *Patriarchal Precedents,* London 1982.

68. Julia Kristeva, *Histoires d'amour,* p. 69.

69. Julia Kristeva, *Powers of Horror,* p. 38 (trans. modified).

70. Julia Kristeva, "Woman Can Never Be Defined," p. 139.

71. Julia Kristeva, *Histoires d'amour,* p. 354.

72. Ibid., pp. 168, 348; Julia Kristeva, "Histoires d'amour—Love Stories," p. 21.

73. Julia Kristeva, "Mémoires," pp. 46–7.

4

Kristeva and Levinas:
Mourning, Ethics, and the Feminine

Ewa Ziarek

"If the status of the phallus is to be challenged, it cannot . . . be
directly from the feminine body but must be by means of a different
symbolic term . . . or else by an entirely different logic altogether"
Jacqueline Rose

"Positing the existence of that other language and even of an other
of language, indeed of an outside-of-language, is not necessarily setting up a preserve for metaphysics or theology"
Julia Kristeva

There are two sets of questions that prompt my preliminary exploration
of the encounter between Kristeva's and Levinas's work. The first one
refers to the possibility of feminist ethics: What would constitute such
ethics and what would it mean in the context of post-structuralism? How
would this ethics intersect with feminist politics? Such conjunction of ethics
and politics orients us toward a signification of female alterity and to the
analysis of violence inherent in thematization of that alterity. The other set
of questions concerns the issue of essentialism that seems to reappear on
the horizon of numerous feminist debates, especially whenever an inquiry
into the specificity of female sexuality is undertaken. In the wake of Lacanian psychoanalysis, attempts to rewrite the symbolic order, to change the
signification of sexual difference, and to retrieve the specificity of female
sexuality from phallic domination seem to risk essentialism (if only strategically), that is, a search for female sexuality outside language and culture.[1]
By juxtaposing Kristeva with Levinas, this paper hopes to articulate female
specificity in ethical terms, to look for ways of thinking female alterity
without essentialism. Although both issues—essentialism and alterity—

orient us toward a certain outside, or a beyond, with respect to the signifying system, they ultimately speak about different locations of exteriority
and give rise to two different kinds of logic. Essentialism posits a true
identity outside a repressive phallocentric system and seeks its eventual
recovery through an undistorted representation. The emphasis on alterity,
however, indicates an outside only as an excess which should not be recuperated within representation. According to Levinas, such desire to represent the other is itself an act of violence rather than recovery.

These two positions become confused with each other—and particularly in the context of Kristeva's work's reception—because a theoretical
framework for thinking about alterity is not always immediately apparent.[2]
In order to draw the ethical and political consequences of Kristeva's
thought, for instance, we need a more radical way of approaching alterity than Lacanian psychoanalysis allows us to do. The problem with Lacan
is not simply that female otherness is always subordinated to the mediation of a third term (in Lacan's language it is the phallus, the paternal
signifier) but that the meaning of the subject and the other is derived from
the symbolic order and, therefore, on the level of the system, if not on the
level of the subject, alterity is reabsorbed within the same. In other words
it is not only the maleness of the phallic signifier that is troubling but,
perhaps even more, its purported neutrality: in either case the signification
of the other issues from and is subordinated to a linguistic structuration.[3]

A more radical approach to alterity emerges from Levinas's ethics. What
interests me in Levinas's philosophy is precisely his attempt to delineate a
signification of the other without, or beyond, the mediation of a third
term, that is, without subordinating alterity to a conceptual or linguistic system. This effort is linked to his redefinition of desire beyond the notion of
a lack or loss. Although I claim that Levinasian philosophy can be very productive for feminist ethics, at the same time I raise questions about the role
of femininity in his own texts. In fact, by comparing psychoanalysis with
the Levinasian ethics, we can see the obverse sides of the same problem:
if psychoanalysis starts with the priority of sexual difference but has considerable difficulties with maintaining female alterity, Levinas asserts the
primacy of the ethical encounter with the other but is then unable to articulate sexual difference in terms of this encounter. By pitting these two discourses against each other, I hope to achieve a solicitation of a figure particularly resistant to thought: the alterity of the maternal body. And such
solicitation inevitably raises a question about the political implications of
the feminist revisions of ethics.

My argument proceeds in three parts: The first one elaborates Levinas's
and Kristeva's ways of approaching alterity beyond essentialism; the sec-

ond part, drawing on Kristeva's discussion of mourning, shows certain limitations of Levinas's ethics in the context of sexual difference and demonstrates why a feminist ethics may encounter difficulties in his thought; the third part returns once again to Levinas's notion of the other in order to reread a signification of maternal alterity in Kristeva's discussion of melancholia. The purpose of this essay is not an assimilation of Kristeva's and Levinas's concerns into a common theoretical framework, but rather a displacement of both positions in order to create a discursive space where the thought of female alterity would be possible.

I.

"It is not I who resist the system . . . it is the other."
Emmanuel Levinas

The fundamental effort of Levinas's thought is to initiate an ethical encounter with the other without reducing it to the order of consciousness or to the totality of a linguistic or philosophical system. The originality of the Levinasian ethics does not lie in a new categorization of alterity, but rather in its obstinate refusal to think the other. Such refusal to think the other does not amount to, however, a renunciation of philosophy; it does not collapse thinking into skepticism or essentialism. Rather, it posits ethics as a critique of ontology—a calling into question of the will to knowledge, in particular the phenomenological model of knowledge, "where thought remains an adequation with the object."[4] Levinas claims that by annulling the difference between the known and the knowing, the activity of thought both grasps and constitutes alterity on its own terms: "It is a hold on being which equals a constitution of that being."[5] "The immanence of the known to the act of knowing is already the embodiment of seizure."[6] Nothing remains exterior or resistant to the appropriating activity of thought. In representing the other to itself, the philosophical consciousness merely closes the circle of its own identification. In thinking its other, the I, like Ulysses, returns to itself.

In opposition to the myth of Ulysses returning home, Levinas proposes an encounter with alterity as an Abrahamic movement without return: "*A work conceived radically is a movement of the same unto the other which never returns to the same.* To the myth of Ulysses returning to Ithaca, we wish to oppose the story of Abraham who leaves his fatherland forever for a yet unknown land."[7] The ethical encounter with the Other, conceived as an Abrahamic movement without return, interrupts the identification of consciousness with itself. By creating an "irremissible disturbance" in the order

of thought, the other dislocates the position of the subject; it puts the subject—to use Kristeva's term—on trial: "The relationship with another puts
me into question, empties me of myself."[8] In the face-to-face relation with
the other, consciousness no longer coincides with itself, no longer returns
to its point of departure.[9]

In order to prevent an assimilation of alterity to the order of representation, thought, or language understood as a totality of signs, Levinas
insists on the exteriority of otherness, which disrupts, or withdraws from,
the mediation of a third term. According to Levinas, "this [relation to the
other] is not a participation in a third term, whether this term be a person, a truth, a work, or a profession. It is a collectivity that is not a com-
munion. It is the face-to-face without intermediary. . . ."[10] Levinas calls
into question the mediation of a third term, because such operation neutralizes alterity by encompassing it within the totality of the conceptual or
linguistic system: "This mode of depriving the known being of its alterity
can be accomplished only if it is aimed at through a third term, a neutral
term, which itself is not a being; in it the shock of the encounter of the same
with the other is deadened."[11] A third term can appear in different forms—
as a category, concept, sensation or, to anticipate Kristeva's critique of
Lacan, as the transcendental signifier, as the phallus—but, according to Levinas, it always neutralizes the shock of the encounter with the other. Yet,
this critique of mediation does not involve an unproblematic return to
immediacy.[12] Rather, what the breakdown of mediation reveals is the
excess of otherness with respect to any totality, whether articulated in
social, conceptual, or linguistic terms. The carefully accumulated cluster of
terms in the Levinasian thought—beyond, excess, transcendence, infinity,
or trace of the other—both perform and preserve this exteriority against
the closure of a phenomenological or linguistic system.[13]

It is this emphasis on the exteriority, or the excess, of the other with
respect to the signifying system that I find particularly illuminating in
thinking about Kristeva's engagement with maternal alterity. In a way
similar to Levinas, although in the context of a different intellectual tradition, Kristeva traces the residues of maternal alterity that disrupt the
mediation of a third term—the paternal law which sets up the signifying
system and the positions of subjects and objects. Indeed, one could look
at the corpus of Kristeva's work from *Revolution in Poetic Language* to
Black Sun as her analysis of different encounters with the other—encounters which can no longer be assimilated to the typography of the sign and
the symbolic totality.

It should be stressed, however, that neither for Levinas nor Kristeva the
exteriority of the other amounts to essentialism. Such alterity does not
constitute a prelinguistic, self-evident identity that should be recovered

through a more faithful representation, but signals itself within a totality of thought only as a trace. The trace announces, for Levinas, a double signifyingness of the other. The other manifests itself always within a cultural and linguistic context, but is not absorbed by it. On the contrary, the other dislocates the context in which it occurs just as it "divests" itself from the very form that manifests it.[14] For Levinas, as for Kristeva, the trace disrupts not only the correlation between the self and the other, the subject and the object, but even more radically, the correlation between the signifier and the signified. Belonging neither to the phenomenological order of appearing nor to the linguistic order of the sign, the trace of the other, "the unrightness itself," signifies only as a disturbance.[15] Yet it is precisely this disturbance that calls the "I" to responsibility for the other.

As Levinas claims, this exteriority and disturbance of the trace of the other should be understood not only in spatial but also in temporal terms. To the primacy of presence, Levinas opposes an insurmountable diachrony as a marker of noncoincidence of the other and the same: "A trace is the insertion of space in time"; "A trace qua trace does not simply lead to the past, but is the very *passing* toward a past more remote than any past and any future which still are set in my time."[16] The trace opens a discontinuous temporality, which marks the exteriority of the future and the past with respect to the present and the presence of the subject. As John Llewelyn argues, this diachrony indicates that the other and the same cannot be brought together, even as a contradiction.[17]

And it is precisely in terms of a spatio-temporal disturbance of the symbolic system that Kristeva articulates the alterity of the maternal. The thought of maternal alterity always brings about a crisis of the symbolic order and of the subject sustained by that order. Yet despite these structural similarities, nothing can be more different than Kristeva's and Levinas's valorizations of this "disturbance": in Kristeva's case, the encounter with the unmediated other bespeaks the necessity of matricide; in Levinas's case, it initiates ethical responsibility for the other and a prohibition of murder. Can it be that this negative or positive valorization of the other has a lot to do with the way alterity is gendered?

II.

"Nothing, however, suggests that a feminine ethics is possible."
Julia Kristeva

So how is alterity gendered in Levinas's philosophy? What happens to the feminine other in his ethics? Many readers have tried to raise this question—Simone de Beauvoir, Luce Irigaray, Catherine Chalier, Tina Chanter, Jacques Derrida, and Simon Critchley, to name only a few.[18] The responses, of course, have varied: from embarrassment to apology, from critique to textual acrobatics (as in the case of Derrida), but all of them indicate a certain "gender trouble" in Levinas's work.[19] This gender trouble occurs already within the founding opposition between Ulysses and Abraham, which, let us recall, indicates for Levinas two different attitudes to alterity. Returning to himself, Ulysses incorporates the other into the order of representation, whereas Abraham's journey without return represents a displacement of the subject in the face-to-face encounter with the other. What is evident, however, is that this paradigm of ethics is incapable of articulating female alterity, say, of Penelope and Sarah. Re-read with respect to female alterity, the terms of the founding opposition between Ulysses and Abraham seem to exchange places. When Levinas describes the erotic relation between the sexes, Abraham in fact becomes Ulysses, always returning to himself. And maybe the greatest challenge for the ethics of sexual difference is to conceive Ulysses as already an Abraham, whose journey home never leads to an identification with himself but to an encounter with Penelope.

Levinas omits the feminine from his discussion of Ulysses and Abraham because he claims that the relation between the sexes should be secondary to ethics. Yet as Derrida and Critchley argue, such "secondary" logic of sexual difference still genders ethics as masculine and sexuality as feminine.[20] Consequently, the priority of ethics means a privilege of the masculine, whereas the ancillary status of sexual difference implies a subordination of the feminine. This double correlation of the masculine with ethics and the feminine with sexuality explains why Levinas insists that feminine alterity should be thought otherwise than the face-to-face relation. For Levinas, sexual difference is not only subordinate to ethics but also coextensive with feminine particularity. In the frequently quoted passage from *Et Dieu Créa la Femme,* Levinas writes that "the particularity of the feminine is a secondary matter. It isn't woman who is secondary, it is the relation to woman qua woman that doesn't belong to the primordial human plan. . . . The problem . . . consists in reconciling the humanity of men and women with the hypothesis of a spirituality of the masculine, the feminine being not his correlative but his corollary; feminine specificity *or the difference of the sexes that it announces* are not straight away situated at the height of the oppositions constitutive of Spirit. Audacious question: How can the equality of the sexes proceed from a masculine property?" [emphasis added].[21]

To Levinas's "audacious" question—"How can the equality between the sexes proceed from a masculine property?"—Derrida responds with an even more audacious question of his own: "How can one mark as masculine the very thing said to be anterior, or even foreign, to sexual difference?"[22] Since sexual difference is not conceived as a difference between the masculine and the feminine but only as the feminine specificity, as the relation to "woman qua woman," this difference marks only the feminine subject and can be overcome in the sameness of humanity. In other words, we risk a hypothesis that only femininity is sexed and gendered while the masculine remains sexually unmarked. As a secondary modification within the human, feminine alterity does not create any dislocations of the masculine economy. Unlike the exteriority of the other, femininity becomes assimilated to the order of the same—to the economy of the human. In Derrida's words, she remains "enclosed within, foreclosed within the immanence of a crypt, incorporated within the Saying which says itself to the wholly other."[23] As Tina Chanter suggests, in Derrida's reading of Levinas, the feminine would occupy a position of Antigone, but only strategically, only to reemerge as the other of the wholly other.[24]

Although there are numerous signs of an enclosure of the feminine within "the immanence of the crypt,"[25] I will mention briefly its most obvious instances. While claiming that the other disturbs my being at home with myself, that the other is never wholly in my site, Levinas thinks the feminine precisely within the structure of the dwelling. The feminine occurs at the site where everything is at the subject's disposal, where, according to Levinas's own terms, "the very alterity of what is only at first other" is suspended and converted into the moments of self-identification.[26] In such a site, she is literally mute. The second way Levinas encloses the other within the immanence of the crypt is by introducing a rigorous distinction between metaphysical desire, understood as the movement toward the other, and sexual desire, which invariably returns the male subject to the order of need and immanence: "It is that by an essential aspect love, which as transcendence goes unto the Other, throws us back this side of immanence." Similarly Levinas writes, "Love remains a relation with the Other that turns into need."[27] Predictably enough, the transcendence of Eros is accomplished eventually not through the love of the beloved but through the coveting of a son.[28] The third moment would refer to the relation between the masculine subject and the maternal body—the moment rarely discussed in Levinas's texts but announced on the level of rhetoric—on the level of metaphors describing the subject's being toward death.

If the assimilation of female alterity into the order of the same means her enclosure "within the immanence of the crypt," then the Levinasian discussion of the feminine is confronted with an unacknowledged task of mourning. Such incorporation of the other into the order of signification, as Kristeva demonstrates in her *Black Sun,* amounts to a negation of the loss of the other, especially, to a forgetting of the loss of the mother. For Kristeva it is the disorder of melancholia that bears a perverse witness to the maternal "Thing" buried within the symbolic order: "Melancholy persons are foreigners in their maternal tongue. They have lost meaning—the value—of their mother tongue *for want of losing the mother.* The dead language they speak . . . conceals a Thing buried alive. The latter will not be translated in order that it not be betrayed." [emphasis added][29] From the Kristevan perspective, the difference between the face of the other and the feminine in the Levinasian texts can be articulated as a difference between ethics and mourning, or more "audaciously" still, as a difference between the epiphany of the other and the negation of its (her) loss. In contrast to the radical exteriority of the other, the signification of mourning points out that the loss of feminine alterity has been overcome through its incorporation into a signifying system.

As I mentioned before, the relation between mourning and ethics is especially evident in Levinas's discussion of death.[30] As "the end of the subject's virility," the anticipation of death creates a moment where a relation to a radical alterity becomes possible.[31] The ethical movement is accomplished, however, when the anguish of the subject's own death gives way to the fear for the death of the other: the Heideggerian being-toward-death gives way to being-for-the-other. Yet by creating a crisis of the subject, the relation to death reveals yet another unacknowledged substratum of ethics—the loss of the maternal body. Such enigmatic resurfacing of the maternal body constitutes death as a repetition of a different kind of an event, as a repetition of birth, announced only on the level of rhetoric:

> My mastery, my virility, my heroism as a subject can be neither virility
> nor heroism in relation to death. There is in the suffering at the heart
> of which we have grasped this nearness of death . . . this reversal of the
> subject's activity into passivity. . . . *To die is to return to this state of irre-*
> *sponsibility, to be the infantile shaking of sobbing.* [emphasis added][32]

What this amazing passage implies is that the event of death is in fact a repetition of an immemorial past: it returns the virile masculine subject to the state of utter passivity, which is figured in terms of a sobbing infant dependent on the maternal body. Beyond the anguish of death, the infant's convulsions of sobbing passionately evoke and erase the absent figure of the mother. Consequently, the figure of death is inscribed in a double temporality: an opening of an absolutely surprising future and a forgetting of an archaic past, a forgetting of birth. The infantile cry, however, is not a simple invocation of the lost mother but betrays a profound ambiguity about maternal alterity: it is already denied and yet unable to be forgotten. As the first figuration of the other evoked in the sobbing of the infant, the absent maternal figure constitutes a forgotten layer of Levinas's ethics. It is to this substratum that Levinas's later work returns in order to articulate maternity as a paradigm of substitution *par excellence*.[33]

III.

> "Now if a contemporary ethics is no longer seen as being the same as morality . . . its reformulation demands the contribution of women."
> *Julia Kristeva*

If, in Levinas's philosophy, mourning constitutes an underside of ethics, can we uncover a possibility of ethics in Kristeva's account of mourning and melancholia?[34] How can the Levinasian nonallergic openness to alterity, how can his signification of the other without a mediation of the third term, assist us in rereading the maternal body in Kristeva's text? By a double displacement of Levinas's insight onto an alien territory—psychoanalysis and the maternal—I hope to approach Kristeva's account of melancholia as a diagnosis of violence inherent in the symbolization of the other.

Kristeva's analysis of melancholia is marked by a profound ambivalence, an ambivalence I want to press further than the confines of Kristeva's argument allow. On the one hand, melancholia is presented as a mental disorder in need of a cure, but, on the other hand, it is a state of supreme lucidity, a "hidden side of philosophy": "In his doubtful moments the depressed person is a philosopher, and we owe to Heraclitus, Socrates, and more recently Kierkegaard the most disturbing pages on the meaning or lack of meaning of Being."[35] This vacillation between mental disorder and philosophical insight is reflected in an uneven attitude to melancholia on Kristeva's part: On the one hand, the predominantly normative, conservative approach concerned with reinstalling the subject into a firm position in the symbolic order proclaims that "matricide is our vital necessity." But on the other hand, the negative label of a "disorder" allows Kristeva to be daring in her description of the irreducible alterity of the mother, alterity that is not accessible to symbolic elaboration. It seems that Kristeva herself deploys strategically Freudian negation (the process that leads the repressed to representation on the condition that it is negated), while her language consistently undoes the work of the negative.

If the melancholy person is not merely a psychotic in need of a cure but also a philosopher, I would imagine her, with a certain degree of audacity of my own, as a philosopher of ethics on the scale of Levinas. And her diagnosis of the "lack of meaning of Being" would issue a profound critique of ontology in order to establish ethics as the first philosophy. With what I take to be a self-ironic gesture, Kristeva, from the outset, reverses the hierarchy between the patient and the therapist and rearticulates it as a more complex exchange between the philosopher and the analyst. If the analyst can proffer a cure, the depressed philosopher resists it and offers in return a critique of psychoanalysis as a philosophy of the subject. Concerned with reinstalling the subject into a firm position in the symbolic order, the conservative analyst proclaims that "matricide is our vital necessity." In response, the patient/philosopher challenges the very nature of this necessity and bears a perverse witness to the excess of maternal alterity overflowing the symbolic system. In the outcome of this exchange, the psychoanalyst admits that the cure might be just a "fantasy of a melancholy theoretician."[36]

What is at stake in melancholia is a complex negotiation of relations between death and eros, hate and love, self and other, absence and presence. In his 1917 essay, "Mourning and Melancholia," Freud defines melancholia as a structure of the ego formation that depends on negotiating the ambivalence about the loss of the other. A certain refusal of loss prompts the subject to absorb alterity within the structure of its own identity: "The narcissistic identification with the object then becomes a substitute for the erotic cathexis, the result of which is that in spite of the conflict with the loved person the love-relation need not be given up. . . . The ego wishes to incorporate this object into itself, and the method by which it would do so, in this oral or cannibalistic stage, is by devouring it."[37] The other becomes embodied, entombed within the self.[38] However, if incorporation of alterity sets up a structure of the self, the other is assimilated at the price of originating a discord and a conflict within the ego. The other is preserved only by creating the "open wound" within the ego.

Extending Freud's insights, Kristeva goes beyond his understanding of melancholia as a kind of cannibalistic imagination: "Far from being a hidden attack on an other who is thought to be hostile because he is frustrating, sadness would point to a primitive self—wounded, incomplete, empty."[39] The signification of melancholia discloses, first of all, an acute awareness of disinheritance, accompanied by a lack of faith in any restoration or recompense for the suffered loss. In this sense, a melancholy person is an atheist, without recourse to a secular or religious economy of salvation. Mourning, on the other hand, provides a way for "disposing" of a loss through an acceptance of the symbolic means of compensation.

This initial contrast between mourning and melancholia allows Kristeva to articulate two very different modes of language acquisition. In Kristeva's revision, mourning for the other becomes the normal condition of learning language, because the possibility of speaking involves an absence of the object. And the first absence that we symbolize is the loss of the mother. According to Kristeva, the task of mourning involves a *negation* of the fundamental loss of the other and an acceptance of the arbitrary linguistic totality as an adequate compensation. In Kristeva's discussion, mourning functions as an economy of losses and compensations, an economy which underlies every order of representation. By correlating the loss of the other with the symbolic compensation in this manner, Kristeva demonstrates in very explicit terms that linguistic mastery is predicated upon the effacement of alterity—in particular, of maternal alterity. Such effacement occurs, we have to add, precisely at the moment when the other is supposed to be recovered, re-presented. Thus, learning language is equivalent to matricide, and the subject's entry into the symbolic system depends upon its ability to carry out the task of mourning in the wake of the symbolic murder:

> Signs are arbitrary because language starts with a *negation* (*Verneinung*) of loss, along with the depression occasioned by mourning. "I have lost an essential object that happens to be, in the final analysis, my mother," is what the speaking being seems to be saying. "But no, I have found her again in signs, or rather since I consent to lose her I have not lost her (that is the negation), I can recover her in language."[40]

According to Kristeva, linguistic mastery depends upon the denial of violence inherent in the symbolic system and upon a spurious faith in the recovery of alterity through the process of representation. Such negation of the loss of the other sets up language as the process of metaphoric translation of the other, but a translation that forgets the heterogeneity of what it translates: "To transpose corresponds to the Greek *metaphorein,* to transport; language is, from the start, a translation, but on a level that is heterogeneous to the one where affective loss, renunciation, or the break takes place."[41] Mourning posits language as a process of distancing from the other and opens a way of neutralizing this alterity through translation. As a result of such symbolic mediation, alterity becomes absorbed in the immanence of linguistic totality.

If mourning is a "normal," or normative, stage in learning language, melancholia registers a certain crisis in symbolic mediation. It undermines the process of translating the other into a linguistic totality, and, as such, it uncovers a different mode of language acquisition. At first, Kristeva defines melancholia as an inability to lose the primordial other but then she immediately qualifies her description as a refusal to accept any compensation for that loss, especially in terms of symbolic mastery. Yet there is a peculiar slippage in the way Kristeva articulates this inability to lose: it can be taken as a denial of the loss itself or as a denial of the possibility of recompense for the loss. If the first instance can lead to a nostalgic fantasy of the reunion with the phallic mother and a refusal of signification, the second case—denial of the negation—evokes an excess of otherness over the signifying system: "The *denial* (Verleugnung) *of negation* would thus be the exercise of an impossible mourning, the setting up of a fundamental sadness and an artificial, unbelievable language, cut out of the painful background that is not accessible to any signifier."[42] The most fundamental questions emerging from Kristeva's discussion of melancholia can be formulated therefore in the following way: What is at stake in thinking about the other in terms of losses and compensations? Does this way of thinking about alterity amount to a certain murder already? Can this way of thinking constitute an ethics of psychoanalysis?

Inspired by Levinas's ethics, we can rearticulate the signification of melancholia as a moment of unusual sobriety (a negative insight, so to speak) which reveals that the symbolic order is established only at the price of a fundamental loss—a loss of maternal alterity. We can reconceive the inability to mourn and overcome this loss as a refusal to master alterity in terms of linguistic proficiency. It is not only a refusal to symbolize the loss, to turn it into an occasion of a virile display of the mastery of the subject—"No I haven't lost; I evoke, I signify through the artifice of signs and for myself what has been parted from me"[43]—but also a refusal to think alterity in terms of losses and compensations.

The inability to trade the loss of the other for the "symbolic triumph" does not strike me necessarily as a disorder of the subject but as a powerful critique of the desire to master alterity through the order of representation. The loss of faith in "valid compensations" for the loss of the mother—"a loss that causes him [the child] to try to find her again, along with other objects of love, first in the imagination, then in words"[44]—implies a critique of the Western tradition of mimesis. Melancholia points to an irreducible excess of alterity disrupting the order of representation. This excess of alterity—being overwhelmed by the other—indicates a breakdown of the mechanism of mediation in the symbolic order. Indeed in the way Kristeva orchestrates her description, melancholia registers an encounter with the other without the intermediary of the third term, understood as a paternal signifier, phallus, or the symbolic order. Although maternal alterity remains in this case unnameable, exterior to the order of signs, it leaves its imprint both on the discourse and on the speaking subject—it signals itself in language as blank spots or dissociation of form. Instead of translating the other into the order of signs, melancholic speech defamiliarizes language itself, affects it with an unnameable strangeness. Such excess of alterity makes both language and the subject "alien to themselves." Indeed, the paradox of melancholy speech is that it turns native speakers into strangers in their own mother tongues.

Although this gesture requires violence directed at Kristeva's text, I suggest that her description of melancholia as a refusal to overcome the loss of the other through symbolic elaboration is similar to the face-to-face encounter in the Levinasian ethics. In both cases, the breakdown of mediation points to the exteriority of the other with respect to the sociolinguistic totality, and, in both cases the other signifies through "disturbance" or excess. To redefine the melancholic disorder as an ethics of otherness would require, however, a displacement from the concern with the subject—its individuation, its anguish, its wounds, its crisis—to alterity ontologically and ethically prior to the subject. In a certain way, melancholia already registers this reversal; the crisis reveals that the subject and its means of representation are always already overwhelmed by the other: "In the tension of their affects, muscles, mucous membranes, and skin, they experience both their belonging to and distance from an archaic other that still eludes representation and naming, but of whose corporeal emissions, along with their automatism, they still bear the imprint."[45] Furthermore, whether it is interpreted negatively as an aggressive devouring or positively as a refusal of compensation for the other's loss, "bearing the imprint of the other" cannot be seen as a result of the subject's initiative. Rather, the mark of alterity points to the subject's indebtedness to the other, to a forgotten maternal gift, which enables our ethical orientation in the world.

In different ways, Kristeva and Levinas attempt to uncover alterity irreducible either to the projections and conceptualizations of the subject or to the regulations of the sociosymbolic order. Shifting priority from identity to otherness, both insist that alterity precedes and displaces the subject. Within the Kristevan psychoanalytic genealogy of the subject this alterity is constituted by the maternal body, whereas the Levinasian ethics is oriented toward the face of a (masculine) He. What the juxtaposition of the work of Levinas and Kristeva helps us to understand, however, is not only the notion of radical alterity but also its gendering. Operating, paradoxically, even prior to the logic of sexual difference itself, such gendering determines, for instance, whether the encounter with the excess of alterity is perceived as a profound ethical posture or as an advent of psychosis. When the face of the (masculine) other in the Levinasian ethics disrupts the correlations between the self and the other, being and knowledge, the signified and the signifier, such disturbance initiates ethical responsibility and respect. Although Kristeva's work, including her analysis of melancholia, consistently demonstrates that the excess of otherness disrupts operations of the symbolic exchange and puts the subject on trial, her valorization of maternal alterity is much more ambivalent. For Kristeva, such resurfacing of maternal alterity can either harbor the seeds of the transformation of the signifying system or lead to the collapse of the subject.

By the time we reach Kristeva's discussion of melancholia in *Black Sun*, the encounter with the maternal other is no longer even ambivalent but seems to be accomplished entirely in negative terms as a psychosis of the subject and a crisis of the symbolic order. Confronted with this crisis, Kristeva herself occupies a defensive position and accepts violence as the only possible response to the mother: "Matricide is our vital necessity, the *sine qua non* condition of our individuation."[46] The ethos of this position only confirms the primacy of identity and its violence in Western metaphysics. Approaching Kristeva's discussion of melancholia wholly "otherwise"—from the position of respect for the other opened by Levinas's work—would require both a recognition of violence inherent in the neutralization of the other and a refusal of the necessity of that violence, without succumbing to a paralysis so characteristic of melancholia. This paralysis stems, I would claim, precisely from an inability to find a different solution to violence other than "putting to death of the self" in place of matricide.[47] Consequently, a refusal of violence would have to transform the suicidal impasse of melancholia into a critique of power relations at the base of the sociolinguistic contrast. These, to my mind, are political tasks confronting psychoanalysis today. However, a refusal of matricide presents an ethical obligation as well. To paraphrase Levinas's insight about the conjunction between death and alterity, I would like to say, in response to Kristeva's worries about the survival of the subject, that the encounter with the (m)other does not automatically spell our suicide but, on the contrary, it is our being-toward-death that might give us a chance to learn respect for alterity. Such respect requires psychoanalysis to make a difficult transition from an ethics of individuation to an ethics of otherness.

Notes

Earlier versions of this paper were presented at "Passions, Persons, Powers" conference, Berkeley, May 1992, and at *Collegium Phaenomenologicum*, Perugia, Italy, July 1992. I am very grateful to the participants of both meetings for insightful comments and suggestions.

1. The phrase "strategic essentialism" is Spivak's and it refers to "the strategic use of an essence as a mobilizing slogan" for political purposes. Gayatri Chakravorty Spivak, "In a Word," *differences* 1, 1989: pp. 126–27. Another example of deploying essentialism for political ends can be found in Diana J. Fuss, "'Essentially Speaking': Luce Irigaray's Language of Essence," *Hypatia* 3 1989: pp. 62–80. For an insightful critique of "strategic essentialism," see Drucilla Cornell, *Beyond Accommodation: Ethical Feminism, Deconstruction, and the Law* (New York: Routledge, 1991), pp. 179–83.

2. Kristeva's work has produced many controversies and debates among feminist critics. On the issue of essentialism in her work, see for instance, Judith Butler, "The Body Politics of Julia Kristeva," chapter 10 of this volume; Ann Rosalind Jones, "Julia Kristeva on Femininity: The Limits of a Semiotic Politic," *Feminist Review* 18 1984: pp. 46–73; Jacqueline Rose, *Sexuality in the Field of Vision* (London: Verso, 1986), pp. 151–7.

3. For a reading of the phallus as a neutral third term and a "structural universal," see Ellie Ragland-Sullivan, "Seeking the Third Term: Desire, the Phallus, and the Materiality of Language," *Feminism and Psychoanalysis*, eds. Richard Feldstein and Judith Roof (Ithaca: Cornell University Press, 1989), pp. 40–64.

4. Emmanuel Levinas, *Totality and Infinity: An Essay on Exteriority*, trans. Alphonso Lingis (Pittsburgh: Duquesne University Press, 1969), p. 27.

5. Emmanuel Levinas, "Ethics as the First Philosophy," trans. Sean Hand and Michael Temple, *The Levinas Reader*, ed. Sean Hand (Oxford: Basil Blackwell, 1989), p. 79.

6. Emmanuel Levinas, "Ethics as the First Philosophy," p.76.

7. Emmanuel Levinas, "The Trace of the Other," trans. A. Lingis, *Deconstruction in Context*, ed. Mark Taylor (Chicago: University of Chicago Press, 1986), p. 348.

8. Emmanual Levinas, "The Trace of the Other," p. 350.

9. For an excellent discussion of the semantics of alterity in the thought of Levinas, see Krzysztof Ziarek, "Semantics Of Proximity: Language and the Other in the Philosophy of Emmanuel Levinas," *Research in Phenomenology* 19 1989: pp. 213–47.

10. Emmanuel Levinas, "Time and the Other," trans. Richard A. Cohen, *The Levinas Reader,* p. 54.

11. Emmanuel Levinas, *Totality and Infinity*, p. 42.

12. Jean Greisch argues persuasively that the signification of the other in Levinas's philosophy disrupts the very opposition of immediacy and mediation as defined by the Hegelian dialectic. "The Face and Reading: Immediacy and Mediation," trans. Simon Critchley, *Re-Reading Levinas,* ed. Robert Bernasconi and Simon Critchley (Bloomington, Ind.: Indiana University Press, 1991), pp. 67–82.

13. For an insightful discussion of the exteriority of the other, see John Llewelyn, "Levinas, Derrida and Others Vis-à-Vis," *Provocation of Levinas: Rethinking the other,* ed. Robert Bernasconi and David Wood (New York: Routledge, 1988), pp. 145–9.

14. Emmanuel Levinas, "The Trace of the Other," p. 358. For further discussion of the discourse of the face to face, see Llewelyn, "Levinas, Derrida and Others Vis-à-Vis," pp. 152–4.

15. The serial interruptions of the trace—the "seriature"—within the structurality of language is at the center of Derrida's deconstructive reading of Levinas in "At This Very Moment in This Work Here I Am," trans. Ruben Berezdivin, *Re-Reading Levinas*, pp. 11–48.

16. Emmanuel Levinas, "The Trace of the Other," P. 358.

17. John Llewelyn, "Levinas, Derrida and others Vis-à-Vis," p. 157.

18. This inquiry was initiated by Simone de Beauvoir's critique in *The Second Sex,* trans. H.M. Parshey (New York: Vintage, 1952), p. xix. For more recent reevaluations of the feminine role in Levinas's ethics, see, in particular, three excellent essays from *Re-Reading Levinas:* Luce Irigaray, "Questions to Emmanuel Levinas: On the Divinity of Love," trans. Margaret Whitford, pp. 109–18; Catherine Chalier, "Ethics and the Feminine," pp. 119–29; and Tina Chanter, "Antigone's Dilemma," pp. 130–48. See also Tina Chanter, "Feminism and the Other," pp. 32–56, and Alison Ainley, "Amorous Discourses: 'The Phenomenology of Eros and Love Stories," pp. 70–82, both in *The Provocation of Levinas: Rethinking the Other.*

19. The phrase "gender trouble" comes from the title of Judith Butler's book, *Gender Trouble: Feminism and the Subversion of Identity* (New York: Routledge, 1990).

20. Jacques Derrida, "At This Very Moment in This Work Here I Am," and Simon Critchley, "'Bois'—Derrida's Final Word on Levinas," both essays are in *Re-Reading Levinas.* Simon Critchley provides an excellent discussion of femininity both in Levinas's work and in Derrida's essay.

21. This passage is quoted and discussed in Derrida's "At This Very Moment in This Work Here I Am," p. 41.

22. Ibid., p. 40.

23. Ibid., p. 43.

24. The suggestion that the figure of Antigone "haunts" Derrida's reading of Levinas comes from Tina Chanter, "Antigone's Dilemma," p. 135.

25. For an interesting reading of representation, death, and otherness in modern philosophical discourse, see Daniel Tiffany, "Cryptesthesia: Visions of the Other," *The American Journal of Semiotics* 6, 1989: pp. 209–19.

26. Emmanuel Levinas, *Totality and Infinity,* p. 38.

27. Ibid., p. 254.

28. For a critique of Levinas's discussion of Eros, in particular, of the way he "substitutes the son for the feminine," see Luce Irigaray, "Questions to Emmanuel Levinas," p. 111.

29. Julia Kristeva, *Black Sun: Depression and Melancholia,* trans. Leon S. Roudiez (New York: Columbia University Press, 1989), p. 53.

30. For Levinas, as for Heidegger, what opens a radical dimension of the unforeseeable future is the subject's relation to death. But unlike the Heideggerian notion of death as the recognition of the finitude leading to the authenticity of *Da-sein,* death for Levinas opens a possibility of alterity.

31. For an interesting interpretation of the ethical obligation coming from the other's death, see Ruben Berezdivin, "3 2 1 CONTACT: Textuality, the Other, Death," *Re-Reading Levinas*, pp. 190–200.

32. Emmanuel Levinas, "Time and the Other," p. 41.

33. See, in particular, Levinas's discussion of maternity in *Otherwise Than Being Or Beyond Essence*, trans. Alphonso Lingis (Hague: Martinus Nijhoff, 1981), pp. 75–81.

34. The project of Kristeva's ethics is discussed by, among others, Eleanor H. Kuyk-endall, "Questions for Julia Kristeva's Ethics of Linguistics," *The Thinking Muse: Feminism and Modern French Philosophy*, ed. Jeffner Allen and Iris Marion Young (Bloomington, Ind.: Indiana University Press, 1989), pp. 180–94; Drucilla Cornell, *Beyond Accommodation*, pp. 36–50; Elizabeth Grosz, *Sexual Subversions: Three French Feminists* (Sydney: Allen & Unwin, 1989), p. 89–91; and Mary Jacobus, "Dora and the Pregnant Madonna," *Reading Woman: Essays in Feminist Criticism* (New York: Columbia University Press, 1986), p. 169.

35. Julia Kristeva, *Black Sun*, p. 6.

36. Ibid., p. 66.

37. Sigmund Freud, "Mourning and Melancholia," *Collected Papers* vol. 4, trans. Joan Riviere (New York: Basic Books, 1959), p. 160.

38. For an excellent reading of melancholia as "denial/preservation of homosexuality in the production of gender within the heterosexual frame" see Judith Butler, *Gender Trouble: Feminism and the Subversion of Identity*, pp. 57–66.

39. Julia Kristeva, *Black Sun*, p. 12.

40. Ibid., p. 43.

41. Ibid., p. 41.

42. Ibid., p. 44.

43. Ibid., p. 23.

44. Ibid., p. 6.

45. Ibid., p. 14.

46. Ibid., pp. 27–8.

47. Ibid., p. 28.

5

Identification with the Divided Mother: Kristeva's Ambivalence

Allison Weir

Given that "identity" is the dirty word of the twentieth century, Julia Kristeva's insistence on the necessity of identification requires some explanation.

In this chapter, "identity" will refer specifically to the identity of the subject, which, paradoxically (or perhaps more to the point, dialectically), entails an identification of the subject with the symbolic order of language. In other terms, the identity of the subject requires an acceptance of the social contract.

Kristeva argues that the critique of this form of identity tends too often to lapse into a *repudiation* of identity and of the symbolic order itself. This amounts to a withdrawal into absence or counteridentification, which leaves the symbolic order untouched, and unchallenged.

For example, in *Revolution in Poetic Language,* Kristeva argues that Derrida's grammatology, in an attempt to free the trace from any dependence on the *logos,* puts it into a space anterior to the *logos,* to the symbolic order—to, indeed, every entity and therefore every position.[1] Because the moment of identity is constantly deferred, negativity is "positivized and drained of its potential for producing breaks."[2] Kristeva argues that the moment of identity is essential to a nonidentity that is neither a pure lack of identity nor a dissolving into endless difference. It is, moreover, essential for the production of contradiction, which is the basis of social and political change.

Similarly, in "Women's Time," her famed and notorious paper on feminism, Kristeva criticizes a tendency within one strain of contemporary feminism, to repudiate and refuse to identify with the given symbolic order, which is equated with the Law of the Father—with, that is, the law which entails the sacrifice of women. Kristeva argues that the refusal to identify with the existing order too often amounts to a refusal to give up the phallic mother. The father is condemned for breaking up the original unity with the mother. What is upheld, then, is an imaginary memory/phantasy of pure gratification, a space imagined as harmonious, continuous, without prohibitions, without breaks or separations. Blaming the father is a way of denying the necessity of separation, and of violence.

This denial is celebrated as a subversive political practice; in fact, it amounts to a counteridentification with the phallic mother . . . with a "fetishist counterpower—restorer of the crises of the self and provider of a *jouissance* which is always already a transgression."[3]

> In this sense and from a viewpoint undoubtedly too Hegelian, modern feminism has been but a moment in the interminable process of coming to consciousness about the implacable violence (separation, castration, etc.) which constitutes any symbolic contract.[4]

The simple repudiation of identification with the Law fails to acknowledge women's desire for the Law. Further, it fails to acknowledge that the attempt to evade the Law and live in a space outside of it, to refuse to speak the language of the given order, is to render oneself aphasic or psychotic, and the political efficacy of psychosis is negligible. Kristeva is insisting, then, that (in Jacqueline Rose's words) "resistance must finally be articulated in a voice which can be heard."[5] Resistance to the given symbolic order requires that we identify with that order, learn its language. It requires, moreover, that we recognize and insist that the symbolic order is not purely "phallic," that it is not an unassailable monolith, but that it is a product of, and constantly changed by, conflicting, heterogeneous processes.

Finally, Kristeva reminds us that the phantasy of complete gratification in the phallic mother is itself a product of the patriarchal order, and is essential to the preservation of that order. Thus, rather than refusing the father and turning to mother (or, in other terms, refusing identity within the symbolic order and turning to nonidentity within a semiotic order), we need to expose the ways in which the order of patriarchy is dependent upon the dream of gratification with the mother. We need to show how the mystique of motherhood serves to appease and contain both men's and women's desires for immediacy, for pleasure. We need to show, also, how the construction of the mother as the all-powerful, all-enveloping womb, as a place of utter peace—and, therefore, death—serves to warn the subject against any attempt at escape from identity and identification with the phallic symbolic order.

What is required, then, is not a repudiation but a reformulation of identity and identification: a reformulation which does not pit mother and father against each other.

I think that Kristeva's insistence on this point is important, and I want to hold onto it. However, it must be admitted—and certainly it has been pointed out often enough— that, against her own warning, she does tend to accept a duality of symbolic and semiotic, father and mother, which is regarded as fundamental to subjectivity. While I do not want to deny that this duality exists in Kristeva's work, I want, in this chapter, to focus on her analysis and critique of this duality as a foundation of our culture. In particular, I want to focus on her analysis of the ways in which identification—and in particular women's identification—with the phallic mother or absolute woman serves the patriarchal order. Finally, I want to discuss Kristeva's attempt to formulate the possibility of a different mode of identification with the mother. I shall discuss, in turn, three of Kristeva's essays: "Stabat Mater," "The Pain of Sorrow in the Modern World: The Works of Marguerite Duras," and "Freud and Love: Treatment and Its Discontents."

In her essay, "Stabat Mater," Kristeva traces the idealization of the mother through the medieval cult of the Virgin Mary. According to Kristeva, the cult of the Virgin served to appease—and to foreclose—the desire for return to the mother, while ensuring both men's and women's identification with the patriarchal social order. This is because the Virgin represents the semiotic order—the order of bodily drives and their rhythms, which is associated with the mother—and reconciles this with the symbolic order under God the Father.

In "Stabat Mater," Kristeva defines the cultural meaning of "the maternal" as:

> the ambivalent principle that is bound to the species, on the one hand, and on the other stems from an identity catastrophe that causes the Name to topple over into the unnameable that one imagines as femininity, non-language or body.[6]

According to this representation, then, motherhood exists on the borderline between nature and culture, body and language. And it is not the mother herself but our memory of relationship to her—the phantasied relationship of primary narcissism[7]—which is idealized in our "consecrated" representations of motherhood.[8] These representations enshrine a memory-phantasy of immediate fusion, pure gratification—a dream of wholeness, prior to the separation of language from body, and hence prior to—and outside of—the Law. Yet the mother's body also serves to *mediate,* for the child, between body and language, nature and culture.[9] Thus, the relationship of primary narcissism exists on the borderline between identity and nonidentity, Name and unnameable. The mother's role as mediator, then, is constituted through not only primal fusion but also its loss. And it is perhaps this borderline condition (and not simply a *lack* of identity, prior to the Law) which, remembered, is projected onto the mother as identity catastrophe.

In "Stabat Mater," Kristeva argues that the medieval cult of the Virgin Mary served to absorb the economy of the maternal—of primary narcissism—into the social order, under the Law of the Father. In other terms, it served to absorb the pagan belief in the Mother Goddess—who represented the economy of the maternal—into Catholicism.

Kristeva argues that by taking up the myth of the Mother Goddess, thereby preserving the maternal order within the jurisdiction of the paternal one, Catholicism was able to maintain "a certain balance between the two sexes":[10]

> the representation of virgin motherhood appears to crown the efforts of a society to reconcile the social remnants of matrilinearism and the unconscious needs of primary narcissism on the one hand, and on the other the requirements of a new society based on exchange and before long on increased production, which require the contribution of the superego and rely on the symbolic paternal agency.[11]

Thus, the Virgin served—in the words of a Church father—as "a 'bond', a 'middle' or an 'interval'"[12] between the unnameable and the Name. And it is through the idealization of the Virgin Mother, who incorporates the dream logic of the semiotic—the heterogeneity of the drives—into a representation which supports and upholds the phallogocentric Western symbolic economy, that Christianity is able to account for what lies outside of that economy, without opening the way for subversion.

> Starting with the high Christly sublimation for which it yearns and occasionally exceeds, and extending to the extralinguistic regions of the unnameable, the Virgin Mother occupied the tremendous territory hither and yon of the parenthesis of language. She adds to the Christian trinity and to the Word that delineates their coherence the heterogeneity they salvage.[13]

This heterogeneity is represented in the figure of the Virgin by the milk and tears which, Kristeva says, became the privileged signs of the Mater Dolorosa. Milk and tears: oral absorption, fusion, and the moment of its loss: symbols of a presymbolic, a nonlinguistic order of relationship.

> Even though orality-threshold of infantile regression is displayed in the area of the breast, while the spasm at the slipping away of eroticism is

translated into tears, this should not conceal what milk and tears have in common: they are the metaphors of non-speech, of a "semiotics" that linguistic communication does not account for. The Mother and her attributes, evoking sorrowful humanity, thus become representatives of a "return of the repressed" in monotheism. They re-establish what is non-verbal and show up as the receptacle of a signifying disposition that is closer to socalled primary processes.[14]

While satisfying the desire for the mother and the heterogeneous order she embodies, the cult of the Virgin also takes care of both man's and woman's desires for self-identification. Man is able to erect himself in triumph over death, through the support of a dreamed/remembered mother's love, now appropriated as his own.

Man overcomes the unthinkable of death by postulating maternal love in its place—in the place and stead of death and thought.[15]

As for women's desires for self-identification, the Virgin was "able to attract women's wishes for identification as well as the very precise inter-position of those who assumed to keep watch over the symbolic and social order."[16] Kristeva argues that the identification of a woman with the Virgin, is a way—and not among the less effective" ways—of dealing with (by both enacting and constraining) "feminine paranoia."[17]

Here, it must be noted that paranoia is a condition produced by the repression of homoerotic desire for the same-sex parent.[18] Thus, feminine paranoia is an effect of the repression of a woman's desire for her mother—and, by extension, for other women. And therefore feminine paranoia is the product of a social order which demands that the female child give up her desire for her mother and turn to her father—give up her desire for other women and turn to men.

Through her identification with the Virgin, woman is able to effect a denial of the other sex (of man) and establish her unique relation with (albeit in subordination to) God. "I do not conceive with *you* but with *Him*."[19] She is thus able to satisfy her paranoid lust for power—while stifling it by "putting it on its knees before the child-god."[20] The Virgin, moreover, "obstructs the desire for murder or devoration" and "assumes the paranoid fantasy of being excluded from time and death."[21] Most importantly, iden-tification with the Virgin facilitates "repudiation of the other woman (which doubtless amounts basically to a repudiation of the woman's mother) by suggesting the image of A Unique Woman."[22] This uniqueness, however, is attained only through "an exacerbated masochism. . . . A bonus, however: the promised *jouissance*."[23]

Of course, the self-identities granted by the Virgin to both men and women are illusions, caught in the realm of the imaginary. The unitary identity, whole and undivided, is a phantasy; one cannot have, nor can one be, the dreamed-of mother.

In the case of women, Kristeva recognizes that it is this identification with the absolute woman, in repudiation of other women, of our mothers, that prevents us from developing singular identities as subjects in relation to other subjects. "The war between mother and daughter," Kristeva notes, was "masterfully but too quickly settled by promoting Mary as universal and particular, but never singular—as 'alone of her sex'."[24] Thus:

> A woman will only have the choice to live her life either *hyper-abstractly* ("immediately universal", Hegel said) in order thus to earn divine grace and homologation with symbolic order; or merely *different,* other, fallen ("immediately particular", Hegel said). But she will not be able to accede to the complexity of being divided, of heterogeneity, of the catastrophic-fold-or-"being" ("never singular", Hegel said).[25]

If we want to accede to a position of singular subjectivity, we need, Kristeva suggests, to open a discourse of motherhood which is not based upon the enforcement of woman's repudiation of the other woman—of her mother. We need, then, to open the possibility of relation to the other woman—to our mothers, as singular subjects, located in their specificity, their difference from the absolute woman. The relation to the mother must be reformulated if we want to reformulate identification.

The cult of the Virgin served to maintain both men's and women's fixations on the archaic mother as absolute woman and thereby served to secure man's place as autonomous individual and woman's as impossible absolute woman. If we want to get beyond these false fixed identities and get to the position of divided subjects-in-process—subjects who can posit ourselves as individuals yet recognize and accept our division—we need to get away from our fixation on the phallic mother.

For the loss of the Virgin Mother as source of this fixed identity has not liberated us from the fixation. In her study of the works of Marguerite Duras, Kristeva analyzes the problematic status of identification, and in particular, of women's identification with their mothers, in the postmodern age of the breakdown of identity. Whereas the subject described in "Stabat Mater" was entrapped in identification, through the Virgin, with the Law, the contemporary subject is left with no God and no Virgin to unify Law and desire, language and body. A great space opens up—a hole where the whole of the subject's identity was. A hole between language and body, now untraversable. The false, fixed identity with the Virgin, under the Law, has given way not to a freedom of difference, an open nonidentity, but to a new trap of emptiness.

For Kristeva, Duras's heroines are borderline cases, trapped in the melancholy of subjects unable to give up their primary attachment to their mothers.

It's not that these women live in illusion. They have learned the language and the terms of the given order all too well. But there is no libidinal or amorous investment in that order; this has "remained in the emptiness of maternal fusion and/or maternal absence."[26] Thus, the desire of these women is void of illusion. They desire completion, but they have been forced, in a world abandoned by God and by the Virgin, to acknowledge that they can never have it. So they live an unendable sadness, a disillusion which is just (to borrow a phrase from Luce Irigaray) as illusory.[27] In a world abandoned by God, the woman abandoned by her mother still wants her—still wants what she can no longer believe in. Resigned to the tragedy, the tragic reality that she cannot have her, she nevertheless wants nothing else.

Duras's sad women are walking memories of the hole left by their abandonment, commemorations of the whole that once was. Bodies holding the void inside them, unable to look away, focused always inward on that hole, these women live the melancholy of impossible mourning. For they cannot give up the mother. They keep her absence in their bodies like a wound. Unable to develop a loving identification with the social symbolic order, Duras's heroines live the postmodern condition of the absence of identity. In the absence of the absolute other there is no One with whom to identify, (or to have in support of one's identity): no self can exist. The truth of division, of fragmentation, of the absence of the self, is laid bare, but rather than forming a tenuous identification with a third party—with the symbolic order—and thereby developing a subjectivity-in-division, accepting their fragmentation, Duras's sad women are fixated upon the emptiness created by the mother's separation.

> This sorrow, expressing an impossible pleasure, is the agonizing sign of frigidity. Holding back a passion that cannot flow, this sorrow is, more profoundly, the prison of an impossible mourning for an ancient love made up wholly of sensation and *autosensation;* it is inalienable, inseparable, and, for that very reason, unnameable. . . . Indeed, at the source of this sorrow, there exists an unassumable abandonment.[28]

And so these daughters remain at the stage of autoerotic immediacy with their mothers, unable to identify with anything outside. Instead of identification there is a reduplication of/with the mother.

> (Re)duplication is a blocked repetition. Whereas repetition extends in time, reduplication is outside of time, a reverberation in space, a game of mirrors with no perspective, no duration. For a while, a double can freeze the instability of the same, give it temporary identity, but eventually it explores the abyss of the same, probing those unsuspected and unplumbable depths. The double is the unconscious depth of the same, that which threatens it, can engulf it.[29]

Caught in the unnameable space of reduplication, preceding, never achieving, identity, Duras's heroines are caught in a choked passion for the other woman—a passion which is endlessly thwarted.

> An echo of the deathly symbiosis with the mother, passion between two women is one of the most intense figures of doubling.[30]

Of course, the mother is as much feared and hated as loved—the hatred and the fear are inextricable from the love, knotted up in the ambivalence of intense desire. And Duras's mothers are all mad women, desired/hated, inaccessible.

> Out of fear of maternal madness, the novelist eliminates the mother, separating from her with a violence no less murderous than that of the mother who beats her prostituted daughter. Destroy, the daughter-narrator seems to say in *The Lover,* but in erasing the figure of the mother, she actually takes her place, substituting herself for maternal madness. She does not kill the mother so much as extend her presence into the negative hallucination of an always loving identification.[31]

Reduplication, then, serves as the "negative hallucination" of an unachieved identification, casting the daughter, like the mother, into the space of the inaccessible woman.

> The mythification of the inaccessible feminine in Duras then contains a certain truth about the female experience of a *jouissance* of sorrow.[32]

Duras's daughters still live the myth of the absolute woman, alone in her sadness. Borderline cases, they reduplicate their mothers' borderline status as *lack* of identity—pure lack, pure sorrow: the truth of division is revealed as pure, beautiful tragedy once more.

Certainly, the reality that underlies the lives of Duras's heroines is the reality of a social order in which the position of the female subject is, to say the least, problematic. Identification with the mother still means reduplication of the universal absolute woman—of, that is, the phallic mother, object of our profoundly ambivalent feelings of intense passion and intense hatred.

If we are going to get rid of the patriarchal order we have to give up the phallic mother. We have to posit ourselves as singular subjects, different from our mothers, and different from the universal absolute woman, the archaic phallic mother of our cultural phantasy.

The question is, however, does this entail accepting our mother's castration and turning from mother to father, or is there a possibility of identification with our singular mothers, nonphallic mothers, within the given social order, and with the capacity of changing that order? Is there, in other words, a possibility of positing ourselves as singular subjects through the acceptance of and identification with a symbolic order which is understood to be not completely phallic?

In her paper, "Freud and Love: Treatment and its Discontents," Kristeva argues that the subjectivity of the subject-in-process requires an identification through or with the divided mother. But she is ambivalent as to how the mother's division is to be constituted. On the one hand, she is apparently arguing, with Freud and Lacan, that the child must accept the mother's castration, or lack of the phallus, and must turn from a state of nondifferentiation with the mother to a tenuous and always-divided identity with the symbolic law of the father—an identity which is always predicated on the lack of the phallus. On the other hand, she seems to be holding out the possibility of identification with a mother who is divided but not lacking.

In "Freud and Love," Kristeva argues for the necessity of identification with what she calls, following Freud, the "imaginary father of individual prehistory,"[33] but the meaning of this phrase is left ambiguous.

Kristeva argues, with Lacan, that the child must accept the mother's division. In other words, the child must accept that (s)he is not the sole object of the mother's desire—that the mother desires something else besides the child. That "something else" is the "imaginary father of individual prehistory."

In places, Kristeva makes it quite clear that what the mother wants—and what the child identifies with—is the phallus. Hence, the accession to the symbolic order entails identification with the mother's lack, with, that is, her castration. This is, of course, quite compatible with the original Freudian-Lacanian position: The child originally identifies with the object of the mother's desire—with the phallus she lacks; but in order to accede to the symbolic order, the child must accept the impossibility of being, or having, the phallus for herself, and so must accept and identify with her lack or division.

> Let me now point out that the most archaic unity that we thus retrieve—an identity so autonomous that it calls forth displacements—is that of the phallus desired by the mother. . . . The imaginary father would thus be the indication that the mother is not complete but that she wants. . . .[34]

So here we are back at the phallus. And if phallus there must be, it had better be the father's. "The archaic inscription of the father seems to me a way of modifying the fantasy of a phallic mother playing at the phallus game all by herself."[35]

Here it seems that Kristeva has reaffirmed the absolute dichotomy between father and mother: the symbolic order belongs to the father, is inherently phallic, and the mother has no place in it except through her dissembling artifice of masquerade as the phallus. We are warned, once again, against identification with "a phallic mother playing at the phallus game all by herself." As if there were no other game to play.

However, in other places Kristeva argues that the imaginary father is simply a metaphor for the third term—something which intervenes between mother and child to introduce the dimension of sociality, to create two where one had been. So that the child is able to leave the immediate unity with the mother and accede to a position of unity, of identity, in separation from her. This movement depends upon the mother's relation to—and positioning within—the symbolic order. Thus, the mother does not exist outside the social order, as its support. Rather, it is the mother's relation to the symbolic order which provides the child with a mode of entry into that order. Yet because the mother's relation to the symbolic coexists with her semiotic relation to the child, she serves as a model of divided subjectivity. Positioned within both the semiotic and symbolic orders, desiring the child and desiring also the world outside, isn't the divided mother the subject-in-process or on-trial with whom the child can identify?

Here, Kristeva is describing a mother quite different from the one who finds her phallus in the child, and quite different from the one locked into the semiotic *chora*.

In a reference to Winnicott, Kristeva remarks:

> nobody knows what the good-enough mother is. I wouldn't try to explain what that is, but I would try to suggest that maybe the good enough mother is the mother who has something else to love besides her child, it could be her work, her husband, her lovers, etc. If for a mother

the child is the meaning of her life, it's too heavy. She has to have another meaning in her life. And this other meaning in her life is the father of prehistory.[36]

The "father of prehistory," is, then, "some sort of archaic occurrence of the symbolic."[37] Identification takes place not with a corporally present object, and not with an actual father, but with a "not-yet-object," a "pattern" or "model"[38]—with that to which the mother's desire refers.

Here, it would seem that in fact the child is to identify with the mother's division, between body and language, fusion and separation. And (s)he identifies not so much with the object of the mother's desire—which is in fact still unknown—as with the mother's desire itself. The child, then, identifies with/as a subject-in-process, represented by the mother. Rather than fixing upon an object, (s)he identifies with the process of subjectivity, a mode of being, characterized by desire for otherness, ordered according to a logic of negativity: constant movement, change.

According to this conception, identification is based on a transferring of "auto-erotic motility" to a "unifying image," such that a "sundered unity" is developed.[39] Kristeva stresses that she wants to "[situate] this unifying guideline within an objectality in the process of being established rather than in the absolute of the reference to the phallus as such."[40]

The concept of the divided mother which I have drawn out of Kristeva's work makes it possible to conceptualize a mode of identification with a symbolic order that is not monolithic, not completely exhausted by the Law of the Father, but which is composed of competing discourses and practices. So, the mother can participate in the symbolic order while maintaining heterogeneity, rather than playing the part of phallic castrated mother within the Law of the Father, or subversive mother on the margins, outside the symbolic order, trapped in the semiotic *chora*.

In closing, I would like to suggest that perhaps there is a good reason for Kristeva's ambivalence between these two positions—between the necessity of accepting the mother's division as castration, lack of the phallus; and the possibility of identification with and through the divided mother as a subject-in-process or on-trial. Perhaps this is the unavoidable ambivalence of a theorist fully cognizant of the situation in which the female subject finds herself in our culture: On the one hand, identification with the given order, acceptance of the given social contract, does entail acceptance of the Law of the Father, and of the mother's—and our own— castration. We do live in a society oriented around the phallus. On the other hand, Kristeva wants to argue that the symbolic order is not absolutely identical with the father's Law—that the mother, for instance, is not merely a victim of, but is also a participant in, the social symbolic order and is capable of representing aspects of symbolic ordering to the child. And, that through identification with her mother, *and* with the symbolic order, a female subject might take up a position as a participant in the given order, and in the creation of a different one.

Notes

1. Julia Kristeva, *Revolution in Poetic Language,* trans. Margaret Waller, (New York: Columbia University Press), p. 143.

2. Ibid., p. 141.

3. Julia Kristeva, "Women's Time," trans. Alice Jardine and Harry Blake, *Signs* 7, 1, 1981: p. 28.

4. Ibid.

5. Jacqueline Rose, "Julia Kristeva—Take Two," chapter 3 in this volume.

6. Julia Kristeva, "Stabat Mater," in *The Kristeva Reader,* trans. Leon S. Roudiez, pp. 161-2.

7. While Kristeva here uses the term "primary narcissism" to refer to the earliest relationship with the mother, in her later theory, she differentiates between the "autoeroticism of the mother-child dyad" ("Freud and Love,: Treatment and Its Discontents," 241) which precedes narcissism, and narcissism as the introjection of an identification with the "father of individual prehistory." These concepts are developed in "Freud and Love," following Freud in *On Narcissism* (Sigmund Freud, *Pelican Freud Library*, 11, see p. 69) and "Identification" in *Group Psychology and the Analysis of the Ego* (Sigmund Freud, *Pelican Freud Library*, 12, see pp. 134-40).

8. Julia Kristeva, "Stabat Mater," p. 161.

9. In *Revolution in Poetic Language,* Kristeva notes that the oral and anal drives, which constitute the primary connections between body, objects, and the protagonists of family—and hence social-structure—are oriented and structured around the mother's body. Thus, the mother's body, as the ordering principle of the *chora,* is what mediates, for the child, the symbolic law organizing social relations. (p. 27).

10. Julia Kristeva, "Stabat Mater," p. 167.

11. Ibid., pp. 181–2.

12. Ibid., p. 163.

13. Ibid., pp. 174–5.

14. Ibid., p. 174.

15. Ibid., p. 176.

16. Ibid., p. 180.

17. Ibid., p. 180.

18. See, for example, Sigmund Freud, "On the Mechanisms of Paranoia," in the case study of Doctor Schreber (Sigmund Freud, *Freud Pelican Library* 9, 196–219) and "A Case of Paranoia Running Counter to the Psychoanalytic Theory of the Disease"

(Sigmund Freud, *Freud Pelican Library* 10, 145–58.)

19. Julia Kristeva, "Stabat Mater," p. 180.

20. Ibid.

21. Ibid., pp. 180–1.

22. Ibid., p. 181.

23. Ibid., p. 181.

24. Ibid., p. 180. Kristeva is referring here to Marina Warner's book, *Alone of All Her Sex. The Myth and Cult of the Virgin Mary* (New York: Knopf, 1976), which was a primary source for Kristeva's "Stabat Mater."

25. Ibid., p. 173.

26. Julia Kristeva, "Freud and Love: Treatment and Its Discontents," p. 266.

27. Luce Irigaray, "Any Theory of the 'Subject' Has Always Been Appropriated by the 'Masculine'," in *Speculum of the Other Woman,* trans. Gillian C. Gill (Ithaca, N.Y.: Cornell University Press, 1985), p. 145.

28. Julia Kristeva, "The Pain of Sorrow in the Modern World: The Works of Marguerite Duras," trans. Katharine A. Jensen, *PMLA* 102, 2 (March 1987): p. 145.

29. Ibid., p. 147.

30. Ibid., p. 148.

31. Ibid., p. 146.

32. Ibid., p. 147.

33. Sigmund Freud, "The Ego and the Id," *Pelican Freud Library* 11, 370.

34. Julia Kristeva, "Freud and Love: Treatment and Its Discontents," p. 256.

35. Ibid., 259.

36. Julia Kristeva, "Julia Kristeva in conversation with Rosalind Coward," in *Desire,* ed. Lisa Appignanesi (ICA Documents, 1984), p. 23.

37. Ibid.

38. Julia Kristeva, "Freud and Love: Treatment and Its Discontents," p. 243.

39. Ibid., p. 247.

40. Ibid.

6

Renaissance Paintings and Psychoanalysis: Julia Kristeva and the Function of the Mother

Mary Bittner Wiseman

The intention of this chapter is to pave the way for a rewriting of Freud's family romance from the point of view of the Madonna, rather than of Oedipus, by calling into question Freud's conceptions of the feminine, based as they are on his admitted ignorance about what goes on in the earliest years of a girl's life and the virtual absence from his writings of any discussion of motherhood or of the mothers of his patients. The laws by which Freud constitutes the feminine, to wit, that everything is always already gendered, that the mother is feminine and every infant masculine, and that one cannot love the same as its self, are challenged by Julia Kristeva's analysis of motherhood. The analysis weaves through her interpretations of the Madonna paintings of Giovanni Bellini and challenges classical psychoanalysis by breaking the conceptual connection posited by Freud between the maternal and the feminine.

This chapter begins in turn-of-the-century Vienna, to see how Madonnas got into psychoanalysis and turns then to Paris of the 1970s, to see how Kristeva theorizes painting, paintings of the Madonna, and motherhood. Finally, it goes to Renaissance Venice, to interpret three paintings by Bellini that themselves interpret a drama scripted by Freud.

Vienna: Two Absences

"She remained *two hours* in front of the Sistine Madonna, rapt in silent admiration."[1]

In 1900 Freud wrote the case history of Dora as an example of a successful application of the theory of dreams. He had deciphered two of her dreams but completed the second only *after* the analysis. He said of the second dream that, since Dora stopped the analysis abruptly, "the whole of it was not cleared up."[2] A clue to why may be found in the way he handled Dora's answer to a question he had asked. Dora had mentioned her first visit to Dresden, and Freud recounts that "not failing, of course, to visit the famous picture gallery . . . [Dora] remained *two hours* in front of the Sistine Madonna, rapt in silent admiration. When I asked what had pleased her so much about the picture she could find no clear answer to make. At last she said: 'The Madonna'."[3] Freud effectively ignored the answer in making only two cursory references to the Madonna in the case history proper. The first is the expression of his intention to make a future investigation into the theme of the virgin mother. The second is made in a footnote in which Freud adds what he calls the supplementary interpretation that Dora is the Madonna. Why? Because "the notion of the 'Madonna' is a favorite counter-idea in the mind of girls who feel themselves oppressed by imputations of sexual guilt" and because had the analysis continued, "Dora's maternal longing for a child would probably have been revealed as an obscure though powerful motive in her behavior."[4] Since the Madonna has neither sexual guilt nor unsatisfied maternal longing, the young girl who imagines herself to be the Madonna has thereby both a child and sexual innocence.

There were other ways for Dora to have put herself into the *Sistine Madonna*, however. She could have wanted to have the Madonna rather than to be her, loving a woman as Freud later discovered she did. She could have wanted to be the child in the Madonna's arms, loving her mother and wanting to be loved by her as once she was. Freud confesses that he had not mastered the serial transferences of Dora's "deepest rooted" feelings. As Peter Gay observes, "with Dora, for reasons of his own, [Freud] failed to build on what he had begun to understand. The case seems to have been the one that largely clarified the issue [of transference] for him—but only after it was over."[5] One of the "reasons of his own" for not building on what he had glimpsed about the analytic bond, and for his interpretative blindness with respect to Dora's encounter with the *Sistine Madonna,* was Freud's difficulty in recognizing a transference that made a woman of him.

The postscript to the case history provides a virtually complete theory of transference, along with the recognition that the deepest current of Dora's unconscious life was her love for a woman. Nonetheless, the absence of the *Sistine Madonna* from the account is striking. Freud interprets Dora's response to the idea of the Madonna, not to Raphael's painting. Yet Dora is captured by the painting, and a work of art cannot be reduced to an idea. Even if it is the subject matter of a work that moves one, the subject is presented in a medium in a certain manner, where the manner extends to the handling of the idea as well as of the material. Freud had spoken of the powerful effect that works of art exercised over him, leading him "to spend a long time before them trying to apprehend them in my own way, i.e. to explain to myself what their effect is due to."[6] Might not Dora have stood in front of the *Sistine Madonna* for the same sort of reason? Julia Kristeva interprets the matter and the manner of Renaissance Madonnas in providing the account of motherhood missing from Freud's writings.

A second striking absence appears in Freud's accounts of female sexuality. They do not explore the time in the life of a girl before the coming of Oedipus. Having said, as late as 1923, that the overcoming of the Oedipus complex was "precisely analogous" in each sex, Freud concluded in 1925 that there was a crucial difference: that the order of the castration and Oedipus complexes differs in girls and boys. The threat of castration followed and "smashed to pieces" the boy's Oedipal desire, whereas the fact of castration preceded and caused the girl's desire for her father, really desire for a child by him.[7] It follows both that the girl's desire for the father is not original and that nothing occurs in the history of the girl to destroy her Oedipal dream as the castration complex destroys that of the boy. Indeed, because the Madonna is the sublime fulfillment of the girl's Oedipal desire, it acts *against* the destruction of the desire. For the Madonna has a child by God, the archetypal father from whom all goods flow, and the child she has by him is what enables all of God's children to regain paradise. There could be no more powerful or desirable father or child. Since there is no heavenly mother of whom Mary need be jealous, she is the archetypal mother. So seductive is the figure of the Madonna that she is what the girl must want to be, and Freud need hardly interpret Dora's response.

In 1931 Freud said that analysis has shown girls' primary attachments to have been to their mothers and that except for the change in the love object there is no difference in their erotic life before and after the coming of Oedipus. He allows that the "insight into this early, pre-Oedipus, phase in girls comes . . . as a surprise, like the discovery, in another field, of the Minoan-Mycenean civilization behind the civilization of Greece."[8] And yet the realization that something happened in the place where the daughter still dreams of her mother did not lead to Freud's trying to uncover what lies buried there. Again Kristeva does what Freud does not do. She excavates the ground of this Minoan-Mycenean civilization, digging down to the residue of what happened in the time before Oedipus brought language, down even into the body of the mother, to where what happens is reenacted in the performances of art by artist and spectator alike. She does this by psychoanalyzing works of art.

Freud may not write the text, but he gives the theoretical permission for the psychoanalysis of works of art. He does not hold that they are to be interpreted in the way that dreams, jokes, and symptoms are. Artworks are neither as direct nor as immediate as are dreams and jokes. Nor are they defenses, as are neurotic symptoms. There is a sense, however, in which artworks are screens behind which lie the forgotten, the repressed, instinctual drives, and on which "alterity becomes nuance, contradiction becomes a variant, tension becomes passage, and discharge becomes peace."[9] In this sense they may be said to have an unconscious that reveals itself in the sometimes powerful effects they have on their viewers. How is this to be theorized? In "Moses and Michaelangelo," Freud claims that the artist intends to produce in his audience "the same mental constellation" that moved him to make the work, and that this intention can be put into words. "To discover his intention, though, I must first find out the meaning and content of what is represented in his work; I must, in other words, be able to *interpret* it."[10] The work is what is to be analyzed and the mind of the artist to be read from it, for the artist is constituted by the work. Freud follows these claims with the example of *Hamlet*, saying that its effect was explained only after "the material of the tragedy had been traced back analytically to the Oedipus theme."[11] This is an example of the effect of an artwork's depending on something not only fundamental to development, as Oedipus is, but also disturbing, as Oedipus is, and this something's being *latent* in the work.

As Freud complicates his theory of the unconscious, it turns out that what is latent may be so not only by having been repressed because disturbing, but also by being instinctual and as such inexpressible or unrepresentable. Since the effects of a work are traceable to the latent content and not to the manifest form or texture of the painting, this content is what must be uncovered in order to account for the effect. Richard Wollheim suggests that the spectator may "use the element of play to divert his attention from the more disturbing or latent content of the work of art," where the play is the Kantian purposeless and disinterested quickening of the faculties of imagination and understanding.[12] In this view, the play diverts the spectator's attention from what the painting represses, and what it represses accounts for its effect on the viewer. Whether or not a painting does express its maker's "intentions and emotional activities," as Freud believed, his crucial observations are that the intention can be discovered only *after* discovery of "the meaning and content of what is represented" and that the manifest content may conceal something disturbing or itself unrepresentable.[13] Freud charts a course he himself could not have run, a course from which are barred no associations with a given artwork or its elements. Kristeva runs the whole of it, implying a theory of interpretation within which the notion of transference accounts for the myriad ways painter and spectator can put themselves into a painting.

The interpretative technique connected with the theory of transference supposes that the spectator or artist transfers certain intentions, beliefs, desires, energies, tendencies, or fantasies onto the painting. The transfer is a return to the painting of precisely what has been called forth and given shape by it. For example, a reader using such an interpretive strategy may assume the role of Dora in front of the painting and put herself into the place of St. Barbara in the *Sistine Madonna*. St. Barbara defied her father and died by his hand rather than recant the faith he abhorred, and Dora, too, would like to defy the father who is trying to pawn her off onto the husband of his mistress and (symbolically) die rather than yield. Transferences are, Freud writes in the postscript to *Dora*, "new editions or facsimiles of the tendencies and phantasies which are aroused and made conscious during the progress of the analysis."[14] Some, he goes on to say, are merely reprints. Others, subject to sublimation, are revised editions. Dora has made of herself a revised edition of Barbara. In the transferences that occur in psychoanalysis, some earlier person is replaced by the person of the physician, whereas in those that occur in the encounter with art, any earlier object or drive or desire aroused and made conscious during the encounter may be replaced by any element of the artwork. Moreover, by a natural extension of the theory, the artist or spectator may replace herself by some other.

Since it was Freud's study of identification that led him to recognize the broader reach of the unconscious, it is plausible to invoke a theory of transference according to which both *subjects,* understood as the nexus of wishes and impulses, drives and desires, beliefs and intentions, and the *objects* of such various mental attitudes and activities are variables capable of assuming sundry values. Wollheim claims that once Freud came to recognize that unconscious operations were not limited either to repression or to "the mode of mental functioning called the primary process," he saw the work of art to be not only expressive but also constructive "in the binding of energy or, what is a theoretically related process, the building up of the ego."[15] While it is true that Freud gave no account of the artwork as a construction of the unconscious mind, the unconscious serving, in Freud's account of art, only "as providing techniques of concealment or possibilities of play," the lineaments of an account can be made out in Kristeva's work.[16]

Paris: The Maternal Function and the Madonna

In "Motherhood According to Giovanni Bellini," Bellini's paintings lead back to the beginning of the human subject, in the time before the appearance of the father thwarted the boy's desire to have the mother and occasioned the girl's desire to be one.[17] Fundamental to classical psychoanalysis is the principle that the mother is always already feminine and her infant masculine and its corollary that a girl becomes a woman by becoming (wanting to become) a mother. Kristeva unties this Freudian knot by freeing the feminine from the maternal and characterizing the mother not as *object* of the child's desire but as a *function,* her body the field on which the genetic code of the species and of the biological individual is written. The woman mother is not the *subject* of motherhood: "[w]ithin the body, growing as a graft, indomitable, there is an other. And no one is present, within that simultaneously dual and alien space, to signify what is going on. 'It happens, but I'm not there.' 'I cannot realize it, but it goes on',"[18] The mother does not become an object of the child's desire until the appearance of the languaged world of figurable and representable objects. The world of named things, including man and woman, masculine and feminine, is fashioned by cuttings, by the markings of differences, but the first split is not, as Freud would have it, between masculine and feminine. It is the splittings that occur in and from the maternal body in which cells split and split again. Maternity itself is neither masculine nor feminine, and what goes on in the body of the woman mother is mimed by the kind of pictorial representation that results in "a shattering of figuration and form in a space of graphic lines and colors, differentiated until they disappear in pure light," the kind of representation of which Bellini was master and with which he initiated the Venetian Renaissance.[19]

The essay begins with a reflection on the maternal body and ends with motherhood's being called nothing but a luminous spatialization, "the ultimate language of a *jouissance* at the far limits of repression, whence bodies, identities, and signs are begotten."[20] How does Kristeva get from the one to the other? Along a path that weaves from the biological phenomenon of gestation to Bellini's transference of the drama of the child's separation from the mother onto his Madonna paintings. The path continues to run through the Renaissance in Venice as Bellini moves the art of painting from the Byzantine portraits of his father, Jacopo, to the nude females of his students, Giorgione and Titian. The maternal body comes to be seen through its painted representations and, finally, through the lines and colors that paintings are, no matter their subject. Insofar as the act of painting is an "indwelling of the symbolic within instinctual drives," it mimes what goes on in the womb.[21] Insofar as the painting exemplifies "the intersection of sign and rhythm, of representation and light, of the symbolic and the semiotic," it is a record made by the unconscious of "those clashes that occur between the biological and social program of the species."[22]

Kristeva introduces Bellini by his difference from Leonardo da Vinci and regards the paintings of Bellini as Freud regards those of Leonardo, namely, as uncanny sublimations of primitive instincts and desires.[23] Freud could not make his way about in the place where the mother is no more than a (bodily) function or in the place where daughter loves mother. He was, therefore, silent about Dora's response to Raphael's Madonna. But since he could easily make his way in the place where son loves mother, he was not silent about Leonardo's Madonna paintings, analyzing them as manifestations of a repressed love for his real and adoptive mothers. In the paintings, the mother exists for the sake of the child, and Leonardo is both beloved child and the mother whose role he assumed as (in her guise) he loved himself in loving boys. Bellini, on the other hand, seems to have been loved by no mother. His father's wife did not acknowledge him, and there is no record of another in his life. Kristeva starts from this apparent fact to claim that the paintings of the two exemplify different economies in Western representation and that the difference follows from their different relations to the mother.

In the early Madonna paintings, Bellini portrays the absence of the mother by the split in the maternal body, between hands that hold the child as close as ever womb held its guest and dreaming, inward-looking face. Her body is there, *she* is not. Later paintings reflect changes in technique, experiments in the composition of light and space as volumes created out of curving light and fragmented space, even as these gain a life of their own. His corpus reenacts both the drama of the separation of child from mother and the transformation of the mother into dazzles of light. In the course of the separation, the seductive mother figured in the earlier paintings becomes space and light, preconditions of seeing the masterable and graspable forms created by Leonardo. The movement is from iconographic Byzantine mother through the seducing mother, the threatening mother, the hostile mother who seems to flee the son, to "the luminous space where she surrogates herself," where Bellini's genius in creating worlds out of nothing but light and its supporting space and air comes to perfection.[24]

Kristeva has revised Freud's account of the human predicament by starting with the maternal function. This starts well before the appearance of the paternal language that constitutes the mother as an object (of desire).

It is a function satisfied by whoever breaks through the symbolic screen of language and culture to reach the semiotic, the instinctual, the primitive, the raw, as it may be supposed Dora did when she remained two hours in front of the *Sistine Madonna,* rapt in silent admiration. The experiences of motherhood and art alike occur in that place where "contradictions become variants," and they are functions in a rather precise sense: They are variables to which indefinitely many values can be assigned; their subjects and the objects are exchangeable by other subjects, other objects.[25] To interpret a painting in the Kristevan way, then, is to do what Freud bid, namely, to find "the meaning and content of what is represented in the work" by giving an account of the manifest in terms of the hidden.[26] The spectator's being powerfully moved by a work of art is a sign of her having reached the work's latent content, where the content is the memory of a time and a place: the time before the mother became an object and the place (in the womb or at the breast) where what would eventually construct an identity (build up an ego) was neither something nor nothing.

The artwork constructs the memory, it does not express it. The construction proceeds by juxtapositions and divisions, whose fusions and fissions produce tiny energy-releasing cataclysms, and the construction is the binding of the released energy. The function of the mother is to stage the "clashes that occur between the biological and social program of the species," to be the body on which is staged the play of language and its other.[27] The biological experience of becoming a mother can register these fusions and fissions, but otherwise "the speaker reaches this limit . . . only by virtue of a particular, discursive practice called 'art'."[28] One division made by Kristeva is that of motherhood into two facets, maternal and paternal. Classical psychoanalysis recognizes only the paternal, in which the desire to be a mother is just desire for a child by the father, and the Madonna stands as the realization, in fantasy, of this desire, doomed by the incest taboo to be realized in fantasy only. The other facet is a material causality, a

> spasm of a memory belonging to the species . . . an excursion to the limits of primal regression [that] can be phantasmatically experienced as the reunion of a woman-mother with the body of her mother. The body of her mother is always the same Master-Mother of instinctual drive. . . . By giving birth . . . a woman is simultaneously closer to her instinctual memory, more open to her own psychosis, and consequently, more negatory of the social, symbolic bond.[29]

This maternal facet is "a whirl of words, a complete absence of meaning and seeing; it is feeling, displacement, rhythm, sounds, flashes, and fantasied clinging to the maternal body as a screen against the plunge."[30] Leonardo is master of the paternal facet of artistic production, Bellini of the maternal.

Venice: Three Paintings

The Lochis Madonna in Bergamo (1475), *Madonna with Two Trees* in Venice (1487), and *Woman with a Mirror* in Vienna (1515) span forty years of Bellini's long painting life, all spent in Venice, where he was born some time after 1433 and died in 1516. His father Jacopo and his brother Gentile were painters, his sister Nicolosia, the wife of Andrea Mantegna. Married by 1485, he had a son who died in 1499, some time after his mother's death. Kristeva suggests that, as a result of his marriage and fatherhood, Bellini replaced the idealized Byzantine and seductive mother portrayed in the *Lochis Madonna* with one who had "the feelings of con-trolled . . . disappointment evident in the *Madonna with Two Trees.*"[31] It is as though paternity were necessary "to find [for the mother] an increas-ingly appropriate language, capable of capturing her specific imaginary *jouissance* . . . beyond, although always coexistent with, the imagery of full, mimetic, and true signs."[32]

Bellini is on the way toward finding what Kristeva considers an appro-priate language in the *Madonna with Two Trees,* of which the art historian Rona Goffen writes, that in it "even the closest forms are defined not by line but by color and ambient light."[33] Leonardo is the master of line, Bellini of color and light. Paintings in which forms are defined solely in Bellini's manner enable their spectators to witness the dissolution of the world into the space and air, color and light, "beyond although always coexistent with" the world of signs.[34] For Kristeva, light and line form a matrix of which the pairs maternal and paternal, semiotic and symbolic, primitive and cul-tured are transformations. Other transformations are freedom and thrall-dom: Bellini's freedom from the mother, encouraged by the simulation in his art of the maternal function; and Leonardo's thralldom to her, encour-aged by the repetition in his art of the fulfillment of the Oedipal fantasy.

Lochis Madonna (1475)

The Madonna and child is the sacred subject most frequently painted by Bellini and the *Lochis Madonna,* (fig. 1) one of dozens of images made by him for private devotion. Until about 1488, mother and child appear alone

Figure 1. Lochis Madonna.

as they do in this painting, whose two figures exhaust its surface. Mary is in the center, her head near the top of the picture plane—as near the top as the front of the parapet on which the child rests is near the bottom. Her right sleeve and his left arm touch the painting's sides. There is no room for a witness to the drama enacted in the shallow space between the flat background panel of dark squares and the ledge on which the child kneels and from which he almost tumbles out of the painting. He does not fall, however, because the Madonna holds him as firmly as the maternal body holds its parasite. But she is not there. Abstracted, inward looking, a beautiful, fragile face beneath the Byzantine wimple, a woman as absent as her maternal hands are present. Face and hands move along different axes. The axis of her body runs from his left knee to the top of her head, the axis of his body moves from his right foot to the top of his head. Her hands are positioned along the axis of his body, which is twisting away from her, whose own body is cut off by the parapet, making of it the partial figure of the icons beloved in Byzantium, icons in which the holy person pictured is supposed actually to be present. No person is present in the *Lochis Madonna,* however. The mother is not there for her son within the painting, but Goffen will articulate a sense in which they are both there for the Renaissance viewer, and Kristeva will assign a sense of an unrepresentable past's being latent in the texture as well as in the content of Bellini's art.

Kristeva and Goffen agree that, within the frame of the painting, Mary is elsewhere but disagree about where the elsewhere is. Goffen submits that it is at the scene of the sacrifice, his crucifixion, foreshadowed in the painting. The child is clad in a white shirt, his left knee rests on the mother's blue mantle. Although his genitals are barely visible between the bottom of his shirt and Mary's basketing robe, they are shown forth in the small frame made by the thumb and index finger of her right hand. His sex is one end of a curve made by the bottom of his shirt whose other end is the blood red of Mary's left sleeve, the color of blood faintly echoed by the color of the parapet. His having genitals and blood, shed at his circumcision and crucifixion, are signs of his humanity. For while divine procreation proceeds from the will alone, human procreation needs an intermediary, and what is passed along through generation(s) is the blood line. And so the course of his life from circumcision to crucifixion is foredrawn.

Whereas Goffen's Madonna is not there for the child because she is contemplating his crucifixion, Kristeva's Madonna is not there because she is experiencing the maternal *jouissance* of which the infant is but efficient and material cause. The mother is in a place where there are no subjects and objects, but only tiny differences like the difference between the instincts of life and death. Kristeva's Madonna looks back, Goffen's looks forward. Each of their elsewheres is out of the human world of languaged forms, however. The Madonna under Kristeva's description, the master mother of instinctual drive, is climbing up and down the genetic tree, while the Madonna under Goffen's description, the Queen of Heaven, is climbing Jacob's ladder. Not only are their Madonnas elsewhere than in the world formed by language, each bridges this world and her elsewhere. According to Kristeva, motherhood bridges raw (primitive) and cultured, real (semiotic) and symbolic, and contains within itself maternal and paternal, for all these pairs are transformations of the matrix of light and line. She describes the body of the mother as the threshold where cyclical nature meets culture and linear time. According to Christian theology, Goffen's text, the Madonna breaches sin and salvation, human and divine; she is the medium between earth and heaven, partaking of both and being (exclusively) neither.

Just as the psychoanalytic and theological explanations of the Madonna's distance from her child are different in content but similar in structure, so too are the accounts of the Madonna and child's presence to the viewer. Goffen's explanation is couched in terms of Renaissance pictorial conventions. In all of the Madonnas painted by Bellini before 1500, Mary is shown half length, and the child is positioned on a ledge or parapet that has the shape of the altar on which the son's sacrifice is repeatedly offered up to his father. The child is always shown on the ledge, thrust toward the viewer, almost out of the picture space, and the Madonna is always immediately behind it.[35] The half figure refers to the Byzantine tradition and the legend of Saint Luke. The legend is that Mary appeared before Luke as he was making a drawing of her, and he was therefore able to produce a portrait.[36] Because it was painted in the presence of the model, the portrait was thought to have greater claim to truth or greater authority than would a picture made from memory or imagination. For example, there was a tradition in Rome that if the emperor were not able to be present to pass judgment as Roman law required, his portrait could be his proxy. Goffen concludes that "we understand, as ancient and Renaissance people did when they made or viewed portraits, that a likeness signifies actual presence."[37]

The half-length figure and the parapet were "a means of asserting the visionary presence of the sacred beings before us" and are gone from the Madonna paintings after 1500.[38] "These implications of presence are [then] replaced by a Western conception of the sacred image as a representation—a painting, not an apparition."[39] Bellini's early Madonna paintings were made for private devotion, and their effectiveness came in part from the viewer's beliefs that God exists, that the child of Mary is God incarnate, and that mother and child are present in their image. This belief was constructed not only from beliefs about the presence of the sacred figures to which Bellini refers, however, but also from his singular contribution to the Venetian Renaissance, namely, the luminous density of color in his paintings. The paintings themselves become fields of color, light, and space in which everything solid melts into air, as does the difference between apparition or image and real thing. Although the Madonna is absent from the child within the painting, she and the child are present to the viewer as the image itself comes to betoken presence. The effect of this realism of the image is to make the painted figures part of the viewer's world, thereby facilitating the viewer's transference onto them of desires aroused and made conscious by the encounter with the painting.

Next to this realism of the image may be put a realism of the becoming-bound-of-instinctual-energy. Rather as Kant's imagination schematizes the manifold of perception, readying percepts for the imposition of concepts (the categories of understanding), so on Kristeva's view, art schematizes the instincts' energy, readying unbound energy for the imposition of symbolic forms (the categories of language). What goes on in the womb and at the breast, before the not-yet-subject has the categories of language through which to express or to represent its experience, binds the subject-to-be to its mother, and separation from the mother requires and begins the schematization of the newly-free energy. In Freud's account, the male child's bond turns into the desire for intimacy with its mother that succumbs to the threat of castration. This is not the case with the girl child, however, and Freud confesses to finding the stage in the girl's life before the bond is loosed a dark continent within which there are no signposts. Nonetheless, he theorizes the matter in such a way that the girl wants to have a child by her father and not to have to contend with her mother as rival. The Madonna satisfies these conditions and is the girl's ideal of what to be and is also the ideal object of the boy's desire. For although the father of the Madonna's child is God, a formidable rival, once the child is born, this father stands aside to let the son take center stage.

Kristeva begins her story before the subject-to-be has become subject-to-desire for the object mother and tells it through art, in which the schematization of the instincts is repeated. Suffering separation from the mother is the beginning of the construction of the subject, the building of the ego, the binding of the energy of the drives. John Lechte has persuasively argued that for Kristeva "art is the means of *identifying* with suffering," or of "putting suffering into the symbolic," and the point can be generalized to whatever is like suffering in that it can be undergone but not said.[40] If the real is supposed to be instinctual energy unbound (directed to no object), then this real is the materiality of language, its rhythm, "the vital, erotic aspect of language . . . the difference between art as drive affect taken in charge, and art denuded of all affect, the art of a pure symbolic form."[41] Bellini's early Madonna paintings take charge of the necessary and impossible bond between mother and child by putting it into signs, assigning a form to what can be suffered but not spoken. He painted its strength and its fragility: for the bond with the mother, like the thread of the spider, is at the same time most strong and most fine. Once the psychic umbilicus is put into signs, it becomes part of what Roland Barthes has called the *studium*, what is conventionally coded in an image, what belongs to culture. The *studium* can be transversed or transgressed by the *punctum*, what leaps up out of the image to pierce, to prick, to touch, to wound its viewer.[42] Kristeva's notion of the instinctual real taken charge of by the symbolic renders Barthes's notion of the intractable real tamed by culture.[43] Tamed but not deadened, for the power of images lies precisely in their being responsive to what can leap up out of them to touch their viewers. Within the world of symbols and culture, the real reasserts itself as energy ever threatening the stability of form, of the coded, the signed. A moment engendered by this threat, a moment of the greatest risk for the infant-becoming-a-subject, is captured in the *Lochis Madonna*. It is when the mother is not there and the forms of the world are not yet, when the instincts are deprived of their natural ends and are not yet redirected to others.

Madonna with Two Trees (1487)

The peril threatening the infant-becoming-a-subject in the early Bellini Madonnas has been overcome by the time of the *Madonna with Two Trees* (fig. 2). The composition is the same, half-length Madonna in front of a curtain and behind a ledge on which the child stands. But there are differences. Behind the dreaming face of the *Lochis Madonna* is her dream, her maternal joy not essentially connected with an object and therefore not with the child. Her self-absorption is seductive: inviting the viewer in, even as it closes her off, it makes the viewer want to be in on Mary's secret. The Madonna in *Madonna with Two Trees* is not self-absorbed but is connected with the child by her look. Whereas the surface of the earlier painting is divided by the diagonal folds of Mary's robe, her dreaming face above the diagonal and her hands and the child they hold below, this painting is divided by the panel of cloth into foreground and background. In the foreground is what occupied all of the earlier painting: cloth, ledge, and two figures. In the background, glimpsed on either side of the centered curtain, is a landscape whose horizon is below the painting's midpoint. The trunks of the two trees of the title appear immediately behind the low parapet on

Figure 2.   Madonna with Two Trees.

which the child stands upright and are interrupted by the sleeves of Mary's mantle. Upright like child, mother, and the cloth whose sides brush and hide their edges, the trees connect background with foreground. Behind the lighted green of the panel edged in red, the horizon dissolves into shimmers of light as meadow gives way to hills bathed in mist that give way, in turn, to infinite-seeming space. The cloth's red borders repeat the strong verticals of figures and trees and, abruptly distinguishing the cloth's lambency from that of the landscape, repeat the red of the mother's gown that is background to the child's bare flesh. Meanwhile, the sky, deeper hued toward the painting's top, curves back from the lustrous depth of the horizon to meet the cloth whose hue it now shares.

In Bellini's Madonna paintings, the "same light and air that suffuse the landscape also surround Mary and Christ. Figures and setting are bound by this enveloping atmosphere, despite the disjunctions of scale, the emptiness of the intermediate space, and the absence of pespectival links between foreground and background. None of these is needed to unite the composition, which is fused, atom by atom, in Bellini's luminous vision."[44] Infinite, light-defined space curves out behind the figures, and light from in front of the painting shines on them, light whose source is implied by the direction of the shadows cast, his head darkening her neck, her head, and the cloth directly behind her. The same light that shines on Madonna and child shines on the spectator, who stands as witness to this scene of successive acknowledgments. The mother acknowledges her child who then acknowledges his relation to an other than his mother by looking out toward the viewer. Each surrenders recent memory and the desire it spawns, only to suffer "the feelings of controlled disappointment" of which Kristeva speaks.[45] The drama of separation is over. The child is free and need not escape the Madonna's grasp. He stands with his feet posed as they will be on the cross, the side of his face touching her neck, his fingers holding hers. The two are branches of the same tree, quietly accepting not only the separation from each other, but also the one foretold by the two trees that flank the child held firm by the mother, as the crosses of the two thieves will flank the man held firm on the cross.

If art is "the intersection of sign and rhythm, of representation and light, of the symbolic and the semiotic," if it takes the instincts in charge by putting them into signs, if it is a construction out of the instinctual energies latent in the manifest "meaning and content of what it represents," then art can break through the myth of the maternal figure that was given its current form by Freud.[46] Part of the myth is that the story of Oedipus tells the truth about the original causes and objects of desire and that all later desires are mere reprints or revised editions of the original. Kristeva suggests that painting plumbs the depths hidden by this myth, in breaking through the screen, the foreground, the obstruction to which she claims the myth is reduced.[47] Her view is that it is a screen behind which the primary processes work and within which lies what has been forgotten or repressed. This is the raw and the unsigned that art takes in charge. This is where motherhood happens. This is where masculine and feminine are not yet.

Woman with a Mirror (1515)

The *Lochis Madonna* refers to the Byzantine world in which the image signified the presence to the viewer of the person imaged. The *Woman with a Mirror* (fig. 3), on the other hand, belongs to the Renaissance world rediscovering the primacy of sight that had yielded to Judeo-Christendom's hidden God, who communicated through signs, not least among them Judaism's written law and Christianity's spoken message. At once more modern and more ancient than the apparitions of Byzantium, the later painting is about looking, not about being in the presence of and suffering separation from what one would keep as one's own. One can be in the presence of something at which one does not look, sensing it through other modalities, but one cannot be a spectator and look at nothing. *Woman with a Mirror* can be said to be about being a spectator, a spectator of images irreducibly separate from the things portrayed.

The composition is familiar. There is a parapet-like table or bench at the bottom of the picture and a dark featureless wall dividing background from foreground as in the *Madonna with Two Trees*. The woman is not behind the parapet as the Madonnas are, but is sitting on it, her legs cropped at the thighs by the bottom of the canvas. They are in front of the parapet that had kept the Madonnas securely within the picture, and the woman seems to hover between our world and the picture plane. Unlike them she is alone, nude, except for a blue and dark green brocade hair covering edged with pearls and a red scarf draped over her right upper arm, around her back, and over her left thigh and pudenda. Along the black, light-absent wall are a window and a round mirror, its top cropped by the painting and its bottom just above her left shoulder. The window occupies three-fourths of the left third of the canvas; on its sill rests a transparent glass vase that holds flowers from the world outside the window and shows light passing through water. Mirrors, window, and water-filled glass comprise a catalogue of media that play light, Venice's genius, by reflecting, transmitting, or refracting it. The left side of the woman's head and her left forearm obscure more than half of the surface of the mirror, which

Figure 3.   Woman with a Mirror.

reflects the back of her head and arm. Finally, in her right hand is a mirror whose glass, unseen by us, reflects the image in the mirror on the wall.

Windows are looked through, mirrors, into. The most distant view in the painting is the one seen through the window which reveals a flat plain and the buildings of a town, behind which rise low hills that give way to higher hills of the same blue as the sky. The horizon vanishes into a horizontal band of brightest yellow-white light above the mountains. Both here and in the *Madonna with Two Trees,* landscape moves the eye into the picture plane back beyond the human figures. Whereas in the earlier painting the shadows cast by the figures' heads posit a source of light in front of the picture plane, opening it up into the space where the spectator stands, here Bellini opens up spaces within the picture plane, "enough to make every cubist dream."[48] The space between the mirror on the wall and the back of her head is one on which there are two perspectives: The spectator sees in the mirror on the wall the back of the woman's head and the forearm that touches the hair covering; the woman sees it in the mirror in her hand. The spectator sees an image in the wall mirror but not in the held one. The woman sees what the spectator does not: the image in the hand mirror of the image in the mirror on the wall.

The viewer's line of sight goes straight through the window to the distant horizon, while the line of sight to the mirror ricochets back toward the viewer through the space between mirror and what it reflects, the woman's arm and head, "producing a bend in representation and engendering a third space. Neither background nor foreground, it is the opening of one vista of the painting towards the viewer. . . . It is a reflexive glance, a circular look, careful to fragment space as much as possible by following the refraction of light rays."[49] This space opens up in front of so unmitigated an absence of light on the rear wall as to render almost irresistible the place where light ricochets between the perpendicular mirrors. Again, within the painting there is the same circular look: the woman looks into the hand mirror to see the image in the wall mirror of her head and arm. The space in the *Lochis Madonna* was shallow and the painting did not point outside to the spectator, who was apt to believe the Madonna to be present in her image and therefore to share his world. In the *Woman with a Mirror,* however, mirror image takes the place of sacred presence, and the painted message is that the spectator sees in the world the same kind of thing that the woman with the mirror sees in the painting, namely, mere reflections. The painting, like a mirror, shows the spectator to himself, shows him to be a viewer of images of images and lures him into the impossible space between image and thing.

The image, the outside, the surface, the skin triumph. The original present thing, its inwardness, its inside, its depth, its womb is forgotten. The separation from the body of the mother, from inside the mother, from the memory of the inside is complete. The body of the mother has become the body of a woman and nothing is hidden, as Mary is from her son in the early Madonna paintings. Kristeva interprets the early Madonna's absence as her dreaming memory of maternal joy and intransitive energy, tied to no object. However this *elsewhere* is to be read, the Madonna's absorption in it, her being taken up in it, has the effect that her attention has no object. Whereas the attention of the Madonna painted after Bellini's marriage and fatherhood has the child as its object, and that of the woman painted in his old age has herself, not as something in which to be absorbed, however, but as something to be seen. No part of the outside of the woman's body is in principle concealed, for the mirrors can do their work and show her all. Her hair and her sex are partially covered but with such a tease of rich brocade and silk as to call attention to them and to prove that it is, after all, what is masked that tempts and has power. So too does what is unconscious, especially where there is no language to represent it, no forms to direct it, or where it has been repressed. Kristeva's thesis, as Lechte elaborates it, is that art gives language and form to what is either disturbing or unrepresentable, inexpressible, unsigned. Once the repressed is re-formed, once the instincts are given form and taken up by systems of signs, of representations, it is the form (the sign, the representation) that is the object of wishes, drives, desires, beliefs, intentions, emotions, energies, tendencies, fantasies.

Nothing seen in the work is *original* because its origin is "a complete absence of meaning and seeing; it is feeling, displacement, rhythm, sounds, flashes," "Heraclitus' flux, Epicurus' atoms, the whirling dust of cabalic, Arab, and Indian mystics."[50] What is seen is not a copy but a representation of what, in its innocence of meaning, cannot be presented. Not an object that can be presented to a subject, the innocent flux or dust can only immerse, surround, subsume, consume the not-yet-subject. Kristevan interpretation is recognition of the transference onto the painting of the primary wishes and impulses, drives and desires, awakened by the painting's giving them form. Transference occurs when instinctual energies become objects of attention for what-is-becoming-a-subject, as its energies are distanced by being represented and (as)signed to it. Freud says of transference that it is "the one thing the presence of which has to be detected almost without assistance and with only the slightest clues to go upon."[51] Yet it cannot be avoided, since "use is made of it in setting up all the obstacles that make the material inaccessible," where resolution of the transference allows the patient to see the validity of the connections constructed during the analysis. The material in question is inaccessible except through interpretation of the transferences, dreams, jokes, symptoms, and body language through which it counterfeits itself, with interpretation of the transferences being the hardest. Rather as the patient in analysis must resolve the transferences she has made in order to understand connections constructed in the course of the analysis, so, in order to explain to herself to what the effects of an artwork are due, the spectator must recognize the transferences the work has made onto its surface of primary processes and primal repressions.

Of the *Woman with a Mirror,* dated and signed the year before Bellini's death in 1516, Goffen says, it "represents the master's final statement on what had been a leitmotif of his oeuvre, the professional self-awareness of the painter and the significance of his art."[52] She ends her study by claiming that with the *Woman with a Mirror* Bellini "reminds us that the purpose of the Renaissance artist is to reflect nature, to mirror and to recreate reality."[53] Icon yields to paragon, Byzantium to Greece, the hidden to the visible, the dark continent to light. But light is not only the necessary condition for the visual perception of form, it is also what reduces form, shatters figuration, dazzles, and blinds. The psychoanalyst is like the Renaissance artist, insofar as he presumes to recreate the reality of the patient, reflecting in his interpretations the unconscious threads that weave themselves through the patient's life, the interpretations mirroring the life. The mirrors show the woman in the painting what she could not otherwise have seen, as analysis shows the patient what would otherwise remain hidden. For this reason, *Woman with a Mirror* may be read as a statement about (the self-awareness and significance of) the art of psychoanalysis as well as of painting, about insight as well as sight, and about blindness.

The unconscious works upon the person to whose system it belongs and is there in that person's life as the Madonna is there in her icon. But the unconscious can be recognized and acknowledged only through its distorting representations, just as the sight of an object is achieved only through some medium that perforce distorts it, more or less. Vision can be shown to be coded, where codes are arbitrary, albeit subject to the constraint of coherence, as is the analyst's interpretations of disguising dreams, transferences, and other constructions of the unconscious. His interpretations diffract these constructions as they themselves diffract the unconscious material of which they are constructions, namely, the unrepresentable energy of drives as well as what has been repressed. Without the interpretations, insight into the unconscious is impossible. The analyst, like the spectator of the *Woman with a Mirror,* can see what the patient and the woman in the painting cannot, the wall mirror or the transference (or any counterfeiting construction). The spectator or analyst *cannot* see what the woman or the patient is seeing, however, and if there is enough of a difference between their points of view, then what analyst and patient (or spectator and woman) see will not be the same. So it was with Dora and Freud. What she might have seen in the *Sistine Madonna* he could not because of his blindness to a feminine not conceptually connected with the maternal, because of his having to interpret the Madonna as an Oedipal ideal, because of his making of woman herself what she is in the *Woman with a Mirror.* What the painting shows is a woman looking at a series of images of herself that is, in principle, unending, where the object of the images is, in principle, unobservable. There is no exit from the loop, as there is no exit for Freud from the story that begins with Oedipus. Kristeva's singular contribution to psychoanalysis is to have begun to tell another story.

Notes

Portions of this article are published elsewhere. The author wishes to thank the following for permission to reprint: Oxford University Press for what appears in "Two Women by Giovanni Bellini," *the British Journal of Aesthetics* 33, no. 3, July 1993; and *Hypatia: A Jour-*

nal of Feminist Philosophy for what appears in "Renaissance Madonna and the Fantasies of Freud," *Hypatia* 8, no. 2 Summer 1993. Also several sections repeat what is forthcoming from Pennsylvania State University Press in "Three Renaissance Madonnas: Freud and the Feminine," *Transformations: The Languages of Personhood and Culture After Theory,* eds. Christie McDonald and Gary Wihl.

1. Sigmund Freud, *Dora: An Analysis of a Case of Hysteria,* ed. Philip Rieff (New York: Collier-Macmillan, 1963). Raphael's *Sistine Madonna* in Dresden (1512) has Mary standing on a billow of clouds between curtains pulled back to reveal her and the child she holds. Two cupids lean on a balustrade at the bottom of the painting, upon which rests the papal tiara of St. Sixtus, who kneels below and to one side of the centered Madonna, while St. Barbara kneels on the other side.

2. Sigmund Freud, *Dora,* p. 114.

3. Ibid., p. 116.

4. Ibid., p. 125.

5. Peter Gay, *Freud: A Life for Our Time* (New York: W. W. Norton, 1988), p. 253.

6. Freud, "Moses and Michaelangelo," *Collected Papers* (New York: Basic Books, 1959), XXI, p. 226.

7. "In boys ... the complex is not simply repressed, it is literally smashed to pieces by the shock of threatened castration." Sigmund Freud, "Some Psychical Consequences of the Anatomical Distinction between the Sexes," *Standard Edition,* Vol. XIX, p. 257.

8. Sigmund Freud,. "Female Sexuality," *Standard Edition,* XXI, p. 226.

9. Julia Kristeva, "Motherhood According to Giovanni Bellini," *Desire in Language,* ed. Leon S. Roudiez (New York: Columbia University Press, 1980), p. 240.

10. Sigmund Freud, "Moses and Michaelangelo," p. 258.

11. Ibid., p. 259.

12. Wollheim, "Freud and the Understanding of Art," *On Art and the Mind* (Cambridge, Mass.: Harvard University Press, 1974), p. 217.

13. Sigmund Freud, "Moses and Michaelangelo," p. 258.

14. Sigmund Freud, *Dora,* p. 138.

15. Richard Wollheim, "Freud and the Understanding of Art," p. 219.

16. Ibid.

17. Julia Kristeva, "Motherhood."

18. Ibid., p. 237.

19. Ibid., p. 269.

20. Ibid.

21. Ibid., p. 240.

22. Ibid., p. 242.

23. Sigmund Freud, *Leonardo da Vinci and a Memory of His Childhood,* intro. Peter Gay (New York: W.W. Norton, 1964).

24. Julia Kristeva, "Motherhood," p. 263.

25. Ibid., p. 240.

26. Sigmund Freud, "Moses and Michaelangelo," p. 258.

27. Julia Kristeva, "Motherhood," p. 242.

28. Ibid., p. 240.

29. Ibid., p. 239.

30. Ibid., pp. 239–40.

31. Ibid., p. 263.

32. Ibid.

33. Rona Goffen, *Giovanni Bellini* (New Haven and London: Yale University Press, 1989), p. 53.

34. Julia Kristeva, "Motherhood," p. 263.

35. Rona Goffen, *Giovanni Bellini*, p. 28.

36. Ibid., p. 59.

37. Nelson Goodman has convincingly argued that *we* should not thus understand the matter on the grounds that ways of looking and seeing have been shown to be conventions and so far from a likeness's signifying the presence of its original, there is at best an arbitrary relation between them, no matter how similar they look. *Languages of Art* (New York: Bobbs-Merrill, 1968).

38. Rona Goffen, *Giovanni Bellini*, p., 65.

39. Ibid., p. 66.

40. John Lechte, "Kristeva and Holbein, Artist of Melancholy," *British Journal of Aesthetics* 30, no. 4, October 1990: p. 346.

41. Ibid., p. 347.

42. Roland Barthes, *Camera Lucida: Reflections On Photography*, trans. Richard Howard (New York: Hill and Wang, 1981), pp. 49–59. 43. Ibid., p. 119.

44. Rona Goffen, *Giovanni Bellini*, p. 52.

45. Julia Kristeva, "Motherhood," p. 263.

46. Sigmund Freud, "Moses and Michaelangelo," p. 258.

47. Julia Kristeva, "Motherhood," p. 260.

48. Ibid., p. 263.

49. Ibid., p. 265.

50. Ibid., pp. 239–40.

51. Sigmund Freud, *Dora,* p. 138.

52. Rona Goffen, *Giovanni Bellini*, p. 252.

53. Ibid., p. 257.

Illustrations

Plate I Giovanni Bellini, *Lochis Madonna*, Galleria dell'Accademia Carrara, Bergamo.

Plate II Giovanni Bellini, *Madonna with Two Trees*, Galleria dell'Accademia, Venice.

Plate III Giovanni Bellini, *Woman with a Mirror*, Kunsthistorisches Museum, Vienna.

7

Abject Strangers:
Toward an Ethics of Respect

Noëlle McAfee

The foreigner presents an uncanny strangeness to natives. No matter how long she remains in a country, she is always relegated to being an outsider. In the United States, African-Americans are still treated as alien, even accused of disrupting the "American" way of life. As I write this, in the wake of the riots in Los Angeles, the explosiveness of this situation is all too apparent. Why is it that we find some people *foreign*, and what makes them so threatening? Why does difference beget fear and violence, and can we ever move to an ethics of respect for those different from us?

In *Strangers to Ourselves*, Julia Kristeva attempts to answer these questions. She links the idea of the foreigner as stranger to the stranger within each of us. She shows how the way we treat foreigners is inherently tied to the way we treat our own unconscious. It is only by coming to terms with the stranger within that we can come to terms with those in our midst. But what does it mean to come to terms with our own unconscious? Does this require eradicating difference and alterity? No, she writes, it means developing an ethics of respect for what cannot be known, for this irreconcilable difference.

As a way toward respecting the radical strangeness of our own unconscious, Kristeva recommends psychoanalysis. And as a means for dealing with foreigners, Kristeva proposes national legal remedies. But still we are left with the problem: radical strangeness is *built in* to our psyches and national identities. Because it is a *constitutive* factor, we need to understand this strangeness ontologically as well as psychoanalytically. As a step in this direction, I shall bring together Kristeva and the late German philosopher Martin Heidegger, from whom part of her approach seems to be drawn.

My first move will be to examine Kristeva's notion of abjection and then show how it functions similarly to Heidegger's notion of the nothing. As I will argue, the import of the nothing makes it problematic to try to reconcile strangeness by trying to do away with abjection. Somehow we have to learn to *live with* and perhaps even *use* abjection. If this were simply a psychoanalytic, i.e. personal, problem, living with abjection could be resolved. Yet the problem becomes a political and ethical one when we see that Kristeva's description of abjection also applies to the foreigner. So if Kristeva's analysis holds, then the foreigner performs a necessary function for subjectivity and political identity.

Here the central question unfolds: is it possible or even desirable to eradicate the abject character of foreignness—that is, to eradicate absolute difference? At issue is the possibility of reconciling difference while retaining subjectivity. Reading Heidegger through Kristeva, I will consider how difference could be seen as an ontological *possibility* for subjectivity—how the dread of the foreigner can be transformed into a welcoming of difference.

II

How does an ego—a demarcated subjectivity—arise out of undifferentiated being? This has, of course, been a core issue for psychoanalysis. Following Freud, Jacques Lacan sought to explain how an infant develops a sense of self, how it breaks itself out of the entirety it experiences with its mother and the whole of the external world. Lacan locates this break in what he calls the mirror stage of an infant's development, the time when an infant begins to recognize its image in a mirror. As he argues, an infant develops a sense of "I" by seeing itself reflected back to it in a mirror (or mirror equivalent). The child identifies with the image, even though it is alien from itself, and mistakenly takes it to be itself. It finds in this image a sense of self-unity that it does not actually experience in itself. This is the way in which an ego is constituted, Lacan's argument goes, through a narcissistic process of identification. Insofar as the ego is created by identification with alien images, the sense of unity is purely fictive.

But, as Kristeva indicates, the mirror stage in itself is insufficient to explain the psychic development of an infant during the pre-Oedipal stage. Kristeva refers to the Lacanian mirror stage as secondary repression, one in which the human being "becomes homologous to another in order to become himself."[1] This mimesis is secondary to an earlier, primal repression of undifferentiated being, or what Kristeva refers to as the *chora*. Going back to Plato, the *chora* means the receptacle. In this state, we might say, the child experiences itself as the receptacle of all being.

The subject/object dichotomy (difference) cannot set in until the child represses the *chora*: this state of being one with all. To do this, the child expels part of itself from itself. Its spits out the warm milk, the mother's body, psychically and physically in order to create itself. "I expel *myself,* I spit *myself* out," Kristeva writes, "I abject *myself* within the same motion through which 'I' claim to establish *myself.*"[2] Through "ab-jecting," the child gives birth to itself as an I.

Before abjection, when the child is immersed in the *chora,* being is undifferentiated. The *chora* is first repressed through abjection—and this makes differentiation possible. The *chora* is repressed in a second way in the mirror stage, creating a second order of difference: within a realm where differentiating is possible, the self/other difference is created.

In primary repression, by expelling—abjecting—the mother's body from its own self, the child begins to form personal boundaries. "I reside here and the abject does not." While this is termed primary repression, it is not a one-time event. Even after abjecting the mother's body, one cannot entirely forget that early *chora,* that state before difference emerged and where being was experienced in entirety. The abject comes back in fleeting encounters, fleeting because we flee, horrified of falling back into the maternal body, where no difference—and thus no subjectivity—is possible. The abject perpetuates the bounds of oneself with the threat "of a reality that, if I acknowledge it, annihilates me." Kristeva writes that abjection arises with a "massive and sudden emergence of uncanniness, which, familiar as it might have been in an opaque and forgotten life, now harries me as radically separate, loathsome. Not me. Not that. But not nothing, either."[3]

Uncanniness, a sensation both Heidegger and Freud have explored, is the telling sign of this radical strangeness. In his essay on the uncanny, Freud argues that one contributing factor of uncanniness is a form of ego-disturbance that harkens back to "particular phases in the evolution of the self-regarding feeling, a regression to a time when the ego had not yet marked itself off sharply from the external world and from other people."[4] Uncanniness results when repressed elements of this earlier experience recur, partly due to the inner "compulsion to repeat" (characteristic of children and neurotics) which is itself perceived as uncanny.[5] Freud argues that "the uncanny is something which is secretly familiar, which has undergone repression and then returned from it. . . ."[6] It is frightening because it is the recurrence of something which has been repressed. Freud sums up his argument with:

> [W]e can understand why linguistic usage has extended *das Heimliche* ["homely"] into its opposite, *das Unheimliche*; for this uncanny is in reality nothing new or alien, but something which is familiar and old-established in the mind and which has become alienated from it only through the process of repression.[7]

The return of the repressed and the concomitant experience of uncanniness is more than a slightly uncomfortable *déjà vu*. Experiencing the uncanny, one feels oneself on the brink of castration and death.[8] As Freud quotes Schelling, "Everything is *unheimlich* that ought to have remained secret and hidden but has come to light."[9] Part of the feeling of uncanniness is dread, horror that castration could cut one off from the symbolic order (the economy of desire) and return one to the maternal *chora*.

Kristeva goes further than Freud by showing how the uncanny strangeness of abjection is not only a side-effect of (primary) repression but is itself a mechanism by which the I is formed and maintained. The abject not only threatens the I, it constitutes it, setting bounds of the self. By pushing one out of the *chora* (undifferentiated being) into the symbolic realm, it allows one to experience difference, where subjectivity becomes possible, where one enters into language and the economy of desire. The uncanny lurks at the border between the *chora* and the symbolic, or, rather, when one strays near the border, one is overcome by uncanniness. *At the precipice, my self dissolves in vertigo.*

III

The state of mind of one experiencing abjection has its parallel in Heidegger's description of the state of encountering the nothing. Both the nothing and the abject present an abyss where one is, as Kristeva writes, "on the edge of nonexistence and hallucination,"[10] where the borders of one's very own self are simultaneously threatened and drawn.

In his essay, "What is Metaphysics?" Heidegger turns the question "What is there in the world?" into the question "What is it that is not?"[11] He asks, "What is it with the Nothing?" In this move, Heidegger shows how presence always coexists with absence, and moreover, that presence is incomprehensible without absence.

As he argues, the difficulty with inquiring into the nothing is that as soon as we ask, "What is the nothing?" we use the existential copula "is." So we end up speaking of nothing as if it were a something. Even saying that the nothing is what "there is not" is misleading, for the problem is not just with our way of speaking but also with our way of thinking. Thinking is "always essentially thinking about something," so in trying to grasp the abyss of the nothing we end up trying to think of the totality of beings and then trying to negate that. But an intellect is in dire straits trying to grasp "the totality of beings," much less the negation of that totality. To make matters worse, the nothing *precedes* beings and the intellect that tries to grasp it. To say that the nothing is the negation of the totality of beings is to speak too late.

The only way to grasp the nothing, Heidegger argues, is in a particular mood, namely *anxiety*. By this Heidegger does not mean fear, because we fear *this or that entity*. While fear is a fear of something, anxiety has no object. And that's just the point. "Anxiety is indeed anxiety in the face of . . . but not in the face of this or that thing."[12] It is impossible to determine what we are anxious about; in fact the striking feature of anxiety is that it brings *indeterminateness* to the fore.

Certainly any human being who is not just sleep-walking through the world has woken early in the morning, disoriented, trying to fathom why she is here, what this *here* means, why she *is* here and when she *might not be* at all. This is anxiety: the mood which reveals the nothing. In anxiety one beholds the nothing, or, to turn a phrase of Kristeva's, in anxiety one encounters the place where all meaning collapses—especially what it means to be an I.

The manner in which Heidegger describes one's encounter with the nothing is very much like the manner in which Kristeva describes the state of abjection. Abjection is the state in which one's foothold in the world of self and other disintegrates. The abject is the symptom of being on the border, pushing toward psychosis where the I blurs and is *not yet*.

Just as encountering the abject blurs the borders between the I and the impossible real, encountering the nothing, as Heidegger writes, makes beings—ourselves and all others—sink into in-difference. This is uncanniness at its height. In anxiety, we say, "one feels ill at ease [*es ist einem unheim-lich*]."[13] But what is it about the slipping away of beings that induces this unease? The abyss is empty; there is no *it* there. In anxiety, beings recede and this receding closes in on us—borders collapse. "We can get no hold on things. In this slipping away of beings only this 'no hold on things' comes over us and remains."[14] Anxiety reveals the nothing. Here we hover while beings as a whole slip away.

In anxiety or abjection—through this overwhelming ill-ease—there can be no differentiating between beings. As Heidegger writes,

> We "hover" in anxiety. More precisely, anxiety leaves us hanging because it induces the slipping away of beings as a whole. This implies that we ourselves . . . in the midst of beings slip away from ourselves. At bottom therefore it is not as though "you" or "I" feel ill at ease; rather it is this way for some "one."[15]

But in this blurring of identity, something (not a thing, really) remains. While our power to differentiate between beings may escape us, while the abyss of not-being (an I?) closes in on us, the other side of not-being rises up. Even though the experience is profoundly unsettling, it produces an awareness of one's being there.

In her own way, Kristeva describes this same experience. For Kristeva, abjection induces violence to the subject—blurring borders of oneself, pushing one toward psychosis where the all-too-real undermines the divisions between self and other and the capacity to differentiate.[16] Yet like Heidegger, Kristeva sees this uncanny encounter in its double aspect: "The time of abjection is double: a time of oblivion and thunder, of veiled infinity and the moment when revelation bursts forth."[17]

Even though encounters with the abject and the nothing arise differently (the experience of abjection is usually triggered by a "something" after all—be it blood, a corpse, excrement), they function analogously, even hand in hand. The abject marks out and sends one reeling into the nothing's territory. In this nowhere, borders dissolve. "The nothing itself nihilates," as Heidegger writes.[18] And here we see how the abject and the nothing are functional equivalents: both nihilate borders and, as a result, *disclose what it is to exist.* "[A]s the repelling gesture toward the retreating whole of beings," writes Heidegger, nihilation "discloses these beings in their full but heretofore concealed strangeness as what is radically other—with respect to the nothing."[19] The other side of nothing is *Dasein.* As Heidegger argues, *Dasein* is none other than "being held out into the nothing." Only through encountering the nothing can one fathom one's own being.

Without "the original revelation of the nothing," writes Heidegger, there is "no selfhood and no freedom."[20] Encountering the nothing makes selfhood possible. So too in an infant's psychic development, abjection makes subjectivity possible.

The experiences of the nothing and the abject are in many respects parallel. Characteristically, both repel us. In encountering both, our very being is questioned. We can hardly speak: vertigo, loss of boundaries. Structurally, the nothing and the abject are encountered in anxiety and create the conditions for subjectivity. "The nothing does not merely serve as the counterconcept of beings," writes Heidegger, "rather it originally belongs to their essential unfolding as such." Even though we can hardly bear the abject and the nothing, it is only by them that we constitute ourselves.

Now we can see how Kristeva goes further than Heidegger, even as she parallels his basic argument. The uncanny strangeness of the abject not only reveals one's existence, it reveals one's existence as an I. Through abjection, the I is formed and renewed. The abject is the vandal *and* the policeman of the self, threatening to dissolve it while simultaneously reinforcing it. Just as the nothing lays the ground for being, the abject lays the ground for being a subject. As Kristeva writes,

If it be true that the abject simultaneously beseeches and pulverizes the subject, one can understand that it is experienced at the peak of its strength when that subject, weary of fruitless attempts to identify with something on the outside, finds the impossible within; when it finds that the impossible constitutes its very *being*, that it *is* none other than abject. The abjection of self would be the culminating form of that experience of the subject to which it is revealed that all its objects are based merely on the inaugural *loss* that laid the foundations of its own being.[21]

Loss inaugurates being-a-subject, and thereafter abjection marks this loss. Uncanniness is the recollection of that inaugural loss, the reminder of the *chora* that one has forgotten/repressed.[22] Bringing together Heidegger and Kristeva we can say: *subjectivity is constituted by being held out into the nothing that abjection heralds.*

IV

In *Strangers to Ourselves*, Kristeva examines the estrangement we feel within ourselves and with the foreigners around us. As she describes the phenomenology of foreignness, she is not discussing xenophobia (fear of strangers) *per se*, for she is not describing a *fear* of foreignness as much as a *dread* of foreignness. Fear signals one sort of encounter of a subject with an object within the realm of differentiation. Dread (or anxiety) signals an encounter that threatens the border between undifferentiated being and subjectivity. Recall Heidegger's distinction: "Anxiety is basically different from fear. We become afraid in the face of this or that particular being that threatens us in this or that particular respect."[23] Anxiety, on the other hand, has no object. Anxiety is the unease of indeterminateness. Is this what the foreigner awakens? It seems so, for there is nothing in particular that makes the foreigner so strange; it's not his or her *being* (as an object) that arouses us. As Kristeva writes:

> [T]he face that is so *other* bears the mark of a crossed threshold that irremediably imprints itself as peacefulness or anxiety. Whether perturbed or joyful, the foreigner's appearance signals that he is "in addition." The presence of such a border, internal to all that is displayed, awakens our most archaic senses through a burning sensation. Vivid concern or delight, set there in these other features, without forgetfulness, without ostentation, like a standing invitation to some inaccessible, irritating journey, whose code the foreigner does not have but whose mute, physical, visible memory he keeps.[24]

Before the foreigner, the native recalls her own incompleteness; she becomes anxious. The body that becomes anxious is both the personal body of the native and the political body of the nation. The foreigner threatens the borders of the symbolic—and national—order.

In fact, Kristeva is describing the foreigner in a way that recalls the abject. While she never explicitly equates the foreigner with the abject, she gives ample room for such a reading: "Confronting the foreigner whom I reject and with whom at the same time I identify," Kristeva writes, "I lose my boundaries, I no longer have a container, the memory of experiences when I had been abandoned overwhelms me, I lose my composure. I feel 'lost', 'indistinct', 'hazy'."[25]

Before the foreigner, Kristeva remarks, we feel this strange uncanniness, *unheimlich,* and as Freud has shown, this means the not-being-home, the familiar unfamiliarity, standing before what we usually cannot know. Drawing on Freud's essay on the uncanny, Kristeva writes:

> In short, if anguish revolves around an *object,* uncanniness, on the other hand, is a *destructuration of the self* that may either remain as a psychotic *symptom* or fit in as an *opening* toward the new, as an attempt to tally with the incongruous. While it surely manifests the return of the familiar repressed, the *Unheimliche* requires just the same the impetus of a new encounter with an unexpected outside element: arousing images of death, automatons, doubles, or the female sex, . . . uncanniness occurs when the boundaries between *imagination* and *reality* are erased.[26]

The foreigner is the return of the abject, our encounter with the nothing—especially insofar as the foreigner is a manifestation of no origin, an other tongue, an abyss or gulf, the frail borders of our psyche, and an encounter with the other within us.

One could object, arguing that the foreigner is simply an other within the realm of difference—an object, not an abject. In other words, one can still ask whether this is a primary or a secondary repression. If it were a primary repression, it would signal a repression/forgetting of undifferentiated being. If it were a secondary repression, it would mark the creation of the difference between self and other. Both repressions make subjectivity possible: the first through creating the *possibility* of difference, the second through *differentiating* subject from object. Recall that Kristeva considers the mirror stage, where the self/other (and subject/object) distinction arises, as a secondary repression. Primary repression occurs earlier, when the not-yet-I abjects itself, giving birth to itself as an I. Throughout *Strangers to Ourselves,* Kristeva refers to the foreigner as other (in the lower case of self/other), indicating that she considers foreignness an aspect of secondary repression. Yet she also refers to the foreigner as someone who disturbs identity, just as the abject disturbs one's always-fragile identity: "[B]y explicitly, obviously, ostensibly occupying the place of the difference, the foreigner challenges both the identity of the group and his own. . . ."[27] No wonder then that we can substitute "alien" for "foreigner," alien being what is so Other (abject?) to a system.

By applying the notion of abjection to the formation of nation-states, we can explain the fascination and horror a nation-state develops toward foreigners. A nation-state constitutes its own boundaries by excluding what is other. But insofar as the other (someone who constitutes/threatens identity) resides *within* the nation state, the foreign *object* becomes the foreign *abject*. The foreigner must be abjected, if not physically, then psychically. As Norma Claire Moruzzi argues, the "familiar foreign(er)" poses a threat to national identity. The foreigner forever haunts the nation's subjective self because it signals the return of the abject—the return of presubjectivity. "For the subjective identity of the nation-state," Moruzzi writes, "this threatened return, that would dissolve the national self into undifferentiatable physical parts, is posed by the stranger. . . ."[28]

The foreigners among us are at the same time fascinating, incoherent, threatening and strange. As Kristeva writes, "[T]he foreigner, from the height of an autonomy that he is the only one to have chosen when the others prudently remain 'between themselves,' paradoxically confronts everyone with an asymbolia that rejects civility and returns to a violence laid bare."[29] But any imagined threat the foreigner poses to national identity pales before the violence that nations can and do commit against foreigners.

National(istic) abjection breeds the worst kind of violence and inhumanity. Racism, fascism, and genocide are the extreme dangers, but even the lesser abjections, such as attempts to legislate a national language, are no more humane. The question we must address is whether it is possible, or even desirable, to rid ourselves of abjection. Without abjection, would personal or political identity (self-same and different from others) be possible?

V

In the preceding sections, I have argued that abjection is a process that makes selfhood possible. This psychological phenomenon has its ontological counterpart: in encountering the nothing *Dasein* unfolds. So, what is radically strange to us performs a function: constituting our being in the world as a subject. Part of our identity is as a member of a nation-state, and to this extent, at least, the foreigner manifests this radical strangeness that lays the ground for our own national identity. The foreigner is also our own projection of the stranger-within-us—our own unconscious— and thus a symptom of our own unease with this inner alterity. So now two dilemmas emerge: (1) we cannot hope to find peace with foreigners because radical strangeness is built into our own psyches; and (2) insofar as being, and being a subject, depends upon an encounter with the abject/nothing (represented by the foreigner), the abject/nothing is neces- sary for being.

Fundamentally, the question before us is whether we are destined to be strangers to ourselves. Kristeva suggests that the answer is yes, but she holds out the possibility that we can come to a reconciliation with this stranger-within-us and so find peace with those in our midst:

> It is through unraveling transference—the major dynamics of otherness, of love/hatred for the other, of the foreign component of our psyche— that, on the basis of the other, I become reconciled with my own oth- erness-foreignness, that I play on it and live by it. Psychoanalysis is then experienced as a journey into the strangeness of the other and of one- self, toward an ethics of respect for the irreconcilable.[30]

There is a contradiction here. On the one hand, Kristeva claims it is pos- sible to become *reconciled* with oneself, but on the other hand, she wants to work toward an ethics of respect for the *irreconcilable*. Kristeva indicates that this strangeness can never be eradicated but that through psycho- analysis it can be ameliorated. We can become more at home with the stranger-within-us so that, as our communities become more multina- tional, we can live in a sort of truce with those strangers among us. "A para- doxical community is emerging," she writes, "made up of foreigners who are reconciled with themselves to the extent that they recognize themselves as foreigners." This is a paradoxical community not only because for- eignness is inherent to it, but also because "community" as she sees it is a by-product of an extreme individualism. "The multinational society would thus be the consequence of an extreme individualism, but conscious of its discontents and limits, knowing only indomitable people ready-to-help- themselves in their weakness, a weakness whose other name is our radi- cal strangeness."[31]

As I have argued, "radical strangeness" is more than a consequence of transferring our own otherness-foreignness. It is also the cause and effect of our own self-formation. If my argument holds, then the task of devel- oping an ethics of respect is that much more problematic. How should we define reconciliation—as coming to accept something unwelcome or as turning conflict into harmony? Or does reconciliation mean defusing conflict altogether? If the latter were the case, then finding reconciliation with our own strangeness would mean dissolving the abject—that which makes subjectivity possible. Nevertheless, we are not destined to be strangers to ourselves; we can *recollect*, if not familiarize, our radical strangeness.

VI

By the end of *Strangers to Ourselves*, Kristeva's solution to this problem takes on the familiar tones of the golden rule or Kant's categorical imperative: we extend to others what we learn to extend to ourselves. "What might be involved, in the final analysis," Kristeva writes, "is extending to the notion of *foreigner* the right of respecting our own foreignness and, in short, of the 'privacy' that insures freedom in democracies."[32] This solution will only work to the extent that every individual respects her own foreignness; and because that is not yet foreseeable, Kristeva suggests legal guarantees that are themselves based on the Kantian formulation. Nations could reciprocate with each other, granting a foreigner the rights she would enjoy in her country of origin. For example, a "double nationality" statute could guarantee a foreigner some of the rights of citizens of the host country as well as the rights the foreigner would enjoy in her native country. In return, the host country's citizens would "carry" their rights with them when they travel to the reciprocating country.

This proposal has some serious flaws. For one, it does not help the foreigner whose native country has a meager notion of rights. Much emigration takes place precisely because people flee repressive countries: they are not only foreigners, they are refugees, seeking rights that exceed those recognized by their native countries. For another, consider the plight of the Palestinian: she has no rights as a Palestinian. Even within her own national borders (Israel), she has no guaranteed right to property, privacy, or liberty. So a reciprocal agreement with her host country would be of no use.

A third problem with Kristeva's proposal is that foreignness does not evaporate after one generation, as any minority within a country can testify. The children and grandchildren of Pakistanis in England, Africans in the United States, Turks in Germany, and Kurds in Turkey may be born nationals of the host country—they may have the same rights *de jure*,[33] but they often are denied rights *de facto*. This, of course, is the extremity of a nation's abjection of foreignness—racism.

In short, the legal remedy Kristeva proposes is useless for those foreigners who need it most: minorities and refugees. As foreigners without a native country, they can only look forward to the rights their hosts grant, which are rarely granted without a struggle. In even the most "civilized" countries, they are shunted aside into ghettoes or refugee camps. So the problem of the foreigners among us remains.

Kristeva recognizes that the juridical arena of legal remedies is secondary to another arena. The "fundamental question . . . belongs to a more psychological or even metaphysical realm."[34] As I discussed above, Kristeva takes the psychological approach, looking at how, in a multinational society, individuals' own moral codes need to be transcended to accommodate others' particularities. One's own moral code can be transcended when—through psychoanalysis perhaps—one recognizes oneself as a foreigner. Here we return to the image of a multinational society composed of atomized individuals, recognizing their own radical strangeness in order to live with others' strangeness. If this seems like a bizarre community it is because here one is first and always communing with one's own (and proper?) strangeness, and only then extending that relationship to others. Here, being-with-others is always uneasy, always co-extensive with the uncanny.

At one point, Kristeva nods to the possibility that psychoanalysis cannot ultimately reconcile uncanniness. In her discussion of Freud and his essay on the uncanny, she mentions how Freud moves (somewhat reluctantly) from looking at the uncanny as manifested in literature to looking at how it is manifested in actual life:

> It is possible, as Yvon Brès said, that Freud's recourse to esthetic works in order to set up the notion of uncanny strangeness was an admission that psychoanalysis could not possibly deal with it. Man would be facing a kind of "existential apriorism," in the presence of which Freudian thought merges with Heidegger's phenomenology.[35]

As an indicator of the origin and a constant companion of being there in the world as a subject, the uncanny has ontological implications. The shortcomings of Kristeva's solutions may be due to the fact that she is looking for a psychoanalytic solution to an ontological problem. Her solutions could work only to the extent that the foreigner is a manifestation of secondary repression. But as a return of the primarily repressed, the abject foreigner presents a far deeper difficulty.

VII

Perhaps one way to restate the problem at hand is to reconsider the state of the person who is being "threatened" by a foreigner. Why is it that someone can be so blind to the stranger within that he or she projects strangeness onto the other? How can this person learn to live with the stranger within?

Heidegger provides an opening to address this question. While he does not write in terms of the unconscious, he does describe the state of being that is hardly conscious of its very own self.[36] Most people pass through this way of being, and many remain there most of their lives. Broadly speaking, this is the state of everydayness, being in an environment in which one is just one among others. In this state, one is always measuring oneself against others. "Is my car as new? Did I come from the right kind of family? Are my political views too outlandish?" When someone is forever asking such questions, Heidegger argues, he or she is disturbing *Dasein*'s Being-with-one-another. When *Dasein* is caught up in everydayness with others, *Dasein* hands over its possibilities to them, as Heidegger terms it, to the "they." This kind of Being-with-one-another "dissolves one's own *Dasein* completely into the kind of Being of 'the Others', in such a way, indeed, that the Others, as distinguishable and explicit, vanish more and more."[37] In this state,

> the real dictatorship of the "they" is unfolded. We take pleasure and enjoy ourselves as *they* take pleasure; we read, see, and judge about literature and art as they see and judge; likewise we shrink back from the "great mass" as they shrink back; we find "shocking" what they find shocking. The "they", which is nothing definite, and which all are, though not as the sum, prescribes the kind of Being of everydayness.[38]

When one is caught up in following the crowd, not only is the specificity or genuineness of all the individuals that make up the they obliterated, so too is one's own. One becomes, as Heidegger terms it, a "they-self." One forfeits oneself by measuring one's distance from others, by accommodating one's actions to others, by disburdening oneself into the they, granting them dominion over one's *Dasein*. "*Everyone is the other, and no one is himself*" [emphasis added].[39]

When one is lost in the they, Heidegger says here, "Everyone is the other. . . ." Through a psychoanalytic lens we can read this as meaning that, under the sway of the they, the difference between self and others is obliterated. *I become you.* The alterity that makes subjectivity possible vanishes in this fiction of the they. Heidegger seems to find this phenomenon untenable, but not for the reason we might, not because it is impossible for a self to remain a self without an other. He finds it untenable because it is a fiction, because it masks the *truth* (as if being an "I" is no less a fiction than the they).

In the state of being lost in the they, "no one is himself." For Heidegger this means that, when one is lost in the they, one is being inauthentic, that is, one has not yet taken up the possibility of becoming one's very own self. From Heidegger's perspective, the challenge is to transform oneself from an anonymous someone whose actions are guided by others to someone who makes her choices in keeping with her very own self—who doesn't just proceed with what the world hands her but who recognizes and uses her own possibilities. But what does it mean to be one's very own self when the self is split, when part of it is necessarily hidden from itself?

While Heidegger's notion of authenticity naively posits a unary subject, we might be able to retain Heidegger's intuition—that when everyone is the other, no one is himself—by considering it in terms of difference and identity. When we live in the fiction that one is (just like) the other, then we obliterate difference. Then of course no one could be herself *because the conditions for subjectivity—namely abjection and difference—would be snatched away.*

In this vein, then, we might try transforming Heidegger's notion of authenticity from one who knows one's true self to one who knows one's self is split. Nietzsche suggested that truth is not self-presence, that unity is impossible; subjectivity requires forgetting this truth. Perhaps Kristeva is calling on us to recollect this—that we are not self-present, that we are split, that alterity is within and without us. And herein lies our problem: how do we recollect this—our own absence—without destroying subjectivity?

In a later essay, "The Age of the World Picture," Heidegger directly addressed the problem of subjectivity in the modern era.[40] As he argued, subjectivism was impossible for the Greeks, for they apprehended the world immediately. The Greeks were *there* in the midst of what disclosed itself to them. That is, Heidegger thought Being was present for the Greeks. Whether or not this is supportable, we can follow Heidegger to the next step: with Descartes and the *cogito,* presence moves behind a veil of re-presentation. As humans begin to re-present the world to themselves, the presence of the world is lost. Instead of truth being presence, truth becomes the certainty of representation. Humans become *subiectum*—the "self-supported, unshakable foundation of truth, in the sense of certainty."[41] "*Subiectum*" has the double force of *substratum* and subject. Humans become subject insofar as they become the ground for representation.

As humans become subjects, the world becomes object: a picture, a view, a representation. In constituting this fundamental difference of self and other, presence evaporates. Or, perhaps, for humans to become subjects, we expel presence. We create a picture of our own making; the world is *our* representation. In forging subjectivity, we become object; we become other to ourselves. Again we see that subjectivity is based upon a loss of presence—the inaugural loss, *a loss whose trace remains as the unconscious*. Can subjectivity remain if this inner alterity is recollected?

In his longing for presence—and in his denial that it was irretrievably lost—Heidegger leaned upon the notion of authenticity. While his notion of authenticity was geared toward recuperating presence, we can take the liberty of translating (or trans-scribing) authenticity as "awareness of one's own strangeness" or the "cognizant split subject." Heidegger also argued that the hallmark of human being-there was *care*—not necessarily a deep concern for others, but at least an inclination to be engaged in the world. When we couple this newly-defined authenticity with the characteristic of care, we come tantalizingly close to a form of subjectivity that recognizes an ethics of respect for irreconcilable difference.

A Heidegger steeped in psychoanalytic theory might argue as follows: An I is the fiction of a unified subjectivity, even though one is always already split. Yet the I can be aware of its own internal difference, in part by seeing others' differences. The subject-in-process creates itself—makes choices for itself—as an ethically existing subject in a world with other *Dasein*s. To this extent, the hallmark of the *cognizant* split subject is *care*: the state of being intentionally engaged in the world. She who is aware of her own strangeness does not care for herself alone—though she must begin with herself—she cares for others, treating them as other subjects-in-process. She does not usurp the other's care for itself; rather, she leaps ahead of the other, giving care "back to [her] authentically as such for the first time." When people are with one another in this manner, working on common affairs, they become inextricably bound together, seeing others in their radical strangeness, freeing the Other in her freedom for herself.[42] Seeing the strangeness of others in this manner she recognizes herself as a split subject.

But how do we turn radical strangeness from a dread of foreigners and an ingredient for racism to this ontological possibility for subjectivity? How does the they-self, whose *Dasein* has dissolved into the they, find itself and take up its capacity for care? How does *Dasein* become an ethically existing subject? To see how Heidegger answers this, I return to the notion of anxiety. As discussed in part three, Heidegger argued that *Dasein* recognizes itself as it is held out into the nothing. The nothing makes sense of being. "Dasein means being held out into the nothing." Now, to move the argument further, we could say that for *Dasein*'s sake, the nothing—or anything that causes such vertigo—is necessary. This nothing (or something that reminds one of the nothing) encountered in uncanniness is needed to shake loose the they-self, to help this person caught up in the denial of difference get a glimpse of her potential as a (split) subject-in-process. Recall Kristeva's comment that this uncanniness is "a *destructuration of the self* that may either remain as a psychotic *symptom* or fit in as an *opening* toward the new, as an attempt to tally with the incongruous." In the midst of uncanniness, there is the potential for seeing difference as an ontological possibility for subjectivity.

Let's see how this works. In *Being and Time*, Heidegger argues that, in experiencing the nothing and nowhere, someone lost in the they may become anxious, which leads to feeling uncanniness. This not-at-home-like feeling is inherently unsettling to someone who is passing through life in the tranquilized assurance of being lost in the they.[43] But in this unsettling uncanniness there is also a promise: "the possibility of a disclosure which is quite distinctive; for anxiety individualizes."[44]

It is through this disclosure that I think we might find a basis for coming to a reconciliation with radical strangeness. In *Being and Time*, Heidegger argues that this disclosure comes through the "call of conscience" that arises in the midst of uncanniness.[45] In the midst of uncanniness, *Dasein* calls to itself. "The caller is Dasein in its uncanniness: primordial, thrown Being-in-the-world as the 'not-at-home'—the bare 'that-it-is' in the 'nothing' of the world."[46] This is not the voice of the superego, not the repository of what *they* have always told us.[47] "The caller is unfamiliar to the everyday they-self; it is something like an *alien* voice."[48] Is this the call of the stranger within us?

As I have suggested, albeit tentatively, Heidegger's notion of the authentic self could be interpreted into psychoanalytic terms as a self embracing its own alterity, its unconscious. So the call of conscience would be the unconscious calling to itself, trying to reclaim itself from the superego—from the *incorporated* they, from the fiction of a unary subject. In Kristeva's terms, we could say that the call of conscience is the *chora* trying to reclaim itself from the monolithic Law of the father—the desire that had been driven underground (and unconscious) when the child left the *chora* for the symbolic realm. And this would explain the double aspect of uncanniness that Freud noted: *unheimlich* means both unhomelike and homelike. It is the eeriness of the forgotten familiar. Not just the intrauterine home that Freud links to death, but the home of the *chora,* where one has not yet differentiated oneself from the entirety of being.

So when one heeds the call of conscience, one takes up the ontological possibility for subjectivity in process. And this can help one reconcile not only internal alterity but the external alterity that has too often degraded into nationalism and racism. Kristeva suggests that the way to subvert nationalism is to question the fiction of unary subjectivity.

[I]t is perhaps on the basis of that contemporary individualism's sub-version, beginning with the moment when the citizen-individual ceases to consider himself as unitary and glorious but discovers his incoherences and abysses, in short his "strangeness"—that the question arises again: no longer that of welcoming the foreigner within a system that obliter-ates him but of promoting the togetherness of those foreigners that we all recognize ourselves to be.[49]

For someone who is attempting to "tally with the incongruous," the for-eigner presents an opportunity and not an abyss. By being shaken loose from the they, this self sees the radical strangeness of others as the continual pos-sibility for being a subject, a split subject whose mirror is always partial. Without completion, possibility thrives.

Notes

1. Julia Kristeva, *Powers of Horror: An Essay on Abjection*, trans. Leon S. Roudiez (New York: Columbia University Press, 1982), p. 13.

2. Ibid., p. 3.

3. Ibid., p. 2.

4. Sigmund Freud, *Complete Works*, volume 17, p. 236.

5. Ibid., p. 238.

6. Ibid., p. 245.

7. Ibid., p. 241.

8. One cause of the uncanny is a result of "anxiety belonging to the castration complex of childhood." Insofar as the threat of castration is a threat of losing the phallus, the threat of castration threatens the symbolic order and language itself.

9. Ibid., p. 225.

10. Julia Kristeva, *Powers of Horror*, p. 2.

11. Martin Heidegger, "What is Metaphysics?" in *Martin Heidegger: Basic Writings* (New York: Harper & Row, 1977).

12. Ibid., pp. 102–3.

13. Martin Heidegger, "What is Metaphysics?" p. 103

14. Ibid.

15. Ibid.

16. I will develop this below.

17. Julia Kristeva, *Powers of Horror*, p. 9.

18. Martin Heidegger, "What is Metaphysics?" p. 105.

19. Ibid.

20. Ibid., p. 106.

21. Julia Kristeva, *Powers of Horror*, p. 5.

22. Recall that Kristeva describes abjection as primary repression. Through the act of abjecting one cuts oneself out of undifferentiated being; one *forgets* life without difference—before subjectivity.

23. Martin Heidegger, "What is Metaphysics?" p. 102.

24. Julia Kristeva, *Strangers to Ourselves*, trans. Leon S. Roudiez (New York: Columbia University Press, 1991), p. 4.

25. Ibid., p. 187.

26. Ibid. p. 188.

27. Ibid., p. 42

28. See Norma Claire Moruzzi's "National Abjects: Julia Kristeva on the Process of Political Self-Identification," chapter 8 of this volume.

29. Julia Kristeva, *Strangers to Ourselves*, p. 7.

30. Ibid., p. 182.

31. Ibid., p. 195.

32. Ibid., p. 195.

33. Of course in many countries descendants of foreigners are still denied *de jure* rights. This serves to show how little the rule of law can be counted on for remedying the problem of foreignness.

34. Julia Kristeva, *Strangers to Ourselves*, p. 195.

35. Ibid, p. 189. A long footnote follows which cites Brès's comparison of Heidegger and Freud's use of the notion of the uncanny.

36. To this extent, at least, Heidegger agrees with Kristeva that the subject is split. For both Kristeva and Heidegger, the subject is not fully self-present and unary, though Heidegger seems to hold out the possibility that self-presence (self-unity, authenticity) can be achieved.

37. Martin Heidegger, *Being and Time*, trans. J. MacQuarne and E. Robinson (New York: Harper & Row, 1962), p. 164.

38. Ibid.

39. Ibid, p. 165.

40. In Heidegger's *The Question Concerning Technology and Other Essays*, trans. William Lovitt (New York: Harper & Row, 1977).

41. Ibid. p. 148.

42. Paraphrasing and altering Heidegger's language in *Being and Time*, pp. 158–9.

43. Ibid., p. 233.

44. Ibid., p. 235.

45. Ibid., pp. 321–2. Also see 'The Age of the World Picture" for Heidegger's notion of "the incalculable" as something that escapes representation. The incalculable is "grasped" through reflection, and this reflection helps point the way (back) to pres-

ence. "Reflection transports the man of the future into that 'between' in which he belongs to Being and yet remains a stranger amid that which is" (p. 136).

46. Ibid.

47. Ibid., p. 335.

48. Ibid., p. 321.

49. Kristeva, *Strangers to Ourselves*, pp. 2–3.

8

National Abjects:
Julia Kristeva on the Process
of Political Self-Identification

Norma Claire Moruzzi

Early on, Julia Kristeva established herself as a theorist of the speaking subject, in-process. Her work stresses the encounter of that subject with those forms of otherness, internal and external, through which identity is established and maintained. In some of her latest works, including *Strangers to Ourselves*[1] and the essays collected in *Lettre ouvert à Harlem Désir,*[2] Kristeva extends the scope of her discussion from the personal to the political. In these writings, Kristeva addresses the problem of the self's confrontation with the "stranger" (as opposed to the other), whether within the constitutive narratives of Western cultural identity, or in the more immediate context of French national political issues. Recognizing that the stranger is always present both within one's (national) borders and within one's (personal) self, Kristeva reasserts the possibility of coming to terms with the condition of our estrangements. In *Strangers to Ourselves,* she examines the consolidation of the presence of the stranger within the Western tradition; in *Lettre ouvert à Harlem Désir,* she suggests a postmodern re-reading and revival of the Enlightenment project, specific to contemporary France.

For France, as for the other European and neighboring nations and states, the issue of nation-state identity has become critical. The difficulties of Western European federation, the problem of immigration (especially by non-European nationals) into the European states, the reunification of the two German states into a single German nation, and the continuing disintegration of state control over various national impulses in Eastern Europe and the former Soviet Union (including the exacerbation of ethnic conflicts within states and the fragmentation of existing states into jealous national communities), all combine to place into question the always-delicate equilibrium that has been the daily working definition of the nation-state. It is in this historical and political context that Kristeva has written her recent work, and it is in this contemporary context, as well as in the theoretical context of her earlier psychoanalytic and literary analyses, that I locate my own discussion of her work.

After introducing the thematic discussions in Kristeva's latest texts, this chapter will concentrate on three particular points of critical comparison. First, I will consider the strange absence of any consideration of racism and racial estrangement in Kristeva's theoretical work, and the way in which this absence shapes her interpretations and her choice of texts.

Second, I will consider Kristeva's *Lettre ouvert à Harlem Désir* (the head of the French human rights organization, S.O.S. Racisme) within the context of recent public debates among French intellectuals, politicians, and activists. Specifically, I will focus on the controversy around what came to be known as *"l'affaire du foulard,"* (the affair of the head-scarves). In October 1989, when three teenage Arab students tried to wear their head-scarves (Islamic modest clothing, or *hejab,* for religious women) to class, they were refused entry to their public college, and the issue became the focus of an enormous public debate over foreigners and principles of national identity, particularly religion, state authority, and secularism. This debate cut across the ordinary political divisions of left and right, making allies of such unlikely pairs as Regis Debray and Le Pen's National Front. Since Kristeva dated her letter to Désir February 24, 1990, and Désir himself was one of the few public figures on the other side of the controversy (supportive of the government decision to allow the young women back into class, with their head-scarves covering their hair), and since *"l'affaire du foulard"* is perhaps an exemplar of the complexity of current questions concerning the public policy of national identity (including, as it does, aspects of gender, race, class, ethnicity, age, religion, and politics), it functions as a referent which destabilizes Kristeva's own reliance on a Montesquieu motto of "enlightened good intentions" as a directive for the country's public schools.

Third, I will compare Kristeva's recent writing, which urges the rational optimism of the Enlightenment, with her own earlier work on abjection. In *Powers of Horror,*[3] Kristeva emphasized the violence and degradation, of the self and others, that is implicit in the consolidation of a self, whether personal or national. In that earlier text, published in 1980, she identified Céline as the writer who best presented the experience of our own abjection, yet ten years later she revives the Enlightenment project and Montesquieu. Certainly, Kristeva's own writing on the integrity of Céline's virulence at least places into question any easy return to a national politics of humanely rationalized French identity.

While Kristeva's work has often been historically framed, it has usually been focused on the more personal politics of psychoanalytic and literary theory. Yet in *Strangers to Ourselves,* Kristeva extends the scope of her discussion to the relationship between personal identity and its public, political signification. In this text, Kristeva considers the role of the stranger in the history of the Western cultural tradition, from the ancient Greeks and the Old Testament Jews through the early Christians, the Renaissance, the Enlightenment, and contemporary postmodernity. Thus, *Strangers to Ourselves* is composed according to the familiar program of histories of (Western) political thought, histories whose retroactive organizing intention is the concept of the nation-state and its development. But Kristeva problematizes this structure by foregrounding, not the triumph, but the breakdown of the nation-state. Her historical analysis traces the recurring presence of the stranger in relation to national communities, whereas most analyses prefer to note the various consolidations of national identity and power.

Throughout her text, Kristeva concentrates on the experiences of a stranger who is not simply an other, but who is defined as an exile, an immigrant, or a foreigner; one who is other by virtue of the laws of the soil and of blood (which are sometimes placed in opposition), disoriented in place and time.[4] Specifically, Kristeva is interested in the internal experiences of the stranger, in relation to the cultural tradition in which that estrangement is made visible and memorable. Thus, Ruth the Moabite, whose story takes up most of Kristeva's discussion of the stranger in Jewish Old Testament history,[5] is known as such because she is both not a Jew, and the matriarch of the line of David (and also, therefore, of Christ)—a woman from elsewhere whose foreign blood will become the maternal origin of the Jewish royal line. But Meursault, the protagonist of Albert Camus's *L'Etranger,*[6] whose story is discussed in the first chapter of Kristeva's book, presents a different kind of estrangement. Meursault is a modern colonial, mourning for and in search of his lost, dead mother, a man for whom the connecting bonds of social experience have become so attenuated that he desires only the full stop of displacement and death.

Although Kristeva does not emphasize this, it is absolutely significant that Meursault is a *pied noir*[7] in Algeria. His story is visible and memorable because it epitomizes the modern personal and political estrangement of the man who has lost his mother, who is also the national who has lost the mother-land of the nation-state. (That Algeria, in 1942, was still considered that colonial extension of France which was also not France, only further displaces the realization of this loss, without in the least substituting a new landed identity. Meursault, in Algeria, remains French; certainly, neither he nor his companions are to be confused with the local Arabs.) Meursault is a stranger in what is asserted to be his own land, a colonial who is an interloper among more clearly defined national identities. He is a character whose displacement is as much a product of apparently unproblematic social and political change (for Camus's novel is not an overt critique of imperialism), as it is of individual trauma or loss, and he provides us with a point of reference for Kristeva's project in the book as a whole. Meursault, alienated as he is, no longer belongs anywhere, because the national system which should sustain and identify him can no longer authenticate its own limits. He is, in his own weird and profoundly unendearing way, a victim of the degeneration of the nation-state system, a degeneration which has been accomplished as much through colonial expansion as through the internal contradictions of the nation-state itself.[8]

But Kristeva's discussion of Meursault is more introductory than substantive. Like the other fictional stranger she discusses in the first chapter of the book, the elusive hero of Vladimir Nabokov's *The Real Life of Sebastian Knight,*[9] Camus's Meursault is a character whose identity has been fractured and misplaced, not only through the personal details of his life, but also by the vague political and social facts among which he, despite himself, has made his life. Yet Kristeva ignores the implications of these political and social circumstances; her emphasis on Meursault's psychoanalytic alienation obscures the specificity of the form in which that alienation is manifested. Meursault is estranged from his mother, from his nation, from his local country, and from himself, yet the happenstance that the man he shoots is not, for instance, his companion Raymond, but is an unnamed Arab, nicely fits the determinations of regional and racial histories. When Kristeva asserts that Meursault, in his hallucinations, shoots "at shadows, whether French or Maghrebian, it matters little,"[10] she elides precisely those larger patterns, involving national identity and power, in which she is attempting to locate the familiarity of the stranger.

Kristeva's analysis of Meursault, coming as it does early in *Strangers to Ourselves,* spreads a sense of unease through her further discussions. Her apparent disregard for the extent to which Meursault's expression of his personal estrangement is perfectly in keeping with the political and social structures which define him (as a young, heterosexual, male *pied noir* in colonial Algeria), indicates a possible inattentiveness to the significance of these issues. In a work which is attempting to trace the integral presence of the stranger in the constitutive texts of the Western cultural narrative, Kristeva's blithely personal approach presents a problem. In her discussion of Meursault, Kristeva's emphasis on the psychoanalytic (the person and the language of his story) elides the political; in her larger discussion, her choice of texts is surprisingly canonical, so that what is missing, estranged from her own text, is not a discussion of formal politics, but an acknowledgment of racial configurations.

Although, for instance, Kristeva carefully explores the authorial self-estrangement of Montesquieu's *Persian Letters,* she never mentions Gobineau's *The World of the Persians,* or, more importantly, his *The Inequality of Human Races.* That Arthur de Gobineau was a disgruntled and somewhat cranky nineteenth-century aristocrat and world traveler would only, presumably, make him more attractive for Kristeva's project. Certainly, Tzvetan Todorov, in *On Human Diversity*[11] a work comparable to Kristeva's *Strangers to Ourselves,* deals significantly with Gobineau. The Bulgarian-born Todorov's work does not focus precisely on the same kind of encounter with the stranger that the Bulgarian-born Kristeva's does; Todorov focuses on the self's consideration of the stranger who is encountered beyond personal or national borders, while Kristeva focuses on the incorporation of the stranger within those borders. But the parallel between the two projects is made clear in their approaches to their individual discussions of Montesquieu. While Todorov approaches Montesquieu only after having examined other French authors whose writing significantly shaped national thought about nation and race (including Gobineau, Tocqueville, and Loti), Kristeva places Montesquieu in a much more eclectic international milieu. Her trajectory of analysis emphasizes the maintenance of an internal estrangement within every effort of self-consolidation, while studiously avoiding dealing with those major French texts which then delineate the ramifications of that (self-)estrangement in its encounter with others, especially racial others. Since Kristeva nonetheless takes that encounter to be fundamental to her discussion of self-estrangement, her elision of any discussion of Gobineau, for instance, is particularly disconcerting, since it seems to result in a somewhat buoyantly simplified national perspective.

Gobineau was a less political and more social theorist than Montesquieu. While Montesquieu's *Persian Letters* are an authorial ploy used to present observations about French culture from the point of view of a (presumed) foreigner, Gobineau's *The World of the Persians* is a description of life in Persia based on the French author's foreign travels. After his return to France, Gobineau sought to explain the differences he had seen abroad and the degeneration he observed at home through speculations on race. He propounded social theories to clarify the estrangement he felt from his class and his nation, while remaining disgruntled, cranky, and estranged. Gobineau cannot match Montesquieu's serene equanimity, but his observant, problematic writing gives an indication of a different French approach to the problem of national identities. Given that Kristeva titles one of her chapter sections with the question "Is Culture French?" it is not a simple issue for her to ignore Gobineau, the (French) writer who is accepted as the originator of racial theories.

Kristeva's preference for Montesquieu over Gobineau is understandable, but her complete exclusion of Gobineau, and of any discussion of race, leads her to present a narrative trajectory of (self-)estrangement that is oddly formal and resolved. By splitting an analysis of formal political theory and history off from the often messier inquiries of social theory and history, Kristeva disembodies her notion of estrangement; in a sense she returns us, apparently, to ourselves. Yet this resolution is specious, as specious as her assertion that Meursault's target need not be specifically embodied as Arab or French.

Faced with an estrangement that is social and racial, Kristeva resorts to the personal and the (formally) political; she resorts to the traditional comforts of Enlightenment humanism. Thus, in *Lettre ouvert à Harlem Désir*, Kristeva repeats a quotation from Montesquieu that she has already used in *Strangers to Ourselves*. In an essay framed as an open letter to Désir, whose organization, S.O.S. Racisme, she specifically commended in *Strangers to Ourselves*, Kristeva proffers Montesquieu's statement as a motto, in troubled times, for the walls of every French classroom:

> If I knew something useful to myself and detrimental to my family, I would reject it from my mind. If I knew something useful to my family but not to my homeland, I would try to forget it. If I knew something useful to my homeland and detrimental to Europe, or else useful to Europe and detrimental to mankind, I would consider it a crime.[12]

Admirable as Montesquieu's statement is, Kristeva's reliance on it is a bit ingenuous. It is a classic statement of enlightened political humanism, but in her letter to Désir, Kristeva proposes it as a philosophic ideal on which to reconstitute the (French national) community, at least the community in the public school classrooms. But some of the most volatile social conditions challenging the French national community are centered around student behavior and attendance, and Montesquieu's ideal, worthy as it is, emphasizes the problem it is currently being proffered to resolve.

Kristeva's letter to Désir is dated February 24, 1990; it was apparently Kristeva's contribution to a forum on the social and political issues associated with immigration and assimilation in France. Certainly immigration and the problematic lack of assimilation of immigrants is an issue that has been gaining attention in France, as elsewhere, for some years now.[13] Often, public concern over these strangers in the midst of the French national community is particularly focused around Islamic immigrants from North Africa, whose religious politics threaten both the Christian right and the secular left.

In the late fall and winter of 1989, just prior to Kristeva's letter, the attention of French politicians and intellectuals, on the right and the left, focused on an incident involving (initially) three young women students from North African families who attended a public college or high school in a depressed industrial suburb outside of Paris: *"l'affaire du foulard."* The young women insisted on wearing head-scarves in the classroom, but their behavior was taken to be a religious (rather than political) challenge to the French national policy of secular education, and they were suspended from school by the local school authorities. The incident was publicized and politicized, the national Minister of Education ordered the young women to be readmitted to school, with or without head-scarves, and that decision was opposed by many French intellectuals, who characterized it as a national acquiescence to religious fundamentalism and a betrayal of French political history and cultural identity. The date of Kristeva's letter to Désir places it in the midst of the larger discussion surrounding this particular incident.[14]

In both *Strangers to Ourselves* and *Lettre ouvert à Harlem Désir*, Kristeva affirms the heterogeneity of national and political communities, but she does so while glossing over the more difficult aspects of social heterogeneity. Her policy suggestions (according foreigners political rights to the extent that their home countries reciprocate) are largely impractical, especially for foreigners from outside of Europe, but her championing of Montesquieu reveals a more disturbing blindness to the implications of our heterogeneity. Montesquieu's orderly hierarchy—self/family/homeland/Europe/Mankind —sounds good if one assumes that a mindfulness of European identity should enclose a mindfulness of national identity. For Kristeva, an immigrant to France from Bulgaria, it makes sense to consider both national communities as participants in a common European identity, and to offer that European identity as the basis for a reconstituted community of nationals. But for the young students from francophone Morocco and Algiers, the European community is not necessarily the most accessible context in which to frame a national identity. For a francophone North African immigrant, for instance, the reservation of European over French interests is a further estrangement. Montesquieu's motto presumes a (French) national identity that is implicitly European, rather than, for instance, Maghrebian. Placing the motto on the wall of every French classroom would only emphasize the insistent exclusivity of French nation-state identity, and the social estrangement, not of (European) nationals and citizens, but of (other) foreigners.

Despite this, Kristeva is sensitive to the contradictions inherent in the formal political identity of the nation-state. Defined by the emergence of a body politic and a national language, the nation-state must continually maintain the legitimacy of its identity as a subject through encounters with an other, strangers either outside or within its borders. This national preoccupation with alterity demands that otherness must constantly be ejected or assimilated, and therefore also continuously recreated and renewed. The process of national consolidation is also a process of ongoing (international and intranational) estrangement. Speaking of the nation-state, Kristeva writes:

> Here one comes up against a paradox. If political regulations or legislation generally speaking define the manner in which we posit, modify, and eventually improve the status of foreigners, they also make up a vicious circle, for it is precisely with respect to laws that foreigners exist. Indeed, without a social group structured about a power base and provided with legislation, that externality represented by the foreigner and most often experienced as unfavorable or at least problematical would simply not exist.[15]

The institutionalization of national identity is accompanied by the institutionalization of the status of the foreigner. If the nation-state can only legitimate itself by establishing its distinction from the foreigners within and outside its given borders, how great, then, will be the disparity between the "rights of man" and the "rights of citizens"?

The conflict between these given concepts—human rights in general and the specific civil rights of the members of a political community—obviously resonates especially profoundly in the context of French history. In August 1789, the Assembly proclaimed a *Declaration of the Rights of Man and Citizen,* which defined "man" (that universal signifier) inclusively, but as members of the nation only. Kristeva points out the deep irony of this definition: "the nation . . . including the poor, workers of all stations, sex and age being indifferent. . . . Never has democracy been more explicit, for it excludes no one—*except foreigners. . . .*"[16] National rights, no matter how democratic, apply only to those who are accepted as members of the nation. But in order to assure national citizens that their rights are being properly regarded, the state must also identify those to whom "the rights of man and citizen" will not be extended, and make sure they do not receive the benefit of those rights. If they did, if foreigners and assorted others were to be included as full beneficiaries and participants in the national community, while still remaining foreigners (to be treated as citizens without having been naturalized as such, for instance) it would be a sign that the integrity of the nation-state itself was breaking down.

This would not necessarily be such a bad thing, and Kristeva herself gestures in this direction several times in *Strangers to Ourselves*. Nonetheless, the contemporary world functions, or dysfunctions, as the case may be, as a system of nation-states, and the prospect of the disintegration of that system is very frightening to very many people, even if the disintegration is already occurring, unacknowledged.

While Kristeva's recent projects explore the relationships that have always existed between strangers and political or national communities, especially nation-states, she does not particularly address the question of the emotional resistance that often accompanies or disrupts this relationship. Given Kristeva's previous work on the violence of the consolidation of psychoanalytic identity, it is odd that she seems to believe in an easily-achieved, generous solution to the problem of national identities. Kristeva's sudden reversion to the tenets of humanism is not only unhelpful, it is, coming from her, also a philosophical about-face and a surprise. In *Strangers to Ourselves*, Kristeva considers the character of the foreigner, and the degree to which the foreigner can only exist in formal relation to a consolidated national or political identity. But to what degree is national identity predicated on an informal, internal dynamic of exclusion and assimilation? If Kristeva has tried to show us that we have always lived with and known the foreigner, that we are indeed familiar with the foreigner, to the extent that we are familiar with ourselves, why then does the presence of the foreigner remain, for the national community, so very deeply fraught? And why, when Kristeva is dealing with the issue of foreigners in France, does she, herself a foreigner, abruptly resort to the soothing mottoes of humanism, when in other circumstances she has been one of the chief critics of humanism's seamless, suffocating philosophy of unification?

For an answer to these questions, we may find it worthwhile to reencounter one of Kristeva's slightly earlier texts, so that her analysis of nation-state identity can be considered in relation to her analysis of the psychoanalytic and/or literary model of the personal subject's process of self-individuation. In *Powers of Horror: an Essay on Abjection*, Kristeva discusses the privately embodied subject's relation with its own borders and excess. The subject abjects itself, and discovers itself in its own abjection; historically, the nation-state establishes itself through the convulsions of a body politic which rejects those parts of itself, defined as other or excess, whose rejected alterity then engenders the consolidation of a national identity. The fragile, all-too-personal political identity of the nation-state offers itself up for a political analysis informed by psychoanalytic and literary theory. In Kristeva's own work the most relevant concept to be applied to her writing on national identity is her own analysis of abjection.

In *Powers of Horror*, Kristeva distinguishes the abject from both the subject and the object. Although her analysis is directed at the development and consolidation of personal, individual identity, it can be applied as well to the development and consolidation of national, political identity. The abject is precisely that which constitutes and opposes the self, whether of the individual or of the nation state. It is that which most confounds the self's boundaries:

> There looms, within abjection, one of those violent, dark revolts of being, directed against a threat that seems to emanate from an exorbitant outside or inside, ejected beyond the scope of the possible, the tolerable, the thinkable. It lies there, quite close, but it cannot be assimilated. . . . Unflaggingly, like an inescapable boomerang, a vortex of summons and repulsion places the one haunted by it literally beside himself.[17]

The abject is that which, although intimately a part of early experience, must be rejected so that the self can establish the borders of its unified subjectivity: the familiar foreign(er) who is suddenly recognized as a threat to (national) identity. This rejection (abjection) of certain aspects of physical immediacy, whether of the personal body or the body politic, is the act which establishes subjective identity, but this act also establishes that identity as a prohibition, and as lacking an earlier bodily continuity. The subjective self, therefore, is always haunted by the possible return of the abject that was a part of presubjective experience. For the subjective identity of the nation-state, this threatened return, that would dissolve the national self into undifferentiatable physical parts, is posed by the stranger, who is both desired and feared. In Kristeva's individual case, changing international relationships involves a possible personal reconfiguration, such that her former identity as a young Bulgarian stranger threatens to return and confound her mature self, a self internationally recognized as a French intellectual.

This self-splitting, a self-abjection, is the quality which makes abjection such a threat. Abjection contradicts the self's (national or individual) claim to unity and knowledge, but this contradiction is so profound precisely because it emerges from the gestures with which the self attempts to assert such a claim: ". . . I expel *myself*, I spit *myself* out, I abject *myself* within the same motion through which 'I' claim to establish *myself*."[18] Who is not in some way individually estranged from the whole of national identity? Abjection blurs the usually clearly marked space between the self and the other which constitutes identity. But abjection does not provide a reconciliation of meaning. Instead, the abject is that which seems to confound the possibility of meaning, its presence threatening a chaos that must be withheld. The self abjects that which is most necessarily inescapable and rejected: the bodily reminders of physical dependence and necessity. (On a national level, how often are those foreigners most despised who have been allowed inside the national borders in order to do those essential jobs disdained by the national population? On the personal level, Kristeva, who has written with great sympathy of her own maternal experiences, finds herself reverting to the respectable truths of humanism when confronted by immigration problems in France and the upheavals in Eastern Europe.) Kristeva writes of the two distinct threats the abject poses to the self's free agency, a free agency that is defined, for the nation, as the achievement of political life over the vaguely inhuman, prepolitical state of nature. "The abject confronts us, on the one hand, with those fragile states where man strays on the territories of the *animal*."[19] In order to attain language and culture, the (human, national) self must differentiate from the (animal, foreign) body. Instead of politics and civilization, however, the abject would drag us back into chaos and bestiality.

The second threat that the abject presents to the distinctly human self and body is one that involves gender. After undermining the supposedly clear separation of human and animal nature, the abject draws us back to a confusion of the boundaries between the self and the mother's body:

> The abject confronts us, on the one hand, and this time within our personal archeology, with our earliest attempt to release the hold of *maternal* entity even before ex-isting outside her, thanks to the autonomy of language.[20]

Kristeva emphasizes the enveloping power of the maternal, which both engenders us and pre-exists a separation of (our) self and other at the earliest conscious stage. Again, although she writes of the relations between individuals, a recollection of her attention to Meursault's multiple maternal estrangements, from his human mother, his mother-land, and, in dealing with the Arabs, from his mother tongue, should remind us that the maternal entity is not only familial. Kristeva's discussion of the maternal abject can be adapted to the context of national identities and their linguistic borders.

This confusion of the self with an animal or maternal (be it familial or national) body provides a deep unease relative to that self's ability to function productively or reproductively as a free adult, or as an autonomous political body. Once the abjected body is reintroduced into the realm of the public and political self, the possibilities for freedom and power recede. One cannot simply continue to make oneself, when confronted with the blunt physiognomy of one's unreformed past. Faced with the return of the abjected body (whether represented by the stranger, or representative of the maternal/national, maternal/familial body) the self can neither sustain its creative attempts nor bring them to fruition. It becomes impotent, and the future, stillborn.

In *Powers of Horror,* the most telling myth concerning the self's reencounter with the abject is that of Oedipus, who, in sleeping with his mother and fathering children by her, confounds, both personally and politically, his filial, paternal, and fraternal roles. His transgression of the conventions of productive and reproductive function initially condemns his kingdom to the plague, and then him and his family to wasteful death and tragedy. Once he knows of his own deep implication with the abject, he can sustain neither his kingly power, nor his generative contribution, and both present and future (as well as, retroactively, the past) are lost.[21]

But Kristeva is not so simply pessimistic about our personal futures, and finally, it is in her discussion of the return of the abject that we may be able to locate a theoretical origin for the strange optimism she brings to her discussion of national futures. While the return of the abject, whether it be through the Oedipal individual's personal encounter or the chaos of a million ethnic refugees within the nation-state, breaks down the clear definition of the subject, Kristeva finds some hope left in this scenario:

> The abject is the violence of mourning for an "object" that has always already been lost. The abject shatters the wall of repression and its judgments. It takes the ego back to its source on the abominable limits from which, in order to be, the ego has broken away—it assigns it a source in the non-ego, drive, and death. Abjection is a resurrection that has gone through death (of the ego). It is an alchemy that transforms death drive into a start of life, of new significance.[22]

In her discussion of abjection, Kristeva recognizes the confounding power of the return of the abject, but identifies it as a dynamic possibility. Given this perspective, we would assume that the disintegration and degeneration of the fixed identity of the nation-state, or the national, need not mean the end of political identity or participation, although it may transform national identity, both individual and collective, as we know it.

Yet Kristeva hesitates before this political implication of her own earlier work. Instead, it seems, when confronted with the very insistent emergence into public view of the formerly hidden bodies of familiar, abject strangers, be they immigrants in France or reawakened nationalists in Eastern Europe, Kristeva retreats to an understandably personal, if personally contradictory (to her own previous theorizations), assertion of humanistic quietude. If abjection, to achieve the generative transformation Kristeva has mentioned, demands the death of the ego, her latest work seems to be asserting, perhaps in spite of herself, that here is one ego that is not yet dead.

At the very least, however, it is an ego divided against itself. Despite her recent predilection for Montesquieu, Kristeva concludes *Strangers to Ourselves* by emphasizing the newly polyglot cosmopolitanism that has overtaken France, the original nation-state. To the extent that the abject has returned, that we live with strangers in our midst, and are strangers to ourselves, we are faced with the task of recreating an international community composed of mutually reciprocating strangers. Perhaps, Kristeva does seem to suggest, the time of the nation-state has passed. By acknowledging this, we may be able to formulate a new model of personal and national identity, one that is less rigid and more open to the inevitability of change. For Kristeva herself, this acknowledgment has grave personal significance, and she is understandably resistant to it, a resistance that, in her case, seems to present itself as nostalgia for the secure perspectives of the Enlightenment. Nonetheless, Kristeva concludes *Strangers to Ourselves* with these remarks:

> A paradoxical community is emerging, made up of foreigners who are reconciled to themselves to the extent that they recognize themselves as foreigners. The multinational society would thus be the consequence of an extreme individualism, but conscious of its discontents and limits, knowing only indomitable people ready-to-help-themselves in their weakness, a weakness whose other name is our radical strangeness.[23]

To the extent that she is a member of this paradoxical community, Kristeva is of course also a stranger to herself. It may not be surprising, then, and is in fact rather encouraging, to note the divisions in her theory, its self-contradictions, all the more evidence, perhaps, of any self's necessary self-contradictions. Ironically enough, Kristeva's recent nostalgia is completely consistent with her own theory of the self's resistance to the return of the abject.

Notes

1. Julia Kristeva, *Strangers to Ourselves,* trans. Leon Roudiez (New York: Columbia University Press, 1991), originally published as *Etrangers à nous-mêmes* (Paris: Fayard, 1989).

2. Julia Kristeva, *Lettre ouvert à Harlem Désir* (Paris: Gallimard, 1991).

3. Julia Kristeva, *Powers of Horror: an Essay on Abjection,* trans. Leon S. Roudiez (New York: Columbia University Press, 1982), originally published in Paris by Editions du Seuil, 1980.

4. Julia Kristeva, *Strangers to Ourselves,* pp. 95–96.

5. Julia Kristeva, *Strangers to Ourselves,* pp. 69–76.

6. Albert Camus, *L'Etranger,* (Paris: Gallimard, 1942).

7. *Pied noir* is the term used to identify French colonial settlers in Algeria, to distinguish them from French visitors and indigenous Arabs.

8. This is not the place to give an extended discussion of the origin or degeneration of the nation-state system, but it may at least be appropriate to indicate one of the main analysts Kristeva herself relies on in her own discussion. For an examination of the contradictions both within nation-state identity, and in the relationship between that identity and the nation-state's function as a colonial power, see Hannah Arendt's various discussions in "Imperialism," the second part of *The Origins of Totalitarianism,* especially the chapters on "The Political Emancipation of the Bourgeoisie" and "The Decline of the Nation-State and the End of the Rights of Man." Hannah Arendt, *The Origins of Totalitarianism* (New York: Harcourt Brace Jovanovich, 1973, originally published 1951), pp. 123–57, 267–302.

9. Vladimir Nabokov, *The Real Life of Sebastian Knight* (New York: New Directions, 1941).

10. Julia Kristeva, *Strangers to Ourselves,* p. 26.

11. Tzvetan Todorov, *On Human Diversity: Nationalism, Racism, and Exoticism in French Thought,* trans. Catherine Porter (Cambridge, Mass.: Harvard University Press, 1993), originally published as *Nous et les autres* (Paris: Seuil, 1989).

12. Charles Louis de Secondat, baron de la Brède et de Montesquieu, *Mes Pensées,* in *Oeuvres complètes,* ed. Roger Caillois, Bibliothèque de la Pléiade (Paris: Gallimard, 1985), p. 1:981, as quoted in *Strangers to Ourselves,* p. 130.

13. A tremendous amount of literature has been appearing dealing with these issues. As an example, published in the United States at about the same time as Kristeva's letter was appearing in France, see for instance the volume subtitled "E Pluribus Unum" of *Telos,* 83, Spring 1990, especially Pierre-André Taguieff, "The New Cultural Racism in France," pp. 109–22, in which Taguieff describes the French right's cooption of the idea of (cultural and racial) difference, and its traduction into a nationalist political platform.

14. The popular press covered the incident extensively while it was going on and immediately afterward, but journal articles appeared, naturally, in the months directly following. See, for example, the issue devoted to "*l'affaire du foulard*" of *le débat* (Paris: Gallimard), No. 58, Jan-Feb 1990.

15. Julia Kristeva, *Strangers to Ourselves,* p. 96.

16. Ibid., p. 149.

17. Julia Kristeva, *Powers of Horror*, p. 1.

18. Ibid., p. 3.

19. Ibid., pp. 12–13.

20. Ibid., p. 13. Kristeva is relying here on a Lacanian model of psychoanalytic development. Before language and the symbolic, linked with the father/the law, intrude a third party into the mother-child dyad, the symmetry of that relationship obscures any absolute claim to a proper division between two physical bodies as separate selves. See Jacques Lacan, "The Mirror Stage as Formative of the Function of the I as Revealed in Psychoanalytic Experience" trans. Alan Sheridan, *Ecrits: A Selection* (New York: Norton, 1977), pp. 1–7. It should be noted here that the maternal is not the same as the individual mother, just as no woman can hold the position of the phallic woman; the psychoanalytic constructs are not identities. For Lacan's own denial of this specification, see for instance Jacques Lacan, "God and the Jouissance of The Woman" trans. Jacqueline Rose, in *Feminine Sexuality: Jacques Lacan and the Ecole Freudienne,* ed. Juliet Mitchell and Jacqueline Rose (New York: Norton, 1982), pp. 137–48.

21. See Julia Kristeva, "From Filth to Defilement" in *Powers of Horror,* pp. 83–89.

22. Julia Kristeva, *Powers of Horror*, p. 15.

23. Julia Kristeva, *Strangers to Ourselves,* p. 195.

9

Des Chinoises: Orientalism, Psychoanalysis, and Feminine Writing

Lisa Lowe

Julia Kristeva's *Des chinoises* occupies a peculiarly paradoxical position within the French orientalist tradition. Emerging, as it did, after the period of French decolonization, Kristeva's text is at once both strikingly different from the earlier French colonial orientalism and yet disturbingly reminiscent of its postures and rhetorics. The principal manner in which Kristeva's "China" differs from the orientalist texts of the eighteenth and nineteenth centuries is that its various deployments of orientalist tropes are meant to represent breaks with colonialist ideology. Indeed, viewing Kristeva's *Des chinoises* in the context of the journal *Tel quel,* to which Kristeva contributed and in which she played a crucial role, the French construction of China in the 1970s was central to a counterideological politics; China was constituted as an object of desire within particular veins of the discourses of semiotics, feminism, psychoanalysis, and French Maoism, whose projects were critical of the ideology of French national homogeneity, centralized state power, and the continuing French subordination of North Africa and Indochina. In this sense, the "post-decolonization" discourse about China appropriated certain orientalist tropes in order to criticize the state apparatus of which the earlier colonialist orientalism was a product. Opposed to, yet in a reactive relation with traditional orientalism, Kristeva's and *Tel quel*'s post-decolonization form of orientalism departed from, yet was determined by, the discursive conditions of the previous orientalism. Perhaps most importantly, the fascination with China and the Chinese Cultural Revolution on the part of French intellectuals must be understood as a response to the student revolts and workers' strikes of May 1968, which demanded radical changes in the authoritarian structures of the university, the factory, and society at large. In the aftermath of 1968, when the revolts had been suppressed and Gaullist power restored, leftist intellectuals in France struggled to explain what had happened, what might have happened, and what remained to be done. In this sense, the figuration of China—as feminist, psychoanalytic, and political utopia—was an indirect response to the thwarted revolution of 1968; a 1970s orientalist recuperation of China as a utopian site of revolution outside of Europe implied a judgment that revolution could never occur in France. The romance with China served as a means for some intellectuals to turn away from the still-demanding struggles in France—struggles not limited to the rebuilding of a fragmented and disillusioned Left but, more important, arising from a growing racial and class stratification in France resulting from the post-decolonization displacements of immigrants from North Africa, Indochina, and the Caribbean.

Des chinoises was written in the context of both the Western Continental feminist debates of the early 1970s and the structuralist and psychoanalytic theoretical debates of the same period; in this sense writing about "*la chinoise*" was an occasion for Kristeva to critique the lack of psychoanalytic sophistication in the French and North American women's movements, as well as a means of providing a feminist critique of the Freudian and Lacanian paradigms of sexual difference.[1] *Des chinoises* invokes the powerful figure of an ancient Chinese matriarch as the disrupting exception to Western patriarchy and psychoanalysis, and the People's Republic of China is praised as a political antithesis to contemporary France. In both senses the examples of China and Chinese women are cited only in terms of Western debates, are invented as solutions to Western political and theoretical problems.

A hierarchical opposition of occidental and oriental is stated in the formal divisions themselves which frame and structure the entire text: a first section, "*De ce côte-ci*," (From this side), and a second section titled "*Femmes de Chine*" (Chinese women). "*De ce côte-ci*" contains five chapters describing the oppression of women in the Western traditions of sexual differentiation and definition: first, the patrilinear monotheistic tradition exemplified by the Old Testament, separating men and women into two races and subjugating "*la femme*" to the privileged identity of "*l'homme*"; and second, the Freudian and Lacanian psychoanalytic explanation of sexual difference. Subsequently, in the section "*Femmes de Chine*," this bipartite narrative about women in Western history is posed against a bipartite narrative about China; with the parallelism of the two cleft narrative reconstructions of Occident and Orient, Kristeva argues that the ancient matriarchal origins of China contrast with the patrilinear monotheism of the Judeo-Christian biblical tradition, whereas the long Confucian period of Chinese history resembles that of the Western psychoanalytic repression of femininity.

In chapter 2 of part 1, "*La guerre des sexes*," Kristeva discusses Western religious and legal discourse; man is genealogically linked to the one God, she argues, whereas woman is excluded from this genealogy.[2] The woman qualifies as human subject only in her relation as "*épouse*," and in her contractual agreement to bear man's children. Within these traditions, man possesses social subjectivity, access to language, and legal and historical presence; woman, Kristeva argues, is constituted by the tradition as the Other, who is mute, powerless, outlawed, ahistorical, and absent. Kristeva's analysis of the Old Testament tradition is a structuralist one, which relies on binary systems of classification (presence and absence, speeched and speechless, man and woman, and so on). In a sense, her interpretation foregrounds the inherent limitations of structuralism as a method of criticism for articulating a feminist project: the fixed nature of the paradigm, and the extent to which structuralism posits and assumes the binary complementarity of the dyad man/woman without providing the tools for an adequate critique of the production of this binary logic: In effect, the structuralist method utilized here constitutes the binary oppositions it ostensibly identifies.[3] In order to find a critical methodology less static than structuralist description, "*De ce côte-ci*" then turns to psychoanalysis as a method that attempts to account for the formation of the subject in language and culture. Yet whereas the theoretical limitations of psychoanalysis are different from the problems of binary reductionism inherent in structuralism, Kristeva's particular use of psychoanalysis in *Des chinoises* implicates its arguments about sexual difference in another set of determined relations.

Psychoanalysis presumes that sexuality is at the center of a subject's identity within family, language, and social arrangements; because the issue of sexuality is central to so many feminist theorists, the attraction to psychoanalysis among feminists is understandable.[4] But the ultimate psychoanalytic revelation that gendered subjectivity is determined by the presence or lack of a penis (in the case of Freud) or the phallus (in the case of Lacan) insistently frustrates the feminist project, to the extent that psychoanalytic explanation of gender tends to rely on an arbitrary assignment of a masculine mark to describe a difference that needs also to be explained by other, more varied methods of analysis and explanation, such as sociology and the construction of sexual difference, economics and the relationship of class and gender, or social history and the production of race and gender.[5] In *Des chinoises*, Kristeva's critique of psychoanalysis consists in revalorizing Freud's formulation of a pre-Oedipal phase by imputing to it certain characteristics extrapolated from Lacan's notion of the Imaginary.[6] In chapter 3 of part 1, "*Vierge du verbe*," Kristeva expands Freud's notion of the pre-Oedipal stage—a period anterior to the legendary castration,

before the child acquires speech and enters into social relations—by stressing the importance of rediscovering the powerful sexuality of the mother.
Following Freud and Lacan, Kristeva adopts the pre-Oedipal as a "prehistory" to Oedipalization, but in contradistinction to Freud and Lacan, for
whom the overwhelming significance lies in the process of Oedipalization,
Kristeva inflects the "regressions" toward pre-Oedipal eroticism for the
mother with a positive value.

> There are two processes in psychoanalysis, one pertaining to the role of
> the mother, the other as a result of language.
>   The first one consists in lifting the repression of the fact that the
> mother is *other,* has no penis, but enjoys pleasure and brings forth chil-
> dren. To lift the repression only to the preconscious, just to imagine that
> she is procreative, but censoring the fact that she has had sexual plea-
> sure in intercourse, in which there was a "primal scene." Further, the
> mother's vagina and pleasure are misrecognized and immediately replaced
> by the circumstances which situate the mother on the side of the
> sociosymbolic community: childbirth, the relationship to the name of the
> father. This operation of false recognition—of misrecognition—of mater-
> nal pleasure is realized according to a process of which Ernest Jones was
> the first to understand the source.[7]

This passage refers to the premises of castration and the repression of
the knowledge of women as both generative and sexual to explain, on the
one hand, the Symbolic appropriation of the woman's body and sexual pleasures, and on the other hand, the exclusion of women from a masculine
model of socialization and subjectivity. Kristeva asserts that the multiple
and nonexclusive sexual pleasures of the mother—"*le vagin et la jouissance*" [emphasis added]—are misrecognized, or repressed, and that psychoanalysis accounts for this misrecognition as necessary for the preservation
of a male order. The implicit reference to castration is significant, for it is
through the drama of castration as the repression of the child's vision of
the mother's sexuality that psychoanalysis explains the formation of masculine identity. Kristeva argues that it is the child's belief in castration that
represses a knowledge of the mother—as sexual, fertile, and vaginal—and
in this belief that the denial and appropriation of women's sexual pleasure,
or *jouissance,* takes place.

Kristeva's refiguration of the pre-Oedipal phase draws somewhat upon
the Lacanian notion of the Imaginary—a hypothetical, specular, preverbal
topos reconstructed from the standpoint of the Symbolic. Lacan's definition of the Imaginary includes a "mirror stage," a hypothetical phase in
which the preverbal child identifies with a specular reflection (or misiden-

tifies, in that it is through identification with images that the subject mis-recognizes itself, and constructs the alienated self, which Lacan calls the *ego* or *moi*). It is termed the Imaginary, because for Lacan the supposition of a period of narcissistic identification and fullness is a mythical stage; it exists only as a recapitulation of an "imaginary" pre-Symbolic state from the standpoint of the subject who is always already within language, the pater-nal order, social hierarchy, and law. Lacan discusses Oedipalization, there-fore, not as Freud's scene in which the child fears castration and identifies with the father's masculinity, but rather as a metaphor for the accession of the subject to the socialized sphere of Symbolic relations. The Lacanian Oedipal phenomenon consists of this initiation into the Symbolic, emblema-tized by the naming/castration of the subject in language, the receipt of the *nom* and the *non* of the father. With the entry of the named subject into language and the social order, the unnamed, repressed desires of the sub-ject are driven underground. This division of the subject in language is cru-cial to the functions of desire and symbolization, for it is in the Symbolic relations of language that the subject attempts to reconstruct the identities and equivalences of the Imaginary. In rewriting the Lacanian notion of the Imaginary as a female pre-Oedipal phase, Kristeva privileges the infant's identification with the mother rather than the specular identification stressed by Lacan: "The child is bound to the mother's body without that body being, as yet, 'other'; rather, her body 'pleasures' with the child's body itself, in a kind of natural/social continuum."[8] Thus, Kristeva expands the notion of the pre-Oedipal/Imaginary in opposition to castration, Oedipalization, and the Lacanian Symbolic; the formulation of the pre-Oedipal represents an attempt to locate a space outside the phallic-dominated Symbolic for a maternal, feminine-dominated phase of psychosexual development.[9]

Kristeva's revalorization of the pre-Oedipal as an absolute state of oth-erness with regard to the paternalistic Symbolic and its systems of signifi-cation is figured in an idealized Other—the Mother—located outside the hierarchical, Oedipalized overdetermination of Western psychoanalysis. But Kristeva does more than idealize this Mother; she "orientalizes" her. In the book's second section, "*Femmes de Chine*," Kristeva constitutes an ancient matrilinear-matrilocal society as the historical analogue to the female-dominated pre-Oedipal *topos*, conflating the matriarch of pre-Con-fucian China with the mother in pre-Oedipal discourse. Both projects place the Mother at the center of their respective paradigms: as the primary fig-ure in child development and gender acquisition, and as the origin of social and economic organization. Both efforts depend on the retrospective inven-tion of a prehistorical moment, an idealized state outside society and his-tory, created from a point located within social arrangements. In the argument that Chinese matriarchy is the antecedent of a twentieth-century revolutionary society, the generalizing narrative, undaunted by the large scope of its project, leaps quickly and simply across two thousand years of Chinese history to propose that, because of China's matriarchal heritage, the communist politics of the People's Republic hold powerful lessons for the French Left in the 1970s. Throughout *Des chinoises* a historical extravagance, which so easily establishes a correspondence between an ancient modality and a contemporary one, lacks an adequately complex appreciation of the heterogeneous and contradictory forces of history; despite an ostensible allegiance to Marxism, Kristeva finds no apparent difficulties in generalizing Chinese history in so undialectical a fashion.

Kristeva first evokes the mother-centered society of pre-Confucian China in chapter 1 of part 2, "*La mère au centre*," in a fantasy description of matrilinear kinship and matrilocal systems of exchange in ancient China. She suggests that genealogy issued from mother to daughter, and that the family groups within each region were organized along maternal lines; that is, the son-in-law moved to the wife's mother's district. In addition, males and females had equal power in the social and political spheres of activity; this is symbolized, she claims, by symmetrically binomial names that include the name of the mother (also the name of the region) as well as the paternal family name. Kristeva employs conditional verb tenses to evoke this ancient system, calling attention to its hypothetical and fictive qualities: "A certain preponderance of women *would be* however logically necessary in this period, and *would explain* a lineage both matrilinear and matrilocal" [emphasis added].[10] Indeed, Kristeva candidly comments on the quality of invention, and of phantasm in her history of the woman-dominated Chinese society—"*hypothétique (utopique? fantasmatique?)*"[11]—and the fact that she selectively chooses this image of matrilinear-matrilocal society from particular, and few, Western sinologists' texts. As with the embellishment of the pre-Oedipal phase in the first section of *Des Chinoises,* in this second section the invented matrilinear-matrilocal society is likewise exploited for its quality of utopia and phantasm; as an Imaginary, and therefore untextualized, Other, the Chinese matriarchy offers the writer of *écriture féminine* a powerful *topos* with which to subvert the narratives of western patrilineality.

Kristeva also justifies the mother-centered theories of the pre-Oedipal phase and the pre-Confucian matriarchy in an "analysis" of Chinese language. She argues that the independence of two linguistic systems—of tonal speech and of written ideogrammatic symbols—is particular to the Chinese language, and that the independent system of tonal speech is a preserved remnant of the matrilinear-matrilocal society, in which the mother and her bodily preverbal tones and rhythms were dominant. Earlier, Kristeva had characterized the pre-Oedipal relationship of infant and mother as one of preverbal "echolalia": "The pre-Oedipal phase corresponds to an intense echolalia, first in rhythm and then in intonation, before the phonologico-syntactic structure is imposed on the sentence."[12] In this discussion of the relationship between written and spoken Chinese, Kristeva suggests that the written language embodies the Oedipal-Confucian suppression of the pre-Oedipal echolalia present in the intoned spoken language.

> The logic of (Chinese) writing ... presupposes, at its base, a speaking, writing individual for whom what seems to us today a pre-Oedipal phase—dependency on the maternal, socio-natural continuum, absence of clear-cut divisions between the order of things and the order of symbols, predominance of the unconscious impulses—must have been extremely important. Ideogrammatic or ideographic writing makes use of this (pre-Oedipal phase) for the ends of state, political, and symbolic power, but without censuring them. A despotic power that has not forgotten what it owes to the mother and the matrilinear family that has certainly preceded it, though not by long. Hypothesis? Fantasy?[13]

In equating the intoned rhythms associated with the pre-Oedipal phase of mother-child union with the ancient, prepatriarchal phase of Chinese history, Kristeva creates a deliberate confusion and conflation of the paradigms of individual psychology and language acquisition, the history of language and civilization. Furthermore, the argument that the intoned quality of Chinese language is evidence that the mother-child union was valued in ancient China is, to say the least, deluded exaggeration; indeed, a great number of contemporary spoken languages are intoned. Although the paradox of an intoned spoken language and a highly coded written language is noteworthy, Kristeva makes extremely speculative use of this paradox in suggesting that the independent system of written ideograms represents a later attempt to repress the ancient maternal tones. Finally, by romanticizing the Chinese language as a system of codes within which one can read about an earlier, tonal, pre-Oedipal society which has survived the later symbolic ordering of written language, Kristeva casts the Chinese linguistic example as the *semiosis* she elsewhere suggests occurs in Western poetics, in which the feminine pre-Oedipal is brought into paternal language.[14] The example of Chinese language, as it is constituted in *Des chinoises,* conveniently serves Kristeva's theory of the semiotic *chora* elaborated at length in *La révolution du langage poétique.* She subjects Chinese language, like Chinese history and culture, to French linguistic and psychoanalytic paradigms; China is constituted as a utopian text (*"Hypothèse? Fantasme?"*)

which illustrates the answers to some pressing theoretical problems for the Western semiotician.

Chapter 2, "*Confucius—un 'mangeur des femmes',*" discusses the Confucian era, generalized and homogenized into a period ranging from 1000 B.C. to the twentieth century (the text does not become less imperializing). In Confucian society, the text argues, an oppressive backlash extensively excluded women by law and social hierarchy. This is compared to the Western biblical and psychoanalytic oppression of Western women, described in the first five chapters of part 1. Absolute language is used to express the oppression of women under Confucianism: "They are subject to authority, they submit themselves to the new authority of parents-in-law and husbands, they owe absolute filial piety and obedience."[15] The bound foot is invoked as an ornate symbol of their profound capacity to obey. The absolute language of persecution calls attention to the polar opposition the text draws between the powerful position of women in the legendary, ancient matriarchy and the extreme oppression of women under Confucianism. The developmental opposition between pre-Confucian and Confucian times puts forth a thesis about the history of Chinese women which is analogous to the paradigmatic splits characterized by the notions of pre-Oedipal and Oedipal phases of human development. If Chinese women formerly had power and coequal status during the ancient period of Chinese civilization, the backlash against Chinese women under Confucianism constitutes a *refoulement* like the psychoanalytic repression of the mother's *jouissance*. Because Chinese women have a point of origin in which they were powerful and dominant, the repressed woman is described as both subject to authoritarian structures of obedience and simultaneously undetermined and outside those structures. Kristeva argues that the Chinese woman is at once within familial and social relations and yet beyond those relations, and that her hysterias, suicides, and pregnancies are statements of her power, and examples of the ways in which the Chinese woman under Confucianism protests her subjection and subverts paternal authority.

Finally, chapters 3–6 discuss the conditions of women in the People's Republic of China. Kristeva concludes that contemporary women in China have liberated themselves and reemerged as fully autonomous political subjects in a restoration of the coequal status and power they had possessed in the original matrilinear and matrilocal society. Because of its matriarchal roots, the Chinese Revolution of 1949, the text asserts, was an antipatriarchal revolution; the socialist revolution in China, Kristeva argues, brought a fundamental revolution in the patriarchal family and in the roles of women. The essential premise is that throughout the history of Chinese women, "her" experience has been completely *other* than the experience of Western women under patriarchy. Confucianism and feudalism are juxtaposed with monotheism and capitalism; Western saints are contrasted with Chinese concubines. For if the Chinese woman is constructed as impenetrably and incomprehensibly different, then it is possible to constitute her as outside Western socialization, not reducible to Western binary and hierarchical classifications. Kristeva rhetorically juxtaposes European and Chinese women, as if in the act of writing an encomium to Chinese women as an exemplary exception to Western oppressions of women her text posits a radical maternal semiotic otherness that surges up through the Symbolic order. The implicit recommendation of the text is that feminine writing ought to regard, praise, and write about Chinese women, for the identification with a position eccentric to Western ideology constitutes a revolutionary political strategy for objecting to that structure.

> The role of the revolutionary (female or male): to refuse all roles, in order, on the contrary, to summon this timeless "truth"—formless, neither true nor false, echoes of our *jouissance*, of our words spoken in delirium, of our pregnancies—into the order of speech and social symbolism. But how do we call it into being? By listening, by recognizing the unspoken in discourse . . . by calling attention at all times to whatever remains unsatisfied, repressed, new, eccentric, incomprehensible, disturbing to the status quo.[16]

The identification and alliance with the eccentric, the Other, the Imaginary, is valorized as a political strategy that challenges the structures of domination in the Western social order. Furthermore, language is considered the material medium of the ideological apparatus, and therefore a material site of political practice and change; writing from a position within Western ideology about a phenomenon outside Western history and ideology is essentialized as a means of displacing that ideology. But in inventing and appropriating the place of "Chinese woman," *Des chinoises* erases the situations of women in contemporary China, the complex interrelation of certain qualified freedoms with remnants of centuries of sexual discrimination and oppression in family, professional, and political life. The Chinese woman is fetishized and constructed as the Other of Western psychoanalytic feminism, a transcendental exception to the overstructured bind of women in western Europe. *Des chinoises* curiously reproduces the postures of desire of two narratives it ostensibly seeks to subvert: the narratives of orientalism and romantic courtship, whose objects are the "oriental" and the "woman."

•

The social production, historical framework, and cultural function of Kristeva's representation of the maternal, imaginary Orient differs greatly from earlier orientalist figurations of the feminine, such as Flaubert's nineteenth-century representations of *"la femme orientale."* Nonetheless, the twentieth-century projection of China as a fiction of absolute cultural and sexual difference from the West is more similar to the earlier orientalist tradition than one might at first imagine. Kristeva's rhetorical posture in the description of her first encounter with the Chinese is reminiscent particularly of Flaubert's famous evocation of the Egyptian courtesan Kuchuk-Hânem in which he writes, "The oriental woman is a machine, and nothing more; she doesn't differentiate between one man and another. . . . We are thinking of her, but she is hardly thinking of us. We are weaving an aesthetic on her account."[17] Kristeva not only duplicates the structure of address that makes the oriental Other an aestheticized object of exchange between occidental writer and receivers, but she also attributes to that otherness similar qualities of silence, inertia, and indifference:

> An immense crowd is seated in the sun; it waits for us without a word, without moving. Calm eyes, not even curious, but slightly amused or anxious, in any case piercing, and certain of belonging to a community with which we will never have anything to do. They don't distinguish among us man or woman, young or old, blonde or brunette, this or that feature of face or body.[18]

The Chinese crowd is homogenized and distanced as Other to the group of French intellectuals traveling in China in 1974. They are still and silent, their collective gaze distant, impenetrable, yet piercing—excluded and excluding—and of one blended character, as if the crowd were like a single mirror reflecting the travelers' *étrangeté*. "They don't distinguish among us man or woman" resonates profoundly with Flaubert's assertion that the oriental woman "doesn't differentiate between one man and another." In both situations the oriental is represented by the French writers as speechless Other, indiscriminate rather than discriminating. The undifferentiating gaze of the French text is displaced and attributed to the gaze of the "undifferentiated" Chinese; that is, the Chinese are constituted as performing the very operation that the textual representation does to them. In both, the French readers are the audience who is interpellated to participate in these orientalist circuits of discourse. This early passage from *Des chinoises*, which reiterates certain generic and rhetorical features of orientalist travel literature, strikes the keynote of the entire text, in which the Chinese, and ultimately Chinese women as inheritors of a matriarchal tradition and maternal culture, are homogenized as the absolute cultural and sexual Others of the occidental tradition.

During the 1970s, Kristeva and other leftist French intellectuals, such as those associated with the journal *Tel quel*, were concerned with criticizing the power of the French state and its ideology, an ideology that justified, among other things, imperialist policies in North Africa and Indochina. In this sense, the construction of China in *Des chinoises* conjured the oriental Other not as a colonized space but as a desired position outside Western politics and signification. Yet a final irony remains: this post-decolonization refiguration of China continued to figure the Orient as the Other, no longer colonized but as utopian, and this romantic regard for China permitted intellectuals in France to disregard the situation of actual post-decolonization peoples residing and laboring in France itself. By the 1950s French colonialism in Africa and Asia had been rigorously challenged by nationalist groups in Algeria, Tunisia, Morocco, and Indochina, as well as by leftist groups within France critical of French politics. Intensification of the anti-French nationalist movements in Morocco and Tunisia forced France to agree to the independence of these countries in the early 1950s. Defeats in Indochina in 1954 and in the Algerian war of the late 1950s marked the decline of French imperial power, and in 1958 De Gaulle was forced to seek an end to the war on the terms of the *Front de libération national* (FLN); Algeria received its independence in 1962. Yet, despite the policies of French decolonization during the late 1960's, it is evident that the French involvement in Asia and the third world continued into the 1970s, even though some of the more overt apparatuses of colonialism had ended. We need only consider the surprising credibility of Jean-Marie Le Pen and the *Front national* (FN) in France to appreciate that even though French colonialism has ended in name in North Africa, the Caribbean, and Indochina, the displaced populations from these regions have not encountered vastly changed relations between "colonizer" and "colonized" in the French metropolis. From this discussion of *Des chinoises,* we understand that even on the Left the orientalist gaze may reemerge, even when the purpose of its project is to criticize state power and social domination; the continuing tendency of projecting revolutionary, cultural, or ethnic purity onto other sites, such as the "third world," must be scrutinized and challenged for its epistemological, political, and discursive relationships to orientalism.[19]

Notes

The editor excerpted this essay from the longer discussion "The Desires of Postcolonial Orientalism: Chinese Utopias of Kristeva, Barthes, and *Tel quel*" which appears in Lowe's book *Critical Terrains: French and British Orientalisms* (Ithaca, N.Y.: Cornell University Press, 1991).

1. The *Mouvement de libération des femmes* (MLF), very active after May 1968, was, in 1974, discussing issues of psychoanalysis, socialism, Marxism, Maoism, and the bearing of these systems of thought and social analysis on the question of women's liberation. By 1977 the MLF had split into at least two factions: those who allied themselves with *"psychanalyse et politique"* and those who allied themselves with *"questions féministes."* The *"psychanalyse et politique"* group, with which Kristeva was associated, concerned itself with women's psycholinguistic position, and explored psychoanalysis as an emancipatory theory of sexual difference. The supporters of *"questions féministes,"* coming out of Simone de Beauvoir's existential feminism, were more concerned with the material conditions of women as a subordinated class. The concerns of Christine Delphy, who, along with de Beauvoir, was one of the founding members of the journal *Questions féministes,* may be considered to have much more in common with the Marxist feminism practiced in the United States. For other discussions of the recent history of French feminism, see Elaine Marks and Isabelle De Courtivron, eds., *New French Feminisms* (Amherst, Mass.: University of Massachusetts Press, 1980); Ann Rosalind Jones, "Writing the Body: Toward an Understanding of L'Ecriture Féminine," *Feminist Studies* 7, no. 2, Summer 1981: pp. 247–63; and Toril Moi, *Sexual/Textual Politics: Feminist Literary Theory* (London: Methuen, 1985). See also the special issues of the journals *Signs* 7, no. 1, Autumn 1981; *Feminist Studies* 7, no. 2, Summer 1981; and *Yale French Studies* 62, 1981, each addressing the question of French and Anglo-American feminism. In particular, see Gayatri Spivak's "French Feminism in an International Frame," in *In Other Worlds* (London: Routledge, 1988), first published in *Yale French Studies* 62, 1981: pp. 154–84, for both its instructive discussion of *Des chinoises* and its equally relevant critique of French feminism.

2. Kristeva observes: "Cut from man, made from that which he lacks, the biblical woman will be wife, daughter or sister. . . . Her function is to ensure procreation . . . she has no direct relationship: God speaks only to man"; p. 21.

3. For example, structural anthropology assumed that the cultural order was founded on the division of society into two sexes: men, who were the social and cultural actors, and women, who were the objects of exchange among men. In Claude Lévi-Strauss's "Language and the Analysis of Social Laws," in *Structural Anthropology* (New York: Basic Books, 1963), the observation that women serve as objects of exchange in culture is offered as "proof" that women are the signifiers of men's roles as producers of culture. The structural paradigm is essentially a description—as opposed to a historical, hermeneutical, or dynamic explanation—that presumes sexual difference as a given binary relationship.

4. As this chapter implies, Freud and Lacan were prominent influences in the formation of French feminist theories, particularly on the work of Luce Irigaray, Hélène Cixous,

Claudine Hermann, and Xavière Gauthier. Feminists in the United States, on the contrary, have been more critical of psychoanalytic theories (unlike English feminists; see, for example, Juliet Mitchell's *Psychoanalysis and Feminism* [New York: Viking, 1974]). In the years since the mid-1970s, however, more American feminists have written about the question of sexual difference from psychoanalytic standpoints; see, for example, Jane Gallop, *The Daughter's Seduction* (Ithaca, N.Y.: Cornell University Press, 1982).

5. Some of these other methods of explication are represented in the works of Rosalind Pechesky (1981) on reproductive rights; Catharine MacKinnon (1987) on the position of women in legal discourse; Nancy Chodorow (1978) on the role of mothering in the social construction of gender; bell hooks (1981) on black women and feminism; and Donna Haraway (1985) on science, technology, and socialist feminism.

6. Although it was Freud who originally described the "pre-Oedipus period" in the lecture "Femininity," in *New Introductory Lectures on Psychoanalysis,* trans. James Strachey (New York: Norton, 1964), as the period of preinfantile sexual attachment of the daughter to her mother before she discovers that she and her mother are "castrated," Freud's references to the pre-Oedipal stage are associated with an interest in describing how female "regressions" into the "prehistory" of the bond between mother and infant affect the development of femininity; see, for example, his theories that jealous paranoia and female homosexuality are conditions "which went back to a fixation in the pre-Oedipus stage" (p. 115). Indeed, Freud suggests in this lecture that the claims of women patients that they had been seduced by their father were "hysterical symptoms," but that the fantasy of seduction by the mother "touches the ground of reality, for it was really the mother who by her activities over the child's bodily hygiene inevitably stimulated, and perhaps even roused for the first time, pleasurable sensations in her genitals" (p. 106).

7. Kristeva, *Des chinoises,* p. 30.

8. Lacan, p. 32.

9. Kristeva adopts yet revalorizes Freud's notion of the pre-Oedipal phase. For Freud, children discover the difference between the father and mother when they observe the father has a penis; assuming that the mother's penis has been cut off, they identify with the father, refusing bonds with the mother, owing to the imagined threat of castration. According to Freud, the imagined castration is all the more important to the male child, for the successful repression of his desire for his mother, through the fear of castration, allows him to adjust to the conditions of adult society, to become socialized as a man. Kristeva suggests that the Oedipal repression must be lifted and the mother rediscovered as the child's object of desire and union.

   The construction of the ego in the mirror stage, as well as the relationship between the Imaginary and the Symbolic realms, is developed in Jacques Lacan's essay "The Mirror Stage as Formative Function of the I as Revealed in Psychoanalytic Experience," in *Ecrits*. The Symbolic, the Oedipal phenomenon, and the naming and splitting of the subject are discussed in "The Agency of the Letter in the Unconscious or Reason since Freud," also in *Ecrits*. Useful exegeses of Lacan's work include Coward and Ellis 1977; Jameson 1977; Lemaire 1977; Wilden 1968; and Mitchell and Rose's preface to Lacan, *Feminine Sexuality,* 1983.

10. Julia Kristeva, *Des chinoise,* p. 51.

11. Ibid., p. 48.

12. Ibid., p. 34.

13. Ibid., p. 61.

14. In *Révolution du langage poétique,* Kristeva discusses the breaking of the Symbolic with the enunciation of "echolalic" or presymbolic tones, associating this phenomenon in avant-garde European poetry with the Chinese system of language. Poetry is described as a process of reinvestment in a maternal, semiotic *chora* that transgresses the symbolic order, or a *genotext* of semiotic processes which interrupts the communicative *phenotext*. Kristeva cites Mallarmé and Joyce as writers who are able to "reach the semiotic *chora*." Julia Kristeva, *Revolution in Poetic Language,* trans. Margaret Waller (New York: Columbia University Press, 1984); see sections 9–12 in "The Semiotic and the Symbolic," pp. 62–89.

    "Women's Time," *Signs* 7, no. 1, Autumn 1981: pp. 13–35, represents a later statement of Kristeva's feminism which is also concerned with a radically different female location outside the masculine linear time of history and politics, and which emphasizes the sociosymbolic materiality of language and writing as well.

15. Julia Kristeva, *Des chinoises,* p. 82.

16. Ibid., p. 43.

17. Gustave Flaubert, "Lettre à Louise Colet (1853)," *Correspondance* in *Oeuvres complètes de Gustave Flaubert* (Paris: Club de l'Honnête homme, 1973).

18. Julia Kristeva, *Des chinoises,* pp. 13–14.

19. For one of the most important discussions of the relationship between "first world" feminism and "third world" women, see Chandra Mohanty, "Under Western Eyes: Feminist Scholarship and Colonial Discourses," in *Third World Women and the Politics of Feminism,* eds. C. Mohanty, A. Russo, and L. Torres (Bloomington, Ind.: Indiana University Press, 1991). For examples of the variety of recent work that renders more complex the representation of women in transnational locations after decolonization, see: Winifred Woodhull, *Transfigurations of the Maghreb: Feminism, Decolonization, and Literatures in French* (University of Minnesota Press, forthcoming); Kumkum Sangari and Sudesh Vaid, eds., *Recasting Women: Essays in Indian Colonial History* (New Brunswick, N.J.: Rutgers University Press, 1990); Kumari Jayawardena, *Feminism and Nationalism in the Third World* (London: Zed Books, 1986); Nanneke Redclift and M. Thea Sinclair, eds., *Working Women: International Perspectives on Labour and Gender Ideology* (London: Routledge, 1991).

10

The Body Politics of Julia Kristeva
Judith Butler

Kristeva's theory of the semiotic dimension of language at first appears to engage Lacanian premises only to expose their limits and to offer a specifically feminine locus of subversion of the paternal law within language. According to Lacan, the paternal law structures all linguistic signification, termed "the symbolic," and so becomes a universal organizing principle of culture itself. This law creates the possibility of meaningful language and, hence, meaningful experience, through the repression of primary libidinal drives, including the radical dependency of the child on the maternal body. Hence, the symbolic becomes possible by repudiating the primary relationship to the maternal body. The "subject" who emerges as a consequence of this repression itself becomes a bearer or proponent of this repressive law. The libidinal chaos characteristic of that early dependency is now fully constrained by a unitary agent whose language is structured by that law. This language, in turn, structures the world by suppressing multiple meanings (which always recall the libidinal multiplicity which characterized the primary relation to the maternal body) and instating univocal and discrete meanings in their place.

Kristeva challenges the Lacanian narrative which assumes that cultural meaning requires the repression of that primary relationship to the maternal body. She argues that the "semiotic" is a dimension of language occasioned by that primary maternal body, which not only refutes Lacan's primary premise, but also serves as a perpetual source of subversion within the symbolic. For Kristeva, the semiotic expresses that original libidinal multiplicity within the very terms of culture, more precisely, within poetic language in which multiple meanings and semantic non-closure prevail. In effect, poetic language is the recovery of the maternal body within the terms of language, one that has the potential to disrupt, subvert, and displace the paternal law.

Despite her critique of Lacan, however, Kristeva's strategy of subversion proves doubtful. Her theory appears to depend upon the stability and reproduction of precisely the paternal law that she sought to displace. Although she effectively exposes the limits of Lacan's efforts to universalize the paternal law in language, she nevertheless concedes that the semiotic is invariably subordinate to the symbolic, that it assumes its specificity within the terms of a hierarchy which is immune to challenge. If the semiotic promotes the possibility of the subversion, displacement, or disruption of the paternal law, what meanings can those terms have if the symbolic always reasserts its hegemony?

The criticism of Kristeva which follows takes issue with several different steps in Kristeva's argument in favor of the semiotic as a source of effective subversion. First, it is unclear whether the primary relationship to the maternal body which both Kristeva and Lacan appear to accept is a viable construct and whether it is even a knowable experience according to either of their linguistic theories. The multiple drives that characterize the semiotic constitute a prediscursive libidinal economy which occasionally makes itself known in language, but which maintains an ontological status prior to language itself. Manifest in language, in poetic language in particular, this prediscursive libidinal economy becomes a locus of cultural subversion. A second problem emerges when Kristeva maintains that this libidinal source of subversion cannot be maintained within the terms of culture, that its sustained presence leads to psychosis and to the breakdown of cultural life itself. Kristeva thus alternately posits and denies the semiotic as an emancipatory ideal. Though she tells us that it is a dimension of language regularly repressed, she also concedes that it is a kind of language which can never be consistently maintained.

In order to assess her seemingly self-defeating theory, we need to ask how this libidinal multiplicity becomes manifest in language, and what conditions its temporary lifespan there? Moreover, Kristeva describes the maternal body as bearing a set of meanings that are prior to culture itself. She thereby safeguards the notion of culture as a paternal structure and delimits maternity as an essentially precultural reality. Her naturalistic descriptions of the maternal body effectively reify motherhood and preclude an analysis of its cultural construction and variability. In asking whether a prediscursive libidinal multiplicity is possible, we will also consider whether what we claim to discover in the prediscursive maternal body is itself a production of a given historical discourse, an effect of culture rather than its secret and primary cause.

Even if we accept Kristeva's theory of primary drives, it is unclear that the subversive effects of such drives can serve, via the semiotic, as anything more than a temporary and futile disruption of the hegemony of the paternal law. I will try to show how the failure of her political strategy follows in part from her largely uncritical appropriation of drive theory. Moreover, upon careful scrutiny of her descriptions of the semiotic function within language, it appears that Kristeva reinstates the paternal law at the level of the semiotic itself. In the end, Kristeva offers us a strategy of subversion that can never become a sustained political practice. In the final section of this paper, I will suggest a way to reconceptualize the relation between drives, language, and patriarchal prerogative which might serve a more effective strategy of subversion.

Kristeva's description of the semiotic proceeds through a number of problematic steps. She assumes that drives have aims prior to their emergence into language, that language invariably represses or sublimates these drives, and that such drives are manifest only in those linguistic expressions that disobey, as it were, the univocal requirements of signification within the symbolic domain. She claims further that the emergence of multiplicitous drives into language is evident in the semiotic, that domain of linguistic meaning distinct from the symbolic, which is the maternal body manifest in poetic speech.

As early as *Revolution in Poetic Language* (1974), Kristeva argued for a necessary, causal relation between the heterogeneity of drives and the plurivocal possibilities of poetic language. Differing from Lacan, she maintained that poetic language was not predicated upon a repression of primary drives. On the contrary, poetic language, she claimed, is the linguistic occasion on which drives break apart the usual, univocal terms of language and reveal an irrepressible heterogeneity of multiple sounds and meanings. Kristeva thereby contested Lacan's equation of the symbolic with all linguistic meaning by asserting that poetic language has its own modality of meaning, which does not conform to the requirements of univocal designation.

In this same work, she subscribed to a notion of free or uncathected energy which makes itself known in language through the poetic function. She claimed, for instance, that "in the intermingling of drives in language . . . we shall see the economy of poetic language," and that in this economy, "the unitary subject can no longer find his place."[1] This poetic function is a rejective or divisive linguistic function which tends to fracture and multiply meanings; it enacts the heterogeneity of drives through the proliferation and destruction of univocal signification. Hence, the urge toward a highly differentiated or plurivocal set of meanings appears as the revenge of drives against the rule of the symbolic which, in turn, is predicated upon their repression. Kristeva defines the semiotic as the multiplicity of drives manifest in language. With their insistent energy and heterogeneity, these drives disrupt the signifying function of language. Thus, in this early work, she defines the semiotic as "the signifying function . . . connected to the modality [of] primary process."

In the essays that comprise *Desire in Language* (1977), Kristeva grounded her definition of the semiotic more fully in psychoanalytic terms. The primary drives that the symbolic represses and that the semiotic obliquely indicates are now understood as *maternal drives,* not only those drives belonging to the mother, but those that characterize the dependency of the infant's body (of either sex) on the mother. In other words. "the maternal body" designates a relation of continuity rather than a discrete subject or object of desire; indeed, it designates that *jouissance* which precedes desire and the subject/object dichotomy that desire presupposes. While the symbolic is predicated upon the rejection of the mother—the refusal of the mother as an object of sexual love—the semiotic, through rhythm, assonance, intonations, sound play, and repetition, re-presents or recovers the maternal body in poetic speech. Even the "first echolalias of infants" and the "glossalalias in psychotic discourse" are manifestations of the continuity of the mother-infant relation, a heterogeneous field of impulse prior to the separation/individuation of infant and mother, alike effected by the imposition of the incest taboo.[2] The separation of the mother and infant effected by the taboo is expressed linguistically as the severing of sound from sense. In Kristeva's words, "a phoneme, as distinctive element of meaning, belongs to language as symbolic. But this same phoneme is involved in rhythmic, intonational repetitions; it thereby tends toward autonomy from meaning so as to maintain itself in a semiotic disposition near the instinctual drive's body."[3]

The semiotic is described by Kristeva as destroying or eroding the symbolic; it is said to be "before" meaning, as when a child begins to vocalize, or "after" meaning as when a psychotic no longer uses words to signify. If the symbolic and the semiotic are understood as two modalities of language, and if the semiotic is understood to be generally repressed by the symbolic, then language for Kristeva is understood as a system in which the symbolic remains hegemonic except when the semiotic disrupts its signifying process through elision, repetition, mere sound, and the multiplication of meaning through indefinitely signifying images and metaphors. In its symbolic mode, language rests upon a severance of the relation of maternal dependency, whereby it becomes abstract (abstracted from the materiality of language) and univocal; this is most apparent in quantitative or purely formal reasoning. In its semiotic mode, language is engaged in a poetic recovery of the maternal body, that diffuse materiality that resists all discrete and univocal signification. Kristeva writes,

In any poetic language, not only do the rhythmic constraints, for example, go so far as to violate certain grammatical rules of a national language . . . but in recent texts, these semiotic constraints (rhythm, vocalic timbres in Symbolist work, but also graphic disposition on the page) are accompanied by nonrecoverable syntactic elisions; it is impossible to reconstitute the particular elided syntactic category (object or verb), which makes the meaning of the utterance decidable. . . .[4]

For Kristeva, this undecidability is precisely the instinctual moment in language, its disruptive function. Poetic language thus suggests a dissolution of the coherent, signifying subject into the primary continuity which is the maternal body:

Language as symbolic function constitutes itself at the cost of repressing instinctual drive and continuous relation to the mother. On the contrary, the unsettled and questionable subject of poetic language (from whom the word is never uniquely sign) maintains itself at the cost of reactivating this repressed, instinctual, maternal element.[5]

Kristeva's references to the "subject" of poetic language are not wholly appropriate, for poetic language erodes and destroys the subject, where the subject is understood as a speaking being participating in the symbolic. Following Lacan, she maintains that the prohibition against the incestuous union with the mother is the founding law of the subject, a foundation which severs or breaks the continuous relation of maternal dependence. In creating the subject, the prohibitive law creates the domain of the symbolic or language as a system of univocally signifying signs. Hence, Kristeva concludes that "poetic language would be for its questionable subject-in-process the equivalent of incest."[6] The breaking of symbolic language against its own founding law or, equivalently, the emergence of rupture into language from within its own interior instinctuality is not merely the outburst of libidinal heterogeneity into language; it also signifies the somatic state of dependence on the maternal body prior to the individuation of the ego. Poetic language thus always indicates a return to the maternal terrain, where the maternal signifies both libidinal dependence and the heterogeneity of drives.

In "Motherhood According to Bellini," Kristeva suggests that, because the maternal body signifies the loss of coherent and discrete identity, poetic language verges on psychosis. And in the case of a woman's semiotic expressions in language, the return to the maternal signifies a prediscursive homosexuality that Kristeva also clearly associates with psychosis. Although

Kristeva concedes that poetic language is sustained culturally through its participation in the symbolic and, hence, in the norms of linguistic communicability, she fails to allow that homosexuality is capable of the same nonpsychotic social expression: The key to Kristeva's view of the psychotic nature of homosexuality is to be understood, I suggest, in her acceptance of the structuralist assumption that heterosexuality is coextensive with the founding of the symbolic. Hence, the cathexis of homosexual desire can only be achieved, according to Kristeva, through displacements that are sanctioned within the symbolic, such as poetic language or the act of giving birth:

> By giving birth, the women enters into contact with her mother; she becomes, she is her own mother; they are the same continuity differentiating itself. She thus actualizes the homosexual facet of motherhood, through which a woman is simultaneously closer to her instinctual memory, more open to her psychosis, and consequently, more negatory of the social, symbolic bond.[7]

According to Kristeva, the act of giving birth does not successfully reestablish that continuous relation prior to individuation, because the infant invariably suffers the prohibition on incest and is separated off as a discrete identity. In the case of the mother's separation from the girl-child, the result is melancholy for both, for the separation is never fully completed.

As opposed to grief or mourning, in which separation is recognized and the libido attached to the original object is successfully displaced onto a new substitute object, melancholy designates a failure to grieve, in which the loss is simply internalized and, in that sense, refused. Instead of negating the attachment to the body, the maternal body is internalized as a negation, so that the girl's identity becomes itself a kind of loss, a characteristic privation or lack.

The alleged psychosis of homosexuality, then, consists in its thorough break with the paternal law and with the grounding of the female ego, tenuous though it may be, in the melancholic response to separation from the maternal body. Hence, according to Kristeva, female homosexuality is the emergence of psychosis into culture:

> The homosexual-maternal facet is a whirl of words, a complete absence of meaning and seeing; it is feeling, displacement, rhythm, sound, flashes, and fantasied clinging to the maternal body as a screen against the plunge . . . for woman, a paradise lost but seemingly close at hand."[8]

For women, however, this homosexuality is manifest in poetic language which becomes, in fact, the only form of the semiotic, besides childbirth, that can be sustained within the terms of the symbolic. For Kristeva, then, overt homosexuality cannot be a culturally sustainable activity, for it would constitute a breaking of the incest taboo in an unmediated way. And yet why is this the case?

Kristeva accepts the assumption that culture is equivalent to the symbolic, that the symbolic is fully subsumed under the Law of the Father, and that the only modes of nonpsychotic activity are those that participate in the symbolic to some extent. Her strategic task, then, is not to replace the symbolic with the semiotic, nor to establish the semiotic as a rival cultural possibility, but rather to validate those experiences within the symbolic that permit a manifestation of the borders that divide the symbolic from the semiotic. Just as birth is understood to be a cathexis of instinctual drives for the purposes of a social teleology, so poetic production is conceived as the site in which the split between instinct and representation coexist in culturally communicable form:

> The speaker reaches this limit, this requisite of sociality, only by virtue of a particular, discursive practice called "art". A woman also attains it (and in our society, especially) through the strange form of split symbolization (threshold of language and instinctual drive, of the "symbolic" and the "semiotic") of which the act of giving birth consists.[9]

Hence, for Kristeva, poetry and maternity represent privileged practices within paternally sanctioned culture which permit a nonpsychotic experience of the heteroegeneity and dependency characteristic of the maternal terrain. These acts of poesis reveal an instinctual heterogeneity that exposes the repressed ground of the symbolic, challenges the mastery of the univocal signifier, and diffuses the autonomy of the subject who postures as their necessary ground. The heterogeneity of drives operates culturally as a subversive strategy of displacement, one which dislodges the hegemony of the paternal law by releasing the repressed multiplicity interior to language itself. Precisely because that instinctual heterogeneity must be re-presented in and through the paternal law, it cannot defy the incest taboo altogether, but must remain within the most fragile regions of the symbolic. Obedient, then, to syntactical requirements, the poetic-maternal practices of displacing the paternal law always remain tenuously tethered to that law. Hence, a full-scale refusal of the symbolic is impossible, and a discourse of "emancipation," for Kristeva, is out of the question. At best, tactical subversions and displacements of the law challenge its self-grounding presumption. But, once again, Kristeva does not seriously challenge the structuralist assumption that the prohibitive paternal law is foundational to culture itself. Hence, the subversion of paternally sanctioned culture cannot come from another version of culture, but only from within the repressed interior of culture itself, from the heterogeneity of drives that constitutes culture's concealed foundation.

This relation between heterogeneous drives and the paternal law produces an exceedingly problematic view of psychosis. On the one hand, it designates female homosexuality as a culturally unintelligible practice, inherently psychotic; on the other hand, it mandates maternity as a compulsory defense against libidinal chaos. Although Kristeva does not make either claim explicitly, both implications follow from her views on the law, language, and drives.

Consider that for Kristeva, poetic language breaks the incest taboo and, as such, verges always on psychosis. As a return to the maternal body and a concomitant de-individuation of the ego, poetic language becomes especially threatening when uttered by women. The poetic then contests not only the incest taboo, but the taboo against homosexuality as well. Poetic language is thus, for women, both displaced maternal dependency and, because that dependency is libidinal, displaced homosexuality as well.

For Kristeva, the unmediated cathexis of female homosexual desire leads unequivocally to psychosis. Hence, one can satisfy this drive only through a series of displacements: the incorporation of maternal identity, i.e. by becoming a mother oneself, or through poetic language which manifests obliquely the heterogeneity of drives characteristic of maternal dependency. As the only socially sanctioned and, hence, nonpsychotic displacements for homosexual desire, both maternity and poetry constitute melancholic experiences for women appropriately acculturated into heterosexuality. The heterosexual poet-mother suffers interminably from the displacement of the homosexual cathexis. And yet, the consummation of this desire would lead to the psychotic unraveling of identity, according to Kristeva. The presumption is that, for women, heterosexuality and coherent selfhood are indissolubly linked.

How are we to understand this constitution of lesbian experience as the site of an irretrievable self-loss? Kristeva clearly takes heterosexuality to be prerequisite to kinship and to culture. Consequently, she identifies lesbian experience as the psychotic alternative to the acceptance of paternally sanctioned laws. And yet why is lesbianism constituted as psychosis? From what cultural perspective is lesbianism constructed as a site of fusion, self-loss, and psychosis?

By projecting the lesbian as other to culture, and characterizing lesbian speech as the psychotic "whirl-of-words," Kristeva constructs lesbian sexuality as intrinsically unintelligible. This tactical dismissal and reduction of lesbian experience performed in the name of the law positions Kristeva within the orbit of paternal-heterosexual privilege. The paternal law which protects her from this radical incoherence is precisely the mechanism that produces the construct of lesbianism as a site of irrationality. Significantly, this description of lesbian experience is effected from the outside, and tells us more about the fantasies that a fearful heterosexual culture produces to defend against its own homosexual possibilities than about lesbian experience itself.

In claiming that lesbianism designates a loss of self, Kristeva appears to be delivering a psychoanalytic truth about the repression necessary for individuation. The fear of such a "regression" to homosexuality is, then, a fear of losing cultural sanction and privilege altogether. Although Kristeva claims that this loss designates a place prior to culture, there is no reason not to understand it as a new or unacknowledged cultural form. In other words, Kristeva prefers to explain lesbian experience as a regressive libidinal state prior to acculturation itself rather than to take up the challenge that lesbianism offers to her restricted view of paternally sanctioned cultural laws. Is the fear encoded in the construction of the lesbian-as-psychotic the result of a developmentally necessitated repression, or is it, rather, the fear of losing cultural legitimacy and, hence, being cast—not outside or prior to culture—but outside cultural legitimacy, still within culture, but culturally "out-lawed"?

Kristeva describes both the maternal body and lesbian experience from a position of sanctioned heterosexuality that fails to acknowledge its own fear of losing that sanction. Her reification of the paternal law not only repudiates female homosexuality, but denies the varied meanings and possibilities of motherhood as a cultural practice. But cultural subversion is not really Kristeva's concern; for subversion, when it appears, emerges from beneath the surface of culture only inevitably to return there. Although the semiotic is a possibility of language that escapes the paternal law, it remains inevitably within or, indeed, beneath the territory of that law. Hence, poetic language and the pleasures of maternity constitute local displacements of the paternal law, temporary subversions which finally submit to that against which they initially rebel. By relegating the source of subversion to a site outside of culture itself, Kristeva appears to foreclose the possibility of subversion as an effective or realizable cultural practice. Pleasure beyond the paternal law can only be imagined together with its inevitable impossibility.

Kristeva's theory of thwarted subversion is premised on her problematic view of the relation between drives, language, and the law. Her postulation of a subversive multiplicity of drives raises a number of epistemological and political questions. In the first place, if these drives are only manifest in language or cultural forms already determined as symbolic, then how is it that we can verify their presymbolic ontological status? Kristeva argues that poetic language gives us access to these drives in their fundamental multiplicity, but this answer is not fully satisfactory. Since poetic language is said to depend upon the prior existence of these multiplicitous drives, we cannot, then, in circular fashion, justify the postulated existence of these drives through recourse to poetic language. If drives must first be repressed for language to exist, and if we can only attribute meaning to that which is representable in language, then to attribute meaning to drives prior to their emergence into language is impossible. Similarly, to attribute a causality to drives which facilitates their transformation into language, and by which language itself is to be explained, cannot reasonably be done within the confines of language itself. In other words, we know these drives as "causes" only in and through their effects and, as such, we have no reason for not identifying drives with their effects. It follows that either (a) drives and their representations are coextensive or (b) representations pre-exist the drives themselves.

This last alternative is, I would argue, an important one to consider, for how do we know that the instinctual object of Kristeva's discourse is not a construction of the discourse itself? And what grounds do we have for positing this object, this multiplicitous field, as prior to signification? If poetic language must participate in the symbolic in order to be culturally communicable, and if Kristeva's own theoretical texts are emblematic of the symbolic, then where are we to find a convincing "outside" to this domain? Her postulation of a prediscursive corporeal multiplicity becomes all the more problematic when we discover that maternal drives are considered part of a "biological destiny" and are themselves manifestations of "a nonsymbolic, non-paternal causality." This presymbolic nonpaternal causality is, for Kristeva, a semiotic, maternal causality or, more specifically, a teleological conception of maternal instincts:

> Material compulsion, spasm of a memory belonging to the species that either binds together or splits apart to perpetuate itself, series of markers with no other significance than the eternal return of the life-death biological cycle. How can we verbalize this prelinguistic, unrepresentable memory? Heraclitus' flux, Epicurus' atoms, the whirling dust of cabalic, Arab and Indian mystics, and the stippled drawings of psychedelics-all seem better metaphors than the theory of Being, the logos, and its laws.[10]

Here, the repressed maternal body is not only the locus of multiple drives, but also the bearer of a biological teleology, one which, it seems, makes itself evident in the early stages of Western philosophy, in non-Western religious beliefs and practices, in aesthetic representations produced by psychotic or near-psychotic states, and even in avant-garde artistic practices. But why are we to assume that these various cultural expressions manifest the self-same principle of maternal heterogeneity? Kristeva simply subordinates each of these cultural moments to the same principle. Consequently, the semiotic represents any cultural effort to displace the *Logos* (which, curiously, she contrasts with Heraclitus' flux), where the *Logos* represents the univocal signifier, the law of identity. Her opposition between the semiotic and the symbolic reduces here to a metaphysical quarrel between the principle of multiplicity that escapes the charge of noncontradiction and a principle of identity based on the suppression of that multiplicity. Oddly, that very principle of multiplicity that Kristeva everywhere defends operates in much the same way as a principle of identity. Note the way in which all manner of things "primitive" and "oriental" are summarily subordinated to the principle of the maternal body. Surely, her description not only warrants the charge of orientalism, but raises the very significant question whether, ironically, multiplicity has become a univocal signifier.

Her ascription of a teleological aim to maternal drives prior to their constitution in language or culture raises a number of questions about Kristeva's political program. Although she clearly sees subversive and disruptive potential in those semiotic expressions that challenge the hegemony of the paternal law, it is less clear of what precisely this subversion consists. If the law is understood to rest on a constructed ground, beneath which lurks the repressed maternal terrain, what concrete cultural options emerge, within the terms of culture, as a consequence of this revelation? Ostensibly, the multiplicity associated with the maternal libidinal economy has the force to disperse the univocality of the paternal signifier, and seemingly to create the possibility of other cultural expressions no longer tightly constrained by the law of noncontradiction. But is this disruptive activity the opening of a field of significations, or is it the manifestation of a biological archaism which operates according to a natural and prepaternal causality? If Kristeva believed that the former were the case (and she does not), then she would be interested in a displacement of the paternal law in favor of a proliferating field of cultural possibilities. But instead she prescribes a return to a principle of maternal heterogeneity which proves to be a closed concept, indeed, a heterogeneity confined by a teleology both unilinear and univocal.

Kristeva understands the desire to give birth as a species-desire, part of a collective and archaic female libidinal drive that constitutes an ever-recurring metaphysical principle. Here Kristeva reifies maternity and then promotes this reification as the disruptive potential of the semiotic. As a result, the paternal law, understood as the ground of univocal signification, is displaced by an equally univocal signifier, the principle of the maternal body which remains self-identical in its teleology regardless of its multiplicitous manifestations.

Insofar as Kristeva conceptualizes this maternal instinct as having an ontological status prior to the paternal law, she fails to consider the way in which that law might well be the cause of the very desire it is said to repress. Rather than the manifestation of a prepaternal causality, these desires might attest to maternity as a social practice required and recapitulated by the exigencies of kinship. Kristeva accepts Levi-Strauss's analysis of the exchange of women as prerequisite for the consolidation of kinship bonds. She understands this exchange, however, as the cultural moment in which the maternal body is repressed rather than as a mechanism for the compulsory cultural construction of the female body as a maternal body. Indeed, we might understand the exchange of women as imposing a compulsory obligation on women's bodies to reproduce. According to Gayle Rubin's reading of Lévi-Strauss, kinship effects a "sculpting of . . . sexuality" such that the desire to give birth is the result of social practices which require and produce such desires in order to effect their reproductive ends.[11]

What grounds, then, does Kristeva have for imputing a maternal teleology to the female body prior to its emergence into culture? To pose the question in this way is already to question the distinction between the symbolic and the semiotic on which her conception of the maternal body rests. The maternal body in its originary signification is considered by Kristeva to be prior to signification itself; hence, it becomes impossible within her framework to consider the maternal itself as a signification, open to cultural variability. Her argument makes clear that maternal drives constitute those primary processes that language invariably represses or sublimates. But perhaps her argument could be recast within an even more encompassing framework: what cultural configuration of language, indeed, of *discourse*, generates the trope of a prediscursive libidinal multiplicity, and for what purposes?

By restricting the paternal law to a prohibitive or repressive function, Kristeva fails to understand the paternal mechanisms by which affectivity itself is generated. The law that is said to repress the semiotic may well be the governing principle of the semiotic itself, with the result that what passes as "maternal instinct" may well be a culturally constructed desire which is interpreted through a naturalistic vocabulary. And if that desire is constructed according to a law of kinship which requires the heterosexual production and reproduction of desire, then the vocabulary of naturalistic affect effectively renders that paternal law invisible. What Kristeva refers to as a "pre-paternal causality" would then appear as a *paternal* causality under the guise of a natural or distinctively maternal causality.

Significantly, the figuration of the maternal body and the teleology of its instincts as a self-identical and insistent metaphysical principle—an archaism of a collective, sex-specific, biological constitution—bases itself on a univocal conception of the female sex. And this sex, conceived as both origin and causality, poses as a principle of pure generativity. Indeed, for Kristeva, it is equated with poesis itself, the activity of making that in Plato's *Symposium* is held to be an act of birth and poetic conception at once.[12] But is female generativity truly an uncaused cause, and does it begin the narrative that takes all of humanity under the force of the incest taboo and into language? Does the prepaternal causality whereof Kristeva speaks signify a primary female economy of pleasure and meaning? Can we reverse the very order of this causality and understand this semiotic economy as a production of a prior discourse?

In the final chapter of Foucault's first volume of *The History of Sexuality*, he cautions against using the category of sex as a "fictitious unity . . . [and] causal principle," and argues that the fictitious category of sex facilitates a reversal of causal relations such that "sex" is understood to cause the structure and meaning of desire:

> [T]he notion of "sex" made it possible to group together, in an artificial unity, anatomical elements, biological functions, conducts, sensations, and pleasures, and it enabled one to make use of this fictitious unity as a causal principle, an omnipresent meaning: sex was thus able to function as a unique signifier and as a universal signified.[13]

For Foucault, the body is not "sexed" in any significant sense prior to its determination within a discourse through which it becomes invested with an "idea" of natural or essential sex. As an instrument and effect of power, the body only gains meaning within discourse in the context of power relations. Sexuality is a historically specific organization of power, discourse, bodies, and affectivity. As such, sexuality is understood by Foucault to produce "sex" as an artificial concept which effectively extends and disguises the power relations responsible for its genesis.

Foucault's framework suggests a way to solve some of the epistemological and political difficulties that follow from Kristeva's view of the female body. We can understand Kristeva's assertion of a "prepaternal causality" as fundamentally inverted. Whereas Kristeva posits a maternal body, prior to discourse which exerts its own causal force in the structure of drives, I would argue that the discursive production of the maternal body as prediscursive is a tactic in the self-amplification and concealment of those specific power relations by which the trope of the maternal body is produced. Then the maternal body would no longer be understood as the hidden ground of all signification, the tacit cause of all culture. It would be understood, rather, as an effect or consequence of a system of sexuality in which the female body is required to assume maternity as the essence of its self and the law of its desire.

From within Foucault's framework, we are compelled to redescribe the maternal libidinal economy as a product of a historically specific organization of sexuality. Moreover, the discourse of sexuality, itself suffused by power relations, becomes the true ground of the trope of the prediscursive maternal body. Kristeva's formulation suffers a thoroughgoing reversal: the symbolic and the semiotic are no longer interpreted as those dimensions of language that follow upon the repression or manifestation of the maternal libidinal economy. This very economy is understood instead as a reification that both extends and conceals the institution of motherhood as compulsory for women. Indeed, when the desires that maintain the institution of motherhood are transvaluated as prepaternal and precultural drives, then the institution gains a permanent legitimation in the invariant structures of the female body. Indeed, the clearly paternal law that sanctions and requires the female body to be characterized primarily in terms of its reproductive function is inscribed on that body as the law of its natural necessity. And Kristeva, safeguarding that law of a biologically necessitated maternity as a subversive operation that preexists the paternal law itself, aids in the systematic production of its invisibility and, consequently, the illusion of its inevitability.

In conclusion, because Kristeva restricts herself to an exclusively *prohibitive* conception of the paternal law, she is unable to account for the ways in which the paternal law *generates* certain desires in the form of natural drives. The female body that she seeks to express is itself a construct produced by the very law it is supposed to undermine. In no way do these criticisms of Kristeva's conception of the paternal law necessarily invalidate her general position that culture or the symbolic is predicated upon a repudiation of women's bodies. I want to suggest, however, that any theory that asserts that signification is predicated upon the denial or repression of a female principle ought to consider whether that femaleness is really external to the cultural norms by which it is repressed. In other words, on my reading, the repression of the feminine does not require that the agency of repression and the object of repression be ontologically distinct. Indeed, repression may be understood to produce the object that it comes to deny.

That production may well be an elaboration of the agency of repression itself. As Foucault made clear, this culturally contradictory enterprise of repression is prohibitive and generative at once and makes the problematic of "liberation" especially acute. The female body that is freed from the shackles of the paternal law may well prove to be yet another incarnation of that law, posing as subversive, but operating in the service of that law's self-amplification and proliferation. In order to avoid the emancipation of the oppressor in the name of the oppressed, it is necessary to take into account the full complexity and subtlety of the law and to cure ourselves of the illusion of a true body beyond the law. If subversion is possible, it will be a subversion from within the terms of the law, through the possibilities that emerge when the law turns against itself and spawns unexpected permutations of itself. The culturally constructed body will then be liberated, not to its "natural past" nor to its original pleasures, but to an open future of cultural possibilities.

Notes

1. Julia Kristeva, *Revolution in Poetic Language,* trans. Margaret Waller (New York: Columbia University Press, 1984), p. 132.

2. Julia Kristeva, *Desire in Language,* trans. Thomas Gora, Alice Jardine, Leon S. Roudiez (New York: Columbia University Press, 1980), p. 135.

3. Ibid.

4. Ibid., p. 134.

5. Ibid., p. 136.

6. Ibid.

7. Ibid., p. 239.

8. Ibid., pp. 239–240.

9. Ibid., p. 240. For an extremely interesting analysis of reproductive metaphors as descriptive of the process of poetic creativity, see Wendy Owen, 1985.

10. Ibid., p. 239.

11. Gayle Rubin, "The Traffic in Women: Notes on the 'Political Economy' of Sex," in *Toward an Anthropology of Women,* ed. Rayna R. Reiter (New York: Monthly Review Press, 1975), p. 182.

12. See Plato's *Symposium,* 209a: of the "procreancy . . . of the spirit", he writes that it is the specific capacity of the poet. Hence, poetic creations are understood as sublimated reproductive desire.

13. Michel Foucault, *The History of Sexuality* vol 1, an introduction, trans. Robert Hurley (New York: Vintage, 1980), p. 154.

11

Kristeva's Politics of Change: Tracking Essentialism with the Help of a Sex/Gender Map

Tina Chanter

Within feminism and within some other discourses, essentialism seems to be a kind of blind spot that won't go away. It hasn't, by and large, been historicized or related to the history of high philosophical essentialisms, but has been invoked to distance and disallow certain kinds of discourses.   *Ellen Rooney*

Essentialism is a loose tongue. In the house of philosophy, it's not taken seriously. You know, it's used by non-philosophers simply to mean all kinds of things when they don't know what other word to use.   *Gayatri Spivak*

Anthropology, and descriptions of kinship systems, do not explain the mechanisms by which children are engraved with the conventions of sex and gender. Psychoanalysis, on the other hand, is a theory about the reproduction of kinship. Psychoanalysis describes the residue left within individuals by their confrontation with the rules and regulations of sexuality of the societies to which they are born.   *Gayle Rubin*

Essentialism: The "Lie" of the Land

"But doesn't that imply a kind of essentialism?"—this oft-repeated feminist refrain has resounded in the halls of the academy for some years. One of the more popular buzz-words of feminist debates in the 1980s, "essentialism" came to embody rifts that established themselves along a variety of interconnecting faults and that structured diverse feminist terrains: the rocky ground on which practice and theory jostle one another; the treacherous territory in which psychoanalysis falls prey to political critique; the slippery slopes on which sexual difference is liable to slide into biological reductionism; the marshy swampland in which any assertion of feminine specificity risks subsiding into a murky pool of universal claims that threaten to immerse feminism in a morass of its own making. Increasingly fancy footwork is required of feminists who negotiate these difficult domains. Among the most tricky maneuvers are those orchestrated by what might be called the "continental divide"—that sometimes polemical division between so-called "French" feminists and "Anglo-American" feminists.

My own position toward the essentialism/anti-essentialism debate is one that has changed over the past few years from incredulity (how could anyone possibly mistake Kristeva or Irigaray as essentialist when their positions were not only diametrically opposed to essentialism, but they explicitly and repeatedly repudiated it?) to an attempt to understand the underlying issues that fostered such interpretations. Gradually replacing my initial disbelief of what I, somewhat arrogantly, simply dismissed as "misreadings," my interest developed not only in the misreadings, themselves, but also in the question of how essentialist readings of the French feminists could gain such prevalence so rapidly despite what seemed to me their obvious falsity. What motivated the wildly divergent readings of the same texts as essentialist or anti-essentialist? My sense was that the divergence could be in large part accounted for by the difference between the philosophical tradition out of which Kristeva and Irigaray were writing and the political pragmatic agendas that formed the background to Anglo-American feminist discourse. French feminists, whatever else their considerable differences, were steeped in a history that took seriously continental philosophy, a tradition that includes thinkers as diverse as Hegel, Nietzsche, Freud, Marx, Heidegger, Derrida, and Lacan. By contrast, the dominant frame of reference for Anglo-American thinkers was a no-nonsense program of reform that centered on arguments for equal rights between the sexes and that tended to look askance upon the continental tradition. The likes of Hegel, Heidegger, and Derrida were regarded, at best, with mild suspicion, and at worst, as charlatans who had little to say about the real world—little more than a series of self-indulgent, esoteric musings. The result was that Kristeva and Irigaray were judged in terms of the liberal discourse of equal rights, and the ideal of sameness that, however inexplicit, tended to accompany it. Not surprisingly, French feminists were found wanting by these standards.[1]

How could the apparently irreconcilable differences between theoretical traditions and cultural backgrounds be addressed? It was hard to know where to begin. Rather than pretentiously assuming that, as a continental philosopher, I simply knew better than those who declared French feminism invalid and essentialist, or elaborating a competing reading that construed the evidence more "adequately," I began to look for cultural explanations and political motivations for the popularity of the often vituperative and apparently gut-level anti-essentialist sentiments that stood in the way of reading French feminists. The extremity of these reactions was not something to be taken lightly. Exploring different versions of anti-essentialism led me to think about how feminists had become invested in certain ideas as to what feminism should be that made them particularly hostile to the French feminists. What is it, I asked myself, that anti-essentialists are so frightened of? Why was French feminism so threatening, what was it that provoked such bitter responses, such swift condemnations, such emotive denunciations? The answer that slowly emerged was this: feminism was afraid of women's bodies. This answer, crude and inadequate in itself, is a short-hand way of expressing a series of connected ideas about the recent history of feminism, its motifs and slogans, its mobilizing forces and characteristics, that I shall spell out in detail.

I: The Essentialist Critique and Its Legacies

The tendency to dismiss with a wave of the hand some feminist theories as "essentialist" is a troubling phenomenon.[2] French feminists, Kristeva among them, have proved to be particularly vulnerable targets of essentialist critiques, charges to which they continue to fall prey—despite the recent appearance of some sophisticated readings of their work.[3] Now Kristeva is getting caught in the crossfire of the debate. Gayatri Spivak, in an interview, urges us to shelve the question of essentialism.[4] Spivak says that she has "no time for essence/anti-essence," while at the same time claiming to be "repelled by Kristeva's politics." She "can't read her seriously anymore [*sic*]" because of Kristeva's "long-standing implicit sort of positivism"—her "naturalizing of the chora."[5] What is it in Kristeva's politics that repels Spivak? Is she repelled according to the same schema within which she objects to the naturalizing of the *chora*? Whatever naturalizing means, does it name anything different from the target of essentialist critiques? Is it certain that the outmoded functioning of the essentialist label as a taboo on the body has not left certain kinds of residues? Can the legacy of the essentialist critique be discerned in Spivak's objection to what she regards as Kristeva's naturalizing?

The answers to such questions remain obscure so long as we fail to pay attention to the convoluted history of essentialism, and to the ways in which feminism itself, in different ways, is both implicated in essentialism, and generates various critiques of essentialism. We need to examine the ways in which the debate over essentialism is situated in terms of other motifs that have guided the development of feminism. We need to provide a history of the various ideological investments feminism has constructed for itself in legislating certain thinkers as essentialist and in attempting to maintain a place for itself outside that alleged essentialism. Otherwise, not only is the sterility of the debate surrounding essentialism that Naomi Schor warns of unavoidable,[6] inevitable too is the tendency of essentialist critiques to reemerge in different guises, as I suspect occurs in Spivak's aversion to Kristeva's "naturalizing of the chora." That is why I do not simply want to put the debate to rest and hope it will go away—I think it has left a legacy that is already being manifested and that the lines of inheritance which are beginning to emerge need to be articulated.

Ahistorical, biologically reductive, psychologically revisionist, universalist—the list of crimes of which Kristeva is found guilty, under the guise of essentialism, abounds. Politically, she fares no better. Her theories are said to be reifying, dogmatic, utopian, elitist, classist, heterosexist, not to mention her reactionary cult of the maternal.[7] The charges of essentialism against Kristeva and those with whom she is frequently associated as a French feminist are familiar enough, and perhaps need not be rehearsed in any detail here.[8] Let me merely cite one example that will serve to indicate the bewildering complexity of phenomena that the word "essentialist" has come to designate. I choose this particular example in order to pursue a question that is central to my concern here—namely the difficulty of being self-conscious about our own situatedness, or the complexity of the role of history in situating ourselves as feminist. As a staunch member of that elite triumvirate, a partner in crime with Hélène Cixous and Luce Irigaray, with whom she has enjoyed the privilege of being so often denounced, Kristeva is accused by Nancy Fraser and Linda Nicholson of endorsing "ahistorical categories like gender identity without reflection as to how, when, and why such categories originated and were modified over time."[9] This version of Kristeva's alleged essentialism is particularly perplexing, given that it is precisely because Kristeva asks how categories such as gender identity originated and were modified over time that she poses a radical challenge to the primacy of gender identity in feminist analyses. In an article that the authors footnote, Kristeva criticizes the tendency to present feminism as if it were a monolithic, hegemonic, unchanging, inflexible body of thought.[10] One might find grounds to disagree with the various conceptual and historical paradigms that Kristeva sees as having characterized feminism throughout this century, but one can hardly reject as ahistorical her explicit attempt to differentiate between phases of feminist history.[11]

Kristeva's concern is not merely to provide a chronology of events, with the purpose of specifying successive periods of feminist activity. She also offers a theory of the temporality of feminism that brings into question the adequacy of the commonplace view of historical time as progressing according to a simple, linear model.[12] The way in which Kristeva thematizes the problem of time suggests the need not only to continually rethink and revise feminist strategies, but also to reconceptualize the idea of history to which we unthinkingly appeal when we dub a certain thinker ahistorical. Kristeva complicates the question of time by introducing sexual difference.[13] It is here that the notion of the semiotic *chora* comes into play for Kristeva. Pursuing the parallel she has begun to develop between twentieth-century European history and a psychoanalytic narrative, and in order to elucidate female spatiality, Kristeva draws upon the terminology of *Revolution in Poetic Language,* where she interprets the Platonic notion of the semiotic *chora* as "an essentially mobile and extremely provisional articulation constituted by movements and their ephemeral stases."[14]

With the publication of *Revolution in Poetic Language* (1974), Kristeva's distinction between the semiotic and symbolic became the hallmark of her work. It is a distinction that has proved to be the stumbling block for many feminists, who see in the attention Kristeva gives to the semiotic a reversion to essentialism. On this view, the semiotic is equated with the biological, instinctual motility of the body. Understood as the precondition of language, as preverbal, the semiotic is assumed to play some kind of foundational role which gives the subject access to the signifying system, or prepares the subject's entry into the symbolic order. The symbolic level at which things take on significance through language—the level at which they become meaningful as objects or signify at all—is also the realm of the law, and as such it is normative, or prescriptive of behavior. The operation of the law is instituted by the prohibiting father-figure, who represents the lack or deprivation experienced by the child when it encounters any refusal or withdrawal of maternal presence. If the influence of culture is introduced through the paternal law, the child's relation to the mother must be prior to the acquisition of language in the symbolic. To the extent that Kristeva seeks to focus upon the maternal experience as a dimension whose significance patriarchal society has tended to overlook, and to the extent that the semiotic is associated with maternity, it is inferred that in embracing the semiotic, Kristeva endorses essentialism. Prior to language, relations between mother and child are assumed to be purely instinctual, based upon the biological needs of the child.

On this account, Kristeva's interest in non-verbal aesthetic expressions, such as rhythm in music and poetry, practices which she identifies with the semiotic, is regarded with suspicion. Does she not thereby endorse a precultural idea of nature, her critics want to know, thereby reverting to an unacceptable naturalism? Such complaints disregard Kristeva's own repeated insistence that the semiotic "is produced recursively" and on the basis of the symbolic break.[15] What has not been sufficiently appreciated is the extent to which the semiotic is a realm that only acquires meaning—or indeed existence—within the realm of the symbolic. The semiotic/symbolic distinction is not offered as a mutually exclusive one. Semiotic meaning can only emerge retroactively, and can only be expressed within the terms of the symbolic. That does not mean that the semiotic can be reduced to the symbolic—it also offers resistance to symbolic expression. It erupts into and explodes onto the symbolic scene. Transgressing and destabilizing the operation of language, the effect of the semiotic cannot be entirely erased, sublated, or canceled out. Its effects will be inscribed in language, but as the other side of language—as traces, residues, marks—rather than as systems, concepts, or meanings. Never entirely recuperated, the semiotic will not signify without loss. Its exoticism will impinge upon language but will not be captured by, submitted to, or circumscribed by the symbolic order. Language remains inadequate to the register of the semiotic, while at the same time signaling, obliquely, its existence, constituting it after the fact.

If Kristeva's elaboration of the semiotic is regarded as collapsing into essentialism, she fares no better in her attempt to acknowledge that, with the subject's entry into language, there is always already present the influence of culture. She is accused of committing the equally grave sin of phallocentrism by accepting the rule of the symbolic. As Butler sees it, "Her strategic task ... is ... to validate those experiences within the Symbolic that permit a manifestation of the borders which divide the Symbolic from the semiotic."[16] For Butler such a task is "self-defeating" precisely insofar as it "concedes that the semiotic is invariably subordinate to the Symbolic."[17] My view is not that Kristeva is making a concession to the symbolic (or paying too much homage to the master-discourse of Lacan—which is, perhaps the underlying point of such critiques), but rather that she acknowledges that it is only through the symbolic, only through the signifying system of language that we can make sense of the semiotic. To acknowledge this is less a signal of Kristeva's lack of radicality, than it is a recognition of the fact that there is no meaning outside the language we have; the subversive moments that feminism can and does achieve may interrupt the equilibrium of dominant power relations, but these disruptions of the system will be momentary. The system will adapt itself to accommodate challenges to its hegemony. The fact that mechanisms of power are not only equipped to cope with attempts to subvert their processes of domination, but can even be said to instigate or create those very attempts, does not mean that we should give up trying to change things. It means that we should remain aware of the limits of such attempts.[18] These limits are due to the tendency of the logic of metaphysics to recuperate whatever transgression it sustains. Just as the desire for a post-metaphysical thinking that would effect a decisive or complete break with metaphysics remains just that—a desire, unfulfilled because ultimately it cannot succeed in expressing itself in terms other than those it inherits from metaphysics itself—so Kristeva admits the impossibility of describing the semiotic in any other terms than those of the symbolic—even if those terms are inadequate to its expression.

One way of explaining the widespread reluctance to accept Kristeva's distinction between the semiotic and the symbolic realms is an unspoken feminist commitment to the ideology of sex and gender, and to a series of connections that the sex/gender distinction is assumed to entail. Kristeva is guilty of mixing up the categories. The story that feminism tells itself is a story in which gender plays the lead role. Once we realized that femininity was culturally constructed, and not inscribed in our natures, we could change the ways in which gender was constructed. Since we can transform culture, whatever natural differences distinguish the sexes become insignificant. In effect, then, sex, nature, biology, and bodies are written out of the feminist picture. What is important for feminism is gender, culture, society, and history. By introducing the distinction between the semiotic and the symbolic, Kristeva seems to be reiterating the sex/gender divide. The symbolic is equated with culture, and the semiotic with nature. The problem is that Kristeva, at least at times, associates the semiotic with the feminine and seems to see it as disruptive of the symbolic (read masculine) order. She thereby appears to subvert the hierarchy between gender and sex that feminism established. This return to nature, this reversion to sex, this celebration of the semiotic can only mean one thing—she must be guilty of essentialism!

But we have not yet finished the story. Recent developments in feminist theory, notably in the area of feminism and science, point toward the need to rethink the distinction between sex and gender. Feminism has been grounded to a great extent in the ideology that gender is historically contingent and socially constructed and is, therefore, capable of change. By contrast, sex has been defined as static and unchanging. Once we take seriously the suggestion that the status of scientific enquiry is up for question, that politics plays a part in defining the agenda of disciplines such as biology, and that women's exclusion from the hard sciences has significantly shaped the "truths" that those sciences have "discovered," it becomes clear that we need to complicate the assumptions that feminism typically makes about sex and gender. We live in an age in which not only the objectivity of the sciences is up for question, but in which medical technology is forcing us to rethink even our most basic assumptions about sex. If previously we took it for granted that conception and reproduction were the exclusive preserve of women, procedures such as *in vitro* fertilization are challenging such apparently obvious truths. It is no longer sufficient to assume that there is a rigid boundary between gender as social, historical, and contingent, and sex as natural, biological, and necessary. Instead, the dichotomy between sex and gender becomes unstable, to borrow Sandra Harding's terminology, and subject to rethinking.[19] In other words, feminism has reached a stage in which it can no longer afford to avoid thinking about sexual difference. This means, among other things, that it is no longer so clear where sex stops and culture starts, since our very definition of sex is always already bound up in cultural assumptions—just as semiotic expression is always already bound up with the symbolic order.

Against the background of the need to rethink the sex/gender distinction as no longer a hierarchical and rigid dichotomy, but rather as a less stable, more fluid, and amorphous difference, Kristeva's distinction between the semiotic and the symbolic cannot be held up as a travesty of feminism. Instead we might see it as having anticipated some of the complications that feminist theorists of science are now confronting in their recognition of the need to revise the sex/gender distinction.

II: Historicizing Essentialism

Kristeva identifies three phases of feminism.[20] During the first phase, feminists focused on the sameness of the sexes, and during the second, they focused on their differences. Neither strategy is without its problems. The first strategy implicitly accepts the patriarchal devaluation of feminine values that it ostensibly challenges. Desperately seeking to elude the grip of history, in this first stage of feminism, women identified with the men who had the authority, the power, and the money. Divesting themselves of their feminine attributes, feminists taught themselves how to command authority, invest power in their own persons, become independent, and earn their own money, instead of obeying the orders of men and living as the financial dependents of their husbands.

If the first strategy bought into the devaluation of women, the second strategy ran the risk of reviving precisely those myths that feminists of the first generation had fought so hard to eliminate: it risked reinscribing the differences between the sexes that earlier feminists had tried to obliterate in arguing for equality. By reinstating the specificity of feminine experience, didn't the second phase of feminism fall into the patriarchal trap? In reevaluating the feminine, didn't feminists, however unwittingly, open the possibility that women's differences from men could be used once again to put women in their place?

For all their surface differences, Kristeva doubts whether the second phase of feminism radically diverged from the first. To be sure, the concrete responses to the problem of sexual inequities are different. The first answer is to prove women are as good as men, and the second answer is to reevaluate their differences from men. But in deeper ways, is the second strategy just a variation on the theme of the first? In both cases, patriarchal authority seems to go unchallenged at a fundamental level. Feminists of the first phase deny their femininity as a way of denying their inferiority, but in doing so they inadvertently subscribe to the view that men were better all along. The second phase rejects patriarchal authority and asserts feminine difference. But in its very attempt to stress difference, this version of feminism confirms male behavior as the standard against which women define their own behavior, albeit a negative standard. Even in rejecting masculinity, feminism preserves it as an ideal insofar as it casts itself in terms of what masculinity is not. While not wanting to deny the continuing usefulness of both strategies in certain contexts, we need perhaps to be aware of the limitations of both. In developing such an awareness, Kristeva suggests we can interweave both strategies, acknowledging the relevance of each approach, depending on the situation, without seeing either as offering an analysis that is comprehensive, totalizing, or absolutely sufficient by itself. However unsatisfactory such an approach may appear, insofar as it is piecemeal, it reflects the contradictions feminists confront. Quite simply, there are times when we need to reassert our right to basic equalities, and in doing so, we appeal to the similarities between women and men; and there are other times when it is the differences between women and men that need to be rehearsed. For example, in order to ensure equal pay for equal work, women need to insist upon the fact that they are worth just as much as men, but because women remain the primary care-takers of children, they need to argue for the right to maternity leave and the right not to be treated prejudicially by employers because of their child-care responsibilities. In some cases, to treat women as if they were identical to men, far from benefitting them, penalizes them.[21] If, in some respects, the differences between the sexes can be considered irrelevant, in other respects they cannot. So long as women remain the primary care-takers of children—whether or not one applauds such a situation—the fact remains that women as a group need special consideration.

Kristeva, among others and better than others, has affirmed that, while the idea of equality still has purchase strategically—in struggles for political, legal, and socioeconomic parity between men and women—we need not confine ourselves to the model of sameness implied by it.[22] It is highly problematic for feminism to limit its vision to the promise of strategic goals such as winning political, social, and economic parity between men and women, without also questioning whether such agendas are not already permeated by revisionist thinking. In other words, simply to abandon all questioning of sexual difference, in our attempt to achieve traditionally masculine virtues, is to accept the premise of the inferiority of the feminine. The constant identification of certain practices as feminine has been used to the detriment of women, but this does not mean that nurturing and caring for others, for example, are bad in themselves. In attempting to distinguish between the cultural imposition of traditionally feminine practices on women, and the value of those practices, feminists have singled out for special attention the practices traditionally associated with women. As a corrective maneuver to the overemphasis of similarities between the sexes, this reorientation was necessary. Of course, to highlight only the differences between men and women, as if there were no commonality at all between them, is just as shortsighted as recognizing only their similarities. When any strategic response is abstracted from the historical event to which it reacts, and represented as an absolute and universal standpoint, it is misrepresented.

Continental Drift: In the Interests of Moving On

I have highlighted the historical contingency of readings that assume Kristeva and her contemporaries are essentialist, critiques which are embedded, I have argued, in the belief that to talk about gender is good, but to talk about sex is suspect for feminists. By underlining the fact that even apparently self-evident categories of sex, nature, and biology are located within particular historical discourses, I hope to have accomplished two things. First, I have suggested that by putting the question of sexual difference back on the feminist map, Kristeva, far from falling into the essentialist trap, reminds us that we cannot afford to neglect the various relations individual women have, as gendered subjects, to their sex. Second, I have suggested that to accept unquestioningly the distinction between sex and gender assumes that both are unproblematically pre-given categories, instead of culturally determined, historically specific concepts which received their current meanings within feminist discourses promoting particular political programs.

The conceptual grid imposed by the differentiation of gender from sex is responsible for composing a powerful network of alliances, the effectiveness of which I do not want to underestimate. I am merely pointing to the tendency of any motif within political discourse to become stultifying unless subjected to critique over time. To retain its effectiveness and relevance, feminism needs to be a vibrant, dynamic, historically self-reflective movement. If the necessity of revising our conception of the sex/gender distinction is being acknowledged by some feminists, the moral grid on which it rests is still in place.[23] Thus Butler can acknowledge that sex might be culturally constructed just as much as gender, but she can still find fault with Kristeva because she allegedly "safeguards the notion of culture as a paternal structure and delimits maternity as an essentially precultural reality."[24] I am suggesting that Kristeva's semiotic/symbolic distinction acknowledges the need not only to unsettle the sex/gender distinction, but also to bring into question received ideas about the difference between nature and culture that often underlie mistaken notions about the ease with which gender can be siphoned off from sex.

Precisely because the philosophical and ethical discourse underpinning the sex/gender map tends to function implicitly rather than overtly, any change in the ethic underlying the configuration of sex/gender relations will be slow to filter through feminist discourse and will do so only indirectly. In the interests of moving on, perhaps feminism needs to be prepared to abandon its nostalgia for gender analyses that proceed in an uncontextualized vacuum, one that regards sex as a taboo subject and the body as out of bounds. Unless we continue to scrutinize the relations between sex and gender, nature and culture, biology and history, we are in danger of ignoring the crucial differences both among women, and between men and women, and their different ways of negotiating their different embodied histories. To deny the importance of sexual difference, or to place it beyond the boundaries of legitimate feminist discussion, is to assume that the sexes are essentially similar to one another, and that any differences between them, at least for the purposes of feminism, do not matter.

Let me end not by reiterating the chasm that divides French feminists from their Anglo-American counterparts, but by recalling the underlying unity that structures the "continental divide." Just as the phenomenon of continental drift is well known to students of plate tectonics, so the underlying substratum of French and Anglo-American feminist thought is capable of shifts. I have tried to exhibit a slow but discernible movement within feminism, namely the shift of strategic significance accorded to the sex/gender distinction. This shift undergirds the continental shelf that both divides and unites French and Anglo-American feminists. Rather than automatically assuming that gender is the central feminist tool of analysis, and sex is the stubborn residue, to be ignored as much as possible, feminism has shown of late an increasing interest in reinvestigating the shifting boundaries of constitutive gender and of sex. Hence the distinction itself is also in question. One of the leitmotifs guiding this analysis has been the (perhaps surprising) alliance between philosophers of science and French feminists. From diverse points of view, figures such as Evelyn Fox Keller and Sandra Harding are approaching the same problems as Kristeva and Irigaray—albeit in different guises. By underlining the continuity between recent investigations of the problematic distinction between sex/gender and the issue of sexual difference, I hope to have delimited at least one area in which there is a common concern. Perhaps productive exchanges, rather than combative polemics, will be the subject of future analyses of the "French connection."

Notes

Epigraphs are from Ellen Rooney, "In a Word," interview with Gayatri Spivak, in *Differences* 1, no. 2, Summer 1989: p. 132; Gayatri Spivak, "In a Word," p. 132; and Gayle Rubin, "The Traffic in Women: Notes on the 'Political Economy' of Sex," in *Toward an Anthropology of Women*, ed. R. R. Reiter (New York: Monthly Review Press, 1975), p. 183.

1. Rosi Braidotti expresses impatience with gestures that distinguish between French and Anglo-American feminisms on the basis that the latter is more pragmatic than the former, *Patterns of Dissonance* (New York: Routledge, 1991). While her impatience is justified to the extent that such characterizations are oversimplistic, my aim here is to refrain from simply brushing aside such generalizations in order to understand how they arose in the first place. I would insist that the specific cultural and historical circumstances by means of which feminists define themselves—and others—provide important information that needs to be considered if we are to understand Kristeva's relation to feminism. My point is not that Anglo-American feminists are atheoretical, but that our theories are perhaps more immediately associated with political positions in a way that predisposes many of us to be wary of theorists such as Kristeva. Consider for example Alison M. Jaggar's classification of feminist theories into "liberal feminism, traditional Marxism, radical feminism and socialist feminism," *Feminist Politics and Human Nature* (Brighton, Sussex: Harvester Press, 1983), p. 8. Kristeva's approach does not easily fit into any of these categories, and to this extent it might appear to be apolitical. I am not suggesting, of course, that the struggle for equal rights plays no part in French feminism. Rather, my point is that both the theoretical and the political heritage of those who thematize the question of sexual difference had the effect of distinguishing French feminist thought from its Anglo-American counterpart. Theoretically, Kristeva's background might be described as a blend of phenomenology, psychoanalysis, and post-structuralism. Politically, theorists who, like Kris-

teva, are interested in questioning sexual difference had good reason to distance themselves from political feminism in France. Dorothy Kaufmann-McCall documents how
the group *Psychanalyse et politique,* led by Antoinette Fouque, attempted to usurp the
feminist platform by gaining a legal right to, and a commercial monopoly on, the term
that identified a diversity of groups comprising the women's movement. They officially
coopted the name MLF (Mouvement de Libération des Femmes), a term that previously had been used as a generic label for identifying various factions of the French
women's movement. This is a good example of the kind of totalizing domination
that can be used in the name of feminism against which Kristeva warns. See Kaufmann-
McCall, "Politics of Difference: The Women's Movement in France from May 1968
to Mitterand," *Signs* 9, no. 2, 1983: pp. 282–93.

   Kristeva rejects politics only insofar as it is totalizing. She maintains a position
that may seem precarious, unstable, risky, even impossible—if one continues to judge
it from a traditional feminist stance. Inasmuch as Kristeva declines to construe feminism in these terms, *either* simply as a struggle for equality, *or* simply as an affirmation
of sexual difference, she challenges both the simplicity of traditional alternatives and
the purity of their logic.

2. My attempt here is to explain the puzzling phenomenon of essentialist critiques of
   French feminism, and for that reason, I have not considered other theorists who have
   been accused of essentialism, such as Mary Daly and Susan Griffin. Let me merely note
   here that, whatever theoretical reservations we may have about endorsing women's
   kinship with nature, such endorsements are, at another level, perfectly understandable
   reactions to excessive confidence in the "progress of science." One can sympathize with
   the motivations of those who question, for example, the naive enthusiasm that most
   of the postindustrial capitalist world displays for technology, and its apparent disregard for environmental concerns. It does not seem unreasonable to suggest that there
   might be connections between the power of patriarchy and the widespread disregard
   for the ecosystem.

3. See, for example, Cynthia Chase, "Desire and Identification in Kristeva and Lacan"
   in *Psychoanalysis and Feminism,* ed. Judith Roof and Richard Feldstein (Ithaca, N.Y.:
   Cornell University Press, 1989), pp. 65–83. Chase assesses Kristeva's use of the Lacanian notion of desire by suggesting parallels between Hegel and Lacan. Also see Miglena
   I. Nikolchina, "Meaning and Matricide: Reading Woolf via Kristeva," Ph.D dissertation, The University of Western Ontario, London, Ontario, January, 1993. Those
   who have discredited the view that Irigaray's work is essentialist include Margaret Whitford. See for example her articles "Luce Irigaray's Critique of Rationality" in *Feminist Perspectives in Philosophy,* ed. Morwenna Griffiths and Margaret Whitford (London: Macmillan, 1988), pp. 109–30, and "Re-reading Irigaray," in *Between Feminism
   and Psychoanalysis,* ed. Teresa Brennan (London: Routledge, 1989), pp. 106–26.
   Updated versions of these articles appear as chapters 3 and 4 in Whitford's book, *Luce
   Irigaray: Philosophy in the Feminine* (London: Routledge, 1991).

4. Gayatri Spivak, "In a Word," p. 147. Later in the same interview, Spivak says that "the
   question of anti-essentialism and essentialism is not a philosophical question," p. 132.

5. To provide some context for her remarks, let me quote Spivak at greater length. She
   says, "I'm repelled by Kristeva's politics: what seems to me to be her reliance on the
   sort of banal historical narrative to produce 'women's time'; what seems to me Chris-
   tianizing psychoanalysis; what seems to me to be her sort of ferocious western Euro-

peanism; and what seems to me to be her long-standing implicit sort of positivism: naturalizing of the chora, naturalizing of the pre-semiotic, et cetera. I'm so put off by this that I can't read her seriously anymore," "In a Word," p. 145. While I disagree with Spivak's reading of Kristeva, I want to affirm the value and importance of her contribution to the debate over essentialism.

6. Naomi Schor, "This Essentialism That Is Not One," *Differences* 1, no. 2, Summer 1989; p. 40.

7. Lynne Segal thinks that Kristeva "succeeds in being disappointingly reactionary—particularly in the light of her forthright homophobia" *Is the Future Female* (London, Virago, 1987), p. 134. Chris Weedon criticizes Kristeva on a more general level, but still for political reasons, claiming that "to take on the Freudian and Lacanian models is implicitly to accept the Freudian principles of psycho-sexual development with their universalist patriarchal implications and their reduction of subjectivity to sexuality," *Feminist Practice & Poststructuralist Theory* (Oxford: Basil Blackwell, 1987), p. 71. Kristeva's involvement with the practice of psychoanalysis is not only greeted with suspicion by feminists who fear that the mere fact of being influenced by psychoanalysis automatically means embracing patriarchy and endorsing the submissive role it accords to women. Kristeva is also criticized on the basis of the specifics of her psychoanalytic terminology. Jacqueline Rose, for example, thinks that Kristeva's emphasis of the semiotic over the symbolic commits her to essentialism. She says "Kristeva has . . . been attractive to feminism because of the way that she exposes the complacent identities of psycho-sexual life. But as soon as we try to draw out of that exposure an image of femininity which escapes the straitjacket of symbolic forms, we fall straight into that essentialism and primacy of the semiotic which is one of the most problematic aspects of her work," "Julia Kristeva—Take Two", chapter 4 of this volume. To acknowledge the effective functioning of the symbolic construction of the subject is not to endorse it in its entirety. On the contrary, Kristeva's project consists precisely in pointing out that which cannot be successfully assimilated within the symbolic, namely the semiotic. Rather than conceding to the invisibility of the semiotic within the symbolic, and far from capitulating to patriarchal modes of thinking, Kristeva attempts to catch sight of the disruptions that the semiotic effects in the symbolic order, disruptions which cannot be cashed out fully in symbolic terms.

8. See Naomi Schor's adumbration of various types of essentialism. She distinguishes four versions of essentialism, which she identifies by elaborating the various critiques of essentialism. These critiques she labels "liberationist" of whom she sees de Beauvoir as representative, "linguistic" (Lacan), "Philosophical" (Derrida and feminist Derrideans), and "Feminist" (those concerned with "very real lived differences." The list of essentialisms she constructs consists of the belief in "an essential difference of woman grounded in the body"; the "naive realist," the essentialist who "fails to acknowledge the play of difference in language and the difference it makes"; and one who endorses a "false universalism," p. 41–2.

9. Nancy Fraser and Linda J. Nicholson, "Social Criticism Without Philosophy: An Encounter between Feminism and Postmodernism" in *Feminism/postmodernism*, ed. Linda J. Nicholson (New York: Routledge, 1990), p. 33.

10. Julia Kristeva, "Le temps des femmes", *33/34 Cahiers de recherche de sciences des textes et documents 5*, winter 1979: pp. 5–19; "Women's Time", trans. S. Hand in *The*

Kristeva Reader, ed. T. Moi (Oxford: Basil Blackwell, 1986), pp. 187–213. Kristeva's essay was previously translated by Alice Jardine and Harry Blake in *Signs: Journal of Women in Culture and Society* 7, no. l, Autumn, 1981: pp. 13–35, and reprinted in *Feminist Theory: A Critique of Ideology,* ed. N. O. Keohane, et. al. (Brighton, Sussex: Harvester Press, 1982), pp. 31–53.

11. In tandem with and parallel to her account of feminism, Kristeva gives a more general political analysis of twentieth-century Europe's historical development. Kristeva distinguishes between the European nation as "reality" and the nation as "dream."

12. I cannot agree with Spivak's objection that Kristeva provides a simple "narrative" of feminism, "In a Word," p. 145 (see note 5, above). Far from simply accepting the narrative convention according to which history proceeds in an orderly and progressive fashion, Kristeva brings into question the teleological model of linear history. By that account, each successive stage of feminism would mark an improvement, each phase would develop as the logical outcome of the previous one, and each period would represent a more or less self-contained unit, so that these units would be mutually exclusive. If at one level, Kristeva concedes to such a narrative, her main concern is to show the inadequacy of it. She supplements the logic of this linear, male account by suggesting that there is another time, a "diagonal" time that cuts across the lines of abstract history, and that moves according to a more circular, rhythmic, female motion.

13. On the question of sexual difference, see Kristeva's comments in a recent interview, where she warns against the dangers of moving toward a future in which the "blurring" or "effacing" of sexual difference leads to "a kind of perpetual androgyny," trans. Katherine Ann Jensen in *Shifting Scenes: Interviews on Women, Writing, and Politics in Post-68 France,* ed. Alice A. Jardine and Anne M. Menke (New York: Columbia University Press, 1991), p. 116. Kristeva goes on to postulate that such a blurring of sexual difference would lead to "the end of a certain kind of desire and sexual pleasure. For, after all, if you level out difference, given that it's difference that's desirable and provokes sexual pleasure, you could see a kind of sexual anesthesia, and this in an incubator society where the question of reproduction will be posed by way of machines and bioscientific methods in order for the species to continue. That's extremely troubling first for the individual's psychic life whose leveling off rules out desire and pleasure and, second, for the individual's creative possibilities," p. 117.

14. Julia Kristeva, *Revolution in Poetic Language,* trans. M. Waller, (New York: Columbia University Press, 1984), p.93.

15. Ibid., p. 69.

16. Judith Butler, *Gender Trouble: Feminism and the Subversion of Identity* (New York: Routledge, 1990), p. 85. The fact that my analysis differs from Butler's does not detract from the overall significance of Butler's argument, particularly her suggestion that Kristeva's view of psychosis "designates female homosexuality as a culturally unintelligible practice" (p. 86). I do not pretend to have solved all the problems that arise from reading Kristeva, and Butler's view that Kristeva designates homosexuality psychotic, and as such culturally unintelligible, clearly demands further discussion.

17. Ibid., p. 80.

18. Butler acknowledges a similar point—although not in relation to Kristeva—in her discussion of the "limits of identity politics," *Gender Trouble*, p. 4. She says, "Obviously, the political task is not to refuse representational politics—as if we could. The juridical structures of language and politics constitute the contemporary field of power; hence, there is no position outside this field, but only a critical genealogy of its own legitimating practices," p. 5.

19. Sandra Harding, "The Instability of the Analytical Categories of Feminist Theory," *Signs* 11, no. 4, Summer 1986: pp. 645–64.

20. In her interview with Spivak, Ellen Rooney asks why essentialism "hasn't, by and large, been historicized or related to the history of high philosophical essentialisms, but has been invoked to distance and disallow certain kinds of discourses," "In a Word," p. 132. I have tried to go some way towards historicizing the feminist discourse on essentialism. To relate it to the history of philosophical essentialisms would not only require another article, it would also be of dubious value in this context. One might begin such a history by establishing how Plato understands "essence" in terms of Platonic Forms, and one might go on to distinguish these Ideal essences from the essential cause that Aristotle identifies as distinct from material, formal and final causes. Already one would have found major differences in the way in which the idea of essence is construed. One could go on to trace the history of the term through to the modern period, turning up a variety of answers as to what philosophers have meant by essence—the "whatness" (*quidditas*) or reality of a thing for example, coming to a stop, perhaps, with Heidegger, who raises the question of whether the tradition has understood what it means by the concept of essence (see "On the Essence of Truth," trans. J. Sailis, in *Martin Heidegger: Basic Writings,* ed. D. F. Krell (London: Routledge, 1978), pp. 117–41. Such efforts may prove superfluous in the end, however, if as Spivak maintains, "the question of anti-essentialism and essentialism is not a philosophical question, that's why there isn't any rebuttal from the house of philosophy. It takes place elsewhere," "In a Word," p. 132. The question is, where, if not in the house of philosophy, does the debate take place? The answer I am suggesting is that it is a debate that has largely played itself out in the political arena, a debate that could be usefully supplemented by some historical and conceptual clarification.

21. For a more detailed discussion of the two approaches indicated here see Alison M. Jaggar, "Sexual Difference and Sexual Equality," in *Theoretical Perspectives on Sexual Difference,* ed. D. Rhode, (New Haven, Conn.: Yale University Press, 1990), pp. 239–54.

22. Julia Kristeva "Women's Time."

23. A variety of overlapping rationales is offered in support of the perceived need to revise or rethink a distinction that has played a central role in articulating feminist agendas. For a good discussion of the issue of sexual difference, in relation to the sex/gender distinction see for example, Moira Gatens, "A Critique of the Sex/Gender Distinction," in *A Reader in Feminist Knowledge* (New York: Routledge, 1991), pp. 139–57. It is within the context of challenging metaphysical notions of identity that Judith Butler casts doubt on the adequacy with which contemporary feminist theory delineates the sex/gender distinction. See *Gender Trouble: Feminism and the Subversion Of Identity* (New York: Routledge, 1990), p. 11. See also Evelyn Fox Keller, "The Gender/Science System: or, Is Sex to Gender as Nature Is to Science?" in *Fem-*

inism & Science, ed. N. Tuana (Bloomington, Ind.: Indiana University Press, 1989), pp. 33–44; originally published in *Hypatia* 2, no. 3, Fall 1987; Ellen Messer-Davidow, "The Philosophical Bases of Feminist Literary Criticisms," in *Gender & Theory: Dialogues on Feminist Criticism,* ed. L. Kauffman (Oxford: Basil Blackwell, 1989), pp. 63–106; Donna J. Haraway, *Simians, Cyborgs, and Women: the Reinvention of Nature* (New York: Routledge, 1991).

24. Judith Butler, *Gender Trouble,* p. 80.

12

Toward a Feminist Postmodern Poléthique: Kristeva on Ethics and Politics

Marilyn Edelstein

Julia Kristeva's recent work can be read as postmodern: part of post-modern philosophy, reflective of postmodernity, and, in some innovative texts, stylistically postmodernist. Just as Kristeva's relations to feminism, ethics, and politics are being hotly debated today, so are the relations of post-modernism to each of these. As I'll argue, understanding Kristeva as a post-modernist can illuminate the intimate relationship between ethics and pol-itics in her later work, clarify her relationship to feminism, and expand our sense of the ethical and political possibilities of postmodernism itself.

Although her emphases have changed throughout her career, Kristeva has always explored the subject's dialogic relations with itself, with others, with language. These relations and her analyses of them are—in the broad-est sense, both ethical and political—concerned with intersubjective prac-tices, practices shaped by power, knowledge, discourse, but also by love or its absence.

Kristeva creates a new term, "*heréthique*," or her-ethics, heretic's ethics, heretical ethics, exemplified by a mother who deals with the other through love.[1] Rather than being an abstract set of moral principles, ethics is, for Kris-teva, a relational, dialogic *practice* in which one acknowledges both the oth-erness of the other and the otherness of the self to itself. Kristeva has not aban-doned politics for ethics; as a feminist and a postmodernist, she has shown that ethics and politics are inseparable. In lieu of metanarratives about "woman," "politics," or "ethics," Kristeva creates a postmodern *poléthique*.

Jean-François Lyotard defines postmodernism itself simply as "incredulity toward metanarratives," which are modernity's grand stories or theories explaining and legitimating human history.[2] Kristeva also asserts that "we have lost faith in One Master Signifier."[3] A critique of universalizing, totalizing the-ories and practices runs through the various species of postmodernism, which also share, as Jane Flax suggests, a skepticism "about beliefs concerning truth, knowledge, power, the self, and language that are often taken for granted within and serve as legitimation for contemporary Western culture."[4]

From the perspective of those, particularly feminists, committed to social and political change, the salient question is whether the postmodern deconstruction of truth, metanarratives, identities can enable rather than hinder such change. Can postmodern micropolitics or ethics be worldtransforming? And can we/does Kristeva live without metanarratives?

One's own narratives about the history and meaning of postmodernism shape one's sense of whether and how there can be such a thing as a postmodern politics or postmodern ethics. Postmodernism in the narrow sense designates the artistic and cultural avant gardes of the last few decades— innovative writing and art characterized by fragmentation, irony, intertextuality, genre-bending, self-reflexiveness. Although such aesthetic practices are not necessarily politically *motivated,* they have political underpinnings and consequences. Kristeva suggests this when she writes that "postmodernism is that literature which writes itself with the more or less conscious intention of expanding the signifiable and thus human realm."[5] In a few innovative texts like "Stabat Mater" and "The Novel as Polylogue," Kristeva herself performs postmodernly, transgressing typographical, textual, and genre boundaries and conventions.[6]

Postmodernism in this sense follows (comes after, develops from, critiques, subverts) modernism as postmodernity follows modernity.[7] Postmodern*ism,* like post-structuralism, is embedded within but not identical to postmodern*ity.*[8] Modernity and postmodernity are broader historical designations, period or *Zeitgeist* markers.[9] Postmodernity is the condition of a post-Enlightenment, post-humanist, and post-Freudian world; for Freud's "discovery" of the unconscious itself called into question the scope and powers of reason as well as the unity of the human subject. The "postmodern condition," as Lyotard calls it, signals the loss of faith in modernity's metanarratives about the powers of reason and the inevitability of progress. In contrast to this nostalgic language of *loss,* we can see postmodernity as *gain,* enabling a proliferation of new meanings, media, narratives, and identities. Kristeva considers postmodernity as a "moment of crisis," in which "something has crumbled, something is rejected, but it is also the moment when new sources appear, and in postmodernity I myself see this aspect of renewal, which interests me."[10]

Since the relations between postmodernism and postmodernity (like those between modernism and modernity) are so complex, and for the sake of simplicity, I'll be using "postmodernism" here to designate both specific contemporary artistic/theoretical avant gardes and the wider social, cultural, discursive, economic, technological, and ideological conditions which they are shaped by and which they, in turn, shape.

But what is postmodernism's own ideology or politics? Theorists of post-modernism debate whether it can be truly critical or political rather than merely self-reflexive and ironic. Postmodernism has been criticized from the right for being relativistic and depthless, from the left (particularly by Marxist theorists) for eliminating all foundations and subjects for liberation.[11]

Other theorists differentiate between positive vs. negative or political vs. playful postmodernisms.[12] In an interview, Kristeva says, "I do not think that there can be a simply ludic and parodic postmodernity. . . . [T]he game for the game—that does not interest anyone."[13] Andreas Huyssen suggests that the newest forms of postmodernism are or should be resistant and critical; he also considers Kristeva's work among the most political (or "politically intended") of recent French theorists.[14] Linda Hutcheon suggests that postmodernism is inevitably political, but that it is "politically ambivalent, doubly encoded as both complicity and critique, so that it can be (and has been) recuperated by both the left and the right, each ignoring half of that double coding."[15] The inevitability of complicity may not be unique to postmodernism, though; as Gayatri Spivak suggests, fem-inist criticism, too, like all forms of critique, "is complicitous with the institution within which it seeks its space," and must recognize this in order to be a force for change.[16]

The complicities or chasms between feminism, which is indisputably political, and postmodernism have only recently begun to be explored.[17] There has been widespread disagreement about whether postmodernism and feminism can make good bedfellows, whether their relationship can be mutually fulfilling and enabling rather than one marked by domination or by effacement of different needs, desires, and goals. Christine di Stefano, among others, argues that political feminism needs the very notions of rationality and subjectivity that postmodernism has decentered. Jane Flax, on the other hand, suggests that feminist theory is itself a form of post-modernism and has much to gain from the postmodern critique of Enlight-enment rationality and the postmodern de-essentializing of gender.[18] Henry Giroux argues that perhaps postmodernism needs feminism even more than feminism needs postmodernism, since "feminism provides postmod-ernism with a politics, and a great deal more."[19]

In my view, postmodernism's rejection of totalizing and universalizing models of and metanarratives about human (read *male*) experience is espe-cially useful for feminists. Passing beyond metanarratives of identity and of gender allows for embracing of difference and a proliferation of possi-ble subject-positions and gender performances.[20] As bell hooks argues, postmodern critiques of essentialism, universalism, and "static over-deter-mined identity" can be as useful for rethinking race as for rethinking gender.[21] Postmodernists and many feminists are justly skeptical of metanarratives, which, as Madan Sarup notes, are "master narratives—narratives of mastery, of man seeking his *telos* in the conquest of nature."[22]

Like other postmodernists, Kristeva has become skeptical of metanarratives, including Marxism, feminism, and traditional ethics when they become monolithic and monologic.[23] She critiques Marxist theory, as many feminists have, for ignoring gender as a category of analysis, and for attending far more to production than to reproduction.[24] She also criticizes Marxist *regimes* for rejecting "all individual stylistic experience that could question or explore the common code and its stereotypes in which ideology must seek shelter in order to dominate."[25]

Kristeva argues in "Women's Time" that feminism, like Marxism, may become trapped in a logic of power and "counter-power"; feminism can become centralized and consolidated just like the universalizing discourses it opposes.[26] For her, feminism, unlike Marxism, is capable of acknowledging particularity and singularity, but only if it resists the siren call of master narratives. Her critiques of feminism seem directed at helping it avoid becoming such a master narrative about Woman.

Kristeva, like other postmodernists, has become especially skeptical about the likelihood of large-scale political movements leading to genuine institutional change. She sees political discourse as a "modern religion: the final explanation," which, in our century has produced "two powerful and totalitarian results: fascism and Stalinism."[27] She argues that "the kind of upheaval now required involves more than a change in class power." Instead, "we must transform the subject in his [*sic*] relationship to language, to the symbolic, to unity, and to history."[28] The postmodern turn from metanarratives to local and specific narratives finds its correlative in a turn from global or national politics to local, community-centered, or even personal politics.[29] The increasing recent interest among postmodern and post-structuralist theorists in the ethical may reflect this localizing impulse, especially if we think of ethics as personal politics. These localizing moves run far less risk than the master narratives did of effacing difference, and of doing violence to the other.

Kristeva makes this postmodernist and feminist move toward the local and specific quite radically. She says in a 1989 interview that "we must try to be the most concrete—I would even say microscopic—that we can. To work at the level of individuals . . . [W]e must not try to propose global models."[30] She asks whether it is possible instead to "make a politics that takes account of the singularities."[31] For Kristeva, ethics is a (political) process through which to explore both singularities and the relations between them.

In her recent work, the increasing emphasis on relations—to oneself, to the Other, to others—is itself an ethical emphasis. Kristeva asserts that it is "relationship with another, from which meaning" and morality derive.[32] Rather than seeing her recent work as renouncing radical politics for liberal individualism, as do critics like Paul Smith and Ann Rosalind Jones, I think we can see it as a postmodernist particularizing of the more broadly social and political concerns in her earlier work.[33]

After all, a focus on relationality is not the same as a focus on the autonomous, unified, individual subject of liberal/modern humanism—the very sort of subject critiqued by postmodernists, post-structuralists, and many feminists. Suzanne Clark and Kathleen Hulley assert that the Kristevan, postmodern subject, "unlike the self-made subject of the American frontier . . . can never be a self-sufficient unity"; instead, it "is an intersection of intertextuality, a subject-in-process."[34] The Kristevan subject is always already social but can *become* ethical.

Kristeva's is an ethics of practice rather than a meta-ethics or metanarrative of ethics. When she proposes "a contemporary ethics," "an heretical ethics separated from morality," she seems to be differentiating between morality as an abstract set of principles and ethics as a practice.[35] Hers is "not the kind of 'ethics' that consists in obedience to laws." Kristeva asserts that "the ethical cannot be stated, instead it is practiced to the point of loss."[36] For her, ethics has more to do with the shattering than the maintenance of codes, more to do with free play than coercion, more to do with love than law.[37]

Kristeva writes that "herethics is undeath, love" (*a-mort* and *amour*); herethics is "perhaps no more than that which in life makes bonds, thoughts, and therefore the thought of death, bearable." She admits that "nothing . . . suggests that a feminine ethics is possible," yet notes that the "reformulation" of contemporary ethics "demands the contribution of women."[38] Kristeva herself contributes to the creation of such a "feminine," (metaphorically) maternal, and postmodern ethics or *heréthique*.

For Kristeva, the ethical consists in "reaching out to the other,"[39] As Elizabeth Grosz puts it, "ethics is a response to the recognition of the primacy of alterity over identity."[40] Kristeva's is a dialogic ethics of practice and process. She borrows the concept of the dialogic from Mikhail Bakhtin, for whom it connotes alterity as well as intertextuality.[41] Kristeva acknowledges that, even before Lacan, Bakhtin introduced her to "the notion of *alterity* and *dialogism*."[42] The relationships between the subject and the other, between the subject and itself, between the semiotic and the symbolic are all dialogic, in Kristevan theory.[43] Dialogism, like postmodernist thought, is relational, dynamic, heterogeneous.

Both maternity and psychoanalysis serve as prime models or metaphors in Kristeva's recent work for potentially ethical, loving relations to the other—dialogic relations which respect and embrace alterity.[44] For Kristeva, a mother is one who can reach out (and in) to the other with love: "maternity is a bridge between singularity and ethics."[45] "Stabat Mater" is a "tale of love," about a mother coming to acknowledge her child as "irremediably an other" and irremediably mortal, but loved because of rather than in spite of these realities.[46] Yet, for Kristeva, not only mothers are capable of ethical practice, nor are all mothers inherently ethical in their relations to others or even to their own children: Kristeva acknowledges that mothers are capable of hate and even infanticide.

As she puts it in "Stabat Mater," her child's birth gives a mother "the possibility—but not the certainty—for reaching out to the other, the ethical."[47] For Kristeva, as I argue elsewhere, the maternal becomes a metaphor for a particular ethical practice.[48]

Psychoanalysis is also an ethical and dialogic practice of love, for Kristeva. She argues that "there is no analysis if the Other is not an Other whom I love."[49] The patient enters analysis for "want of love," and if analysis is successful, if transference and countertransference occur, then the patient is able to love (since transference is "a synonym for love") and also able to distance herself or himself from the analyst. For Kristeva, "the ordeal of analysis requires, at a minimum, that I (analyst or analysand) accept the existence of an other," who can remain both other and loved.[50]

Many feminists, like Grosz and Domna Stanton, have critiqued Kristeva's privileging of maternity and motherhood, arguing that she either essentializes women by idealizing the maternal—thus reinscribing cultural stereotypes—or effaces the bodies and differences of real women.[51] I think Kristeva, like other postmodernists, de-essentializes gender; she treats the *maternal* as metaphorically available to both men and women, but also considers *maternity* as a physiological experience shared by many women. Psychoanalysis itself, practiced by both men and women, becomes, in Kristeva's analyses, a maternal activity, as does much transgressive art. Yet, clearly, her discussions of maternity—including conception, gestation, childbirth, from the mother's point of view—acknowledge the embodiedness, the pain and *jouissance* of real women.

Kristeva's increasing commitment to psychoanalysis has also provoked criticism from some feminists, like Eleanor Kuykendall, who assert that she too uncritically appropriates Freudian or Lacanian psychoanalysis, with all their universalizing, phallogocentric, and ahistorical assumptions.[52] I think Kristeva engages in a creative, non-agonistic re-reading of both Freud and Lacan, even though she is not fully self-critical of her own commitment to psychoanalysis. Just as Lyotard may be creating a *grand récit* about the loss of *grands récits*, as Sarup astutely notes,[53] so Kristeva may be replacing the master narrative of Marxism or some feminisms with that of psychoanalysis. If a master narrative is one that believes it explains the fundamentals of human behavior, then psychoanalysis is certainly a master narrative. It even has a foundational assumption—the existence of the unconscious (much as most post-structuralist theory makes language virtually foundational). I agree with Spivak that Kristeva seems to posit "truth" in psychoanalysis;[54] Kristeva even claims psychoanalysis is the "antidote" to political discourse.[55] But this failure to maintain complete postmodern skepticism may simply reveal all theorists' (if not all humans') need for metanarratives.

Kristeva seems to see psychoanalytic *practice*, though, as a *micro*narrative and a local politics. She believes her "work as an analyst is political work, to take it in a microscopic and individual sense,"[56] and it is. But some critics have a very different view of the relations between politics and psychoanalysis. Spivak, for instance, asserts that "Kristeva makes an unproblematic analogy between the single-person situation of analysis and the vastly multitudinous, multiracial, and multinational . . . political arena."[57] I agree with Spivak that psychoanalytic work or interpersonal ethics is not the same as, and cannot replace, global politics. But one can hardly claim that (Kristevan) psychoanalysis is a "single-person situation," since it involves at least a dyad—two persons in conversation, with far more voices and subjects at play in the dialogue. Psychoanalytic, familial, amorous, and friendly relations are more narrowly social than, but also part of, the broader sociosymbolic, political spheres. Practices within such relations may serve either to replicate or to challenge and change existing social practices.

Both ethics and politics involve relationships to the Other. Psychoanalysis, motherhood, love, and religion—subjects of Kristeva's recent work—are all social, dialogic, and, finally, political practices. Like any politics, they can be liberatory, just, and ethical—or not. Rhetorics and metanarratives of liberation or emancipation suggest a teleology, an end at which liberation or emancipation will be achieved. But liberatory practices, like ethics and like subject-formation, are ongoing, heterogeneous, recursive processes which can never reach an end.

I agree with Kristeva "that there can be no socio-political transformation without a transformation of subjects: in other words, in our relationship to social constraints, to pleasure, and more deeply, to language."[58] Such transformation of subjects and of their ethical practices toward others is a necessary but not sufficient condition for broader sociopolitical change. Foucault, a more explicitly political theorist, makes a similar point: "We have to promote new forms of subjectivity through the refusal of this kind of individuality which has been imposed on us for several centuries."[59] Kristeva, too, talks about the power of refusal, of negativity, of rejection, in fact asserting "that a feminist practice can only be negative, at odds with what already exists."[60] But Kristeva may hold out more transformative possibilities than Foucault, since she suggests love and ethical practice as positive gestures which can follow this refusal.

Can such a postmodern ethics and/as politics be allied with or useful for feminists? Not everyone would agree with me that it can.[61] Hutcheon believes that postmodernism is quite distinct from feminisms, since postmodernism "has no theory of positive action on a social level" or a theory of agency, whereas "all feminist positions do" and must.[62] Alcoff critiques post-structuralists for neither theorizing nor allowing for agency, since they believe in "a total construction of the subject," which eliminates "the subject's ability to reflect on the social discourse and challenge its determinations."[63] Kuykendall levels a similar charge specifically against Kristeva: "Despite the apparent centrality of the feminine in her writings on maternity, Kristeva's ethics of linguistics is not, finally, feminist . . . in that it is avowedly Freudian and leaves no place for a feminine conception of agency."[64] Although these are apt criticisms of some postmodernist and post-structuralist theory, I do not believe they really apply to Kristeva.

In all of her work, and especially recently, Kristeva "insists on the individual as the site of subversion and ethical possibility."[65] For Kristeva, the split subject—positioned at the intersections of language and the unconscious, the symbolic and the semiotic, word and flesh—is able to "get pleasure from . . . renew . . . even endanger" the sociosymbolic system.[66] Kristeva argues that "we must maintain the autonomy of discourse with respect to the social level, because it is a level of autonomy that guarantees freedom. We can speak in a different manner than our familial and social determination."[67] Since, for Kristeva, the subject can transgress or subvert the "socio-symbolic system," can speak (and be) differently, he or she must be capable of individual agency.

But can such transgressive practices by individual subjects enable, accompany, or merely reflect changing ethical or political practices? Toril Moi argues that Kristeva assumes "the disruption of the subject" in avant-garde texts "prefigures or parallels revolutionary disruptions of society," but that "her only argument in support of this contention is the rather lame one of comparison or homology."[68] Rita Felski suggests that Kristeva fails to explain "the ultimate nature of the relationship between textual and political revolution."[69] Jones argues that for Kristeva it is "a curiously private revolution: the poet, solitary, original and unique, and the critic/semiotician are the only participants it requires."[70]

Yet, in my view, for Kristeva, neither writers nor readers (nor any subjects) are "solitary." Since the Kristevan subject is created in and through language, at the place where word and flesh meet,[71] and since language is a social practice, the subject and the social cannot be separated. Although not all recent Kristevan texts provide "materialist analysis of social relations"[72] all her theories of the speaking subject are, finally, social.

But if they are social, are they truly political? Aesthetic transgression of the sort Kristeva usually discusses *can be* a form of political transgression. Kristeva has often argued that one cannot refuse the symbolic without becoming psychotic,[73] but one can transgress the symbolic—the order of culture and language—from within it, through the semiotic, with which it is always in dialogic relation. The semiotic—the realm of the body, the drives, the unconscious—can express itself in avant-garde discourses and in the maternal. But the semiotic need not be identified with the maternal or the feminine, since the pre-Oedipal archaic mother with which it is associated includes or transcends both masculine and feminine.[74] Kristeva's work both suggests and demonstrates the possibility of conscious, agentic transgressions, as well. Although many of her critics do not think so, Kristeva presents the symbolic as challengeable rather than hegemonic.

Although Hutcheon argues that "art forms cannot change unless social practices do,"[75] I agree with Kristeva that changing artistic and representational practices can enable as well as reflect sociopolitical changes.[76] Without *speaking*—and hearing—differently, we cannot *be* differently. As Grosz argues, "The struggle for the right to write, read and know differently is not merely a minor or secondary task within feminist politics [but] ... it cannot replace the other forms of struggle in which feminists are engaged."[77] As many feminists today would agree, multiple feminist practices are both inevitable and desirable.

To sever subjective or aesthetic from political transgression is to have a modernist view of the autonomy of selves and art—the very view that postmodernists like Kristeva reject.[78] Kristeva argues that "a literary text does not live in an autistic fashion, closed on the interior of itself," but always borrows from other texts and discourses. Kristeva has a Bakhtinian conception of the dialogic relations between aesthetic discourses and political/public ones. She even argues that fiction is "a form of atomized politics, ... in the sense of the atomizer, 'the spray'." Similarly, she says the individual "is not an atom closed on herself" but is "a process."[79]

If neither subjects nor texts are atoms—autonomous and discrete—they are nonetheless, as Kristeva often argues, singular. Kristeva notes the political problem in France (as elsewhere) of "how to arrange it such that this aspect of singularity does not become isolation, but that there is nevertheless a kind of communication among singularities."[80] For Kristeva, both literature and ethics are such "politics of singularity" and alterity. The problem is how to create ethical and liberatory intertextual and intersubjective practices, at both a micro- and a macro- level. Cultivating dialogic communities of singular subjects aware of their own alterity may be one method.

Kristeva's interests in ethics, politics, psychoanalysis, and not only the sociosymbolic contract but social policy merge in her recent book *Strangers to Ourselves*. Her analysis there of xenophobia and immigration suggests what a *poléthique* might be—a political ethics or ethical politics. Ethics is always political, but, as we all know, *un*ethical politics (and politicians) are all too common, in the everyday sense of "unethical" as well as in the Kristevan sense of seeing others as the enemy. For Kristeva, "the ethical decision alone appears able to transcend the narrow needs of national politics."[81] An ethical politics would enable both more loving and more just treatment of those seen and valued as different; such a politics is especially crucial now as national borders are increasingly fluid, as immigration expands internationally, and as countries like the U.S. and France become increasingly ethnically diverse.[82]

Whether borders/boundaries are psychological or geographical, we all must learn how to negotiate their transgression. For Kristeva, psychoanalysis is perhaps the best way to "think about the question of the other." This is so "because the Freudian message, to simplify things, consists in saying that the other is in me. It is my unconscious. And instead of searching for a scapegoat in the foreigner, I must try to tame the demons which are in me."[83] Of course, acknowledging our own stranger/strangeness within may be a necessary but is hardly a sufficient condition for eradicating racism and xenophobia.

Nations, states, cities, communities, and individuals must deal increasingly with difference and otherness. But the concept of "foreigner" for Kristeva doesn't merely apply to those of a different race, ethnicity, or nationality. She refers to men and women as "these foreigners . . . to one another."[84] Even these foreigners need not be at war with each other, however. Kristeva imagines the possibility of a time, a third generation of feminism, in which "the very dichotomy man/woman as an opposition between two rival entities may be understood as belonging to *metaphysics*."[85]

Kristeva often argues that women have a special access to outsideness or foreignness, more because of their position within the existing sociosymbolic order than because of their "nature" (although, in her analyses, bearing children reinforces women's sense of the "foreign" within). As she says, "I am very attached to this idea of the woman as irrecuperable foreigner. But I know that certain American feminists do not think well of such an idea, because they want a positive notion of woman. But one can be positive by starting with this permanent marginality, which is the motor of change."[86]

Yet, Kristeva sees *both* women and men as irrecuperably foreign to themselves. As she puts it in *Strangers to Ourselves,* "the foreigner is neither a race nor a nation. . . . Uncanny, foreignness is within us: we are our own foreigners, we are divided."[87] She asks, "How could one tolerate a foreigner if one did not know one was a stranger to oneself?" For her, psychoanalysis is a "journey into the strangeness of the other and of oneself, toward an ethics of respect for the irreconcilable,"[88] but love is also such a journey.

Clearly, not all human beings can afford or would want to undergo actual psychoanalysis; perhaps those most in need of achieving the loving respect for otherness it makes possible (although not inevitable) are the very ones least likely to seek it. But psychoanalysis is not the only relation or practice of transference, love, or ethics, even if for Kristeva it is an exemplary one. Human relations with others, with ourselves, with language, and with sociality can all become sites for ethical engagement and for embracing of alterity. As Kelly Oliver argues, what unites Kristeva's recent concerns with maternity, poetic language, and psychoanalysis is that each of these calls into question "the identity of the unified subject" and "points to the alterity within identity." As Oliver suggests, "This strangeness in identity can found a new ethics and politics."[89]

I've coined the term *"poléthique"* to suggest the inseparability of ethics and politics for Kristeva and other postmodernists. As Grosz argues, one can only oppose ethics to politics if one assumes "that politics is social and collective, while ethics only pertains to the behaviour of individuals." For French feminists like Kristeva, however, "ethics is not opposed to politics but is a continuation of it within the domain of relations between self and other."[90] Politics can also become a continuation of ethics in a broader public arena. Just as self and other are always in dialogic relation, so are ethics and politics.

Kristeva's deconstruction of the seeming binary opposition between ethics and politics is a postmodernist but also a feminist move, in keeping with other feminist critiques of traditional oppositions between public and private, or between the personal and the political. Kristeva's postmodern critiques of identity and autonomy, her foregrounding of ethical *practice,* her (re-)valuing of the maternal, her emphasis on acknowledging and respecting one's own and others' alterity can enrich the burgeoning field of feminist ethics and wider debates about both subjectivity and agency. Her work also enables us to reconceive postmodernism, to see that it can be both ethical and political. Her work may be problematic in some respects, but she is a major thinker doing important work at the intersections of feminism, psychoanalysis, postmodernism, political theory, and ethical theory. Kristeva's *heréthique* becomes a fertile space from which can emerge a feminist, postmodern *poléthique*.

Notes

I'd like to thank Diane Jonte-Pace and Karen Bryce Funt for valuable advice on this chapter; a shorter version of it was presented at the 1992 International Conference on Narrative.

1. This term was used in the original title for her essay later translated as "Stabat Mater" (the name of a Latin hymn on Mary's suffering at the Crucifixion) and collected in *Tales of Love*. "Heréthique de l'amour" first appeared in *Tel Quel* in 1977 and then was renamed upon inclusion in *Histoires d'amour*.

2. Jean-François Lyotard, *The Postmodern Condition: A Report on Knowledge,* trans. Geoff Bennington and Brian Massumi (Minneapolis: University of Minnesota Press, 1984), p. xxiv.

3. Julia Kristeva, *Powers of Horror: An Essay on Abjection,* trans. Leon S. Roudiez (New York: Columbia University Press, 1982), p. 209.

4. Jane Flax, "Postmodernism and Gender Relations in Feminist Theory," *Signs* 12, 1987: p. 624.

5. Julia Kristeva, "Postmodernism?" *Romanticism, Modernism, Postmodernism,* ed. Harry R. Garvin, spec. issue of *Bucknell Review* 25, 1980: p. 137.

6. "Stabat Mater" is Kristeva's first essay leaving the dense, philosophical style of her early semiological writing for a more playful, personal, postmodern style. Kristeva argues that postmodernist texts explore both literary/linguistic limits and "the typical imaginary relationship, that to the mother ("Postmodernism?" pp. 137, 139–140); it is thus significant that Kristeva's first postmodern essay is about motherhood. As I suggest in "Metaphor, Meta-narrative . . ." "Stabat Mater" may be in part a parody of *écriture feminine,* which Kristeva has criticized for a reliance on a "belief in Woman, Her power, Her writing," from which it needs to "break free." Julia Kristeva, "Women's Time," trans. Alice Jardine and Harry Blake, *The Kristeva Reader,* ed. Toril Moi (New York: Columbia University Press, 1986), p. 208. Parody is itself emblematic of postmodernism.

7. I am using "modernism" here to designate the literary/artistic avant gardes of the late nineteenth and early to mid-twentieth centuries, which stressed aesthetic autonomy, impersonality, and innovation. The complex relationship between postmodernism and modernism, like that between modernity and postmodernity, has been a major focus in both descriptive and evaluative discussions of postmodernism. For a useful summary of these debates, see Linda Hutcheon, *The Politics of Postmodernism* (London: Routledge, 1989), pp. 23–29. Kristeva is perhaps being more "postmodern" than I am here by using "avant-garde," "modern," and "postmodernist" almost interchangeably to describe innovative and transgressive literary and artistic practices. As Alice Jardine notes, "the word 'postmodern,' as commonly used in the United States . . . perhaps most accurately corresponds to what the French name *la modernité* . . . those writing self-consciously from within the (intellectual, scientific, philosophical, religious, literary) *epistemological crisis* specific to the postwar period." Alice Jardine,

"Opaque Texts and Transparent Contexts: The Political Difference of Julia Kristeva," chapter 1 of this volume.

8. Hutcheon also criticizes the conflation, by theorists like Fredric Jameson, of postmodernity and postmodernism. For her, postmodernism is a "cultural notion," while postmodernity designates "a social and philosophical period or 'condition'." Linda Hutcheon, *The Politics of Postmodernism,* pp. 23–24. But for her, culture "responds" to "ground," p. 26. This question of the relation between culture and ground is a version of Marxist debates about base/superstructure relations. I agree with Raymond Williams that these relations are neither simple nor unidirectional (which Hutcheon implies). Raymond Williams, "Base and Superstructure in Marxist Cultural Theory," *Problems in Materialism and Culture*(London: Verso, 1980), pp. 31–49. I believe that postmodernity both shapes and is shaped by postmodernism. I also want to avoid the conflation of postmodernism and post-structuralism, which is part of but not equivalent to postmodernism, and of deconstruction, which is, in turn, a part of but not equivalent to post-structuralism. Such metonymies have characterized much recent metatheoretical discourse. Huyssen argues that postmodernism and post-structuralism could not be "identical or even homologous," since "poststructuralism is primarily a discourse of and about modernism." Andreas Huyssen, *After the Great Divide: Modernism, Mass Culture, Postmodernism* (Bloomington, Ind.: Indiana University Press, 1986), p. 207. Some texts by Kristeva, Cixous, Irigaray, and others are simultaneously post-structuralist, (post)modernist, and deconstructive.

9. It is important to keep in mind that (meta)narratives of modernity and postmodernity, as of modernism and postmodernism, are primarily based on Euro-American white, elite intellectual and social history (more recently, Japanese). For example, frequently made claims about the impact of television and computers in shaping postmodern life have little validity outside the context of industrialized, if not postindustrial, societies.

10. Suzanne Clark and Kathleen Hulley, "An Interview with Julia Kristeva: Cultural Strangeness and the Subject in Crisis," *Discourse* 13, 1990–91; p. 165.

11. Jürgen Habermas, for instance, believes postmodernism has prematurely rejected the incomplete liberatory project of modernity, along with Enlightenment metanarratives of reason and progress. For Habermas, post-structuralism, a species of postmodernism, is a form of neoconservatism. Jürgen Habermas, "Modernity—An Incomplete Project," trans. Seyla Ben-Habib, *The Anti-Aesthetic: Essays on Postmodern Culture,* ed. Hal Foster (Seattle: Bay Press, 1983). Terry Eagleton argues that postmodernism eliminates the possibility of ethical and political resistance. Terry Eagleton, "Capitalism, Modernism and Postmodernism," *New Left Review* 152, 1985: pp. 72–73. Jameson wonders whether "postmodernism replicates or reproduces—reinforces—the logic of consumer capitalism" but suggests it might also resist that logic. Fredric Jameson, "Postmodernism and Consumer Society," *Postmodernism and Its Discontents: Theories, Practices,* ed. E. Ann Kaplan (London: Verso, 1988), p. 29.

12. As Jameson argues, all cultural texts "are social and political." Fredric Jameson, *The Political Unconscious: Narrative as a Socially Symbolic Act* (Ithaca, N.Y.: Cornell University Press, 1981), p. 20. But some cultural texts foreground the political far more than others do. Of course, a refusal to "be political" or acknowledge one's politicalness is itself a political statement.

13. Suzanne Clark and Kathleen Hulley, "An Interview with Julia Kristeva," p. 177.

14. Andreas Huyssens, *After the Great Divide*, p. 208.

15. Linda Hutcheon, *The Politics of Postmodernism*, p. 168.

16. Gayatri Spivak, "Imperialism and Sexual Difference," *Oxford Literary Review* 8, 1986: p. 225. Clearly, differing degrees of complicity are possible—from cooptation or absorption to intended, if incomplete, rejection. Some degree of complicity within a discourse may be not only inevitable but desirable if one wishes to influence it: one must speak the language to converse with its "native" speakers.

17. As recently as 1986, Huyssen could claim "it is somewhat baffling that feminist criticism has so far largely stayed away from the postmodernism debate which is considered not to be pertinent to feminist concerns." Andreas Huyssen, *After the Great Divide*, p. 198. Craig Owens noted in 1983 "the absence of discussions of sexual difference in writings about postmodernism, as well as the fact that few women have engaged in the modernism/postmodernism debate." Craig Owens, "The Discourse of Others: Feminists and Postmodernism," *The Anti-Aesthetic*, pp. 57–82. The situation has changed dramatically in the last few years, with the publication of essays and books by Flax, Linda J. Nicholson, Patricia Waugh, Henry Giroux, and others. Debates about feminism and postmodernism sometimes center on the absence of women writers in the postmodernist canon or of women theorists of postmodernism, rather than on feminist theory's relation to postmodernist theory.

18. Christine Di Stefano, "Dilemmas of Difference: Feminism, Modernity, and Postmodernism," *Feminism/Postmodernism*, ed. Linda J. Nicholson (New York: Routledge, 1990), pp. 63–82. Jane Flax, "Postmodernism and Gender Relations," pp. 621–43. Owens makes a similar point. Flax's essay in *Signs* and Daryl McGowan Tress's reply embody the debate between critics and advocates of Enlightenment rationality and individualism. Daryl McGowan Tress, "Comment on Flax's 'Postmodernism and Gender Relations in Feminist Theory,'" *Signs* 14, 1988: pp. 196–200. Nancy Fraser and Linda Nicholson suggest that a *cautious* alliance between feminism and postmodernism can be productive for both but believe feminists need not forswear metanarratives or grand theory. They do argue that postmodern-feminist critique must be historically specific, pragmatic, cross-cultural, nonuniversalist, and based on a politics of alliance rather than shared identity or essence. Nancy Fraser and Linda Nicholson, "Social Criticism without Philosophy: An Encounter between Feminism and Postmodernism," *Feminism/Postmodernism*, ed. Linda J. Nicholson (New York: Routledge, 1990), pp. 34–35.

19. Henry Giroux, "Introduction. Modernism, Postmodernism, and Feminism: Rethinking the Boundaries of Educational Discourse," *Postmodernism, Feminism, and Cultural Politics: Redrawing Educational Boundaries,* ed. Henry A. Giroux (Albany, N.Y.: State University of New York Press, 1991), p. 33.

20. Judith Butler persuasively argues for the political usefulness of moving beyond essentialist "identity politics"; see, esp., her "Conclusion" in *Gender Trouble: Feminism and the Subversion of Identity* (New York: Routledge, 1990). Giroux also notes that postmodernisms share a "rejection of absolute essences." Henry Giroux, "Modernism, Postmodernism, and Feminism," p. 18: see also Diana Fuss's *Essentially Speaking: Feminism, Nature & Difference* (New York: Routledge, 1989), and bell hooks's review of it, "Essentialism and Experience," *American Literary History* 3, 1991: pp. 172–83. Flax and Toril Moi also welcome postmodernism's rejection of totalizing metanarratives.

21. bell hooks, "Postmodern Blackness," *Yearning: Race, Gender, and Cultural Politics* (Boston: South End Press, 1990), p. 28

22. Madan Sarup, *An Introductory Guide to Post-structuralism and Postmodernism* (Athens, Ga.: University of Georgia Press, 1989), p. 132. Owens, too, notes the similarity between master and meta-narratives: "Master narrative—how else to translate Lyotard's *grand récit?*" Craig Owens, "The Discourse of Others," p. 65. He suggests that feminists, like postmodernists, reject the idea that there can be one total explanatory theory of history or of gender relations. The term "master narrative" is Fredric Jameson's, who uses it to refer to "allegorical narrative signifieds" that are "deeper, underlying ... hidden," inscribed both in texts and in "our collective thinking and collective fantasies about history and reality." Fredric Jameson, *The Political Unconscious*, p. 34, 28). Jameson's own primary master narrative is Marxism, one of the main metanarratives rejected by postmodernists like Lyotard and Kristeva.

23. Of course, both Marxists and feminists often critique Kristeva; see, especially Grosz, Rose, Stanton, Moi, Smith, Fraser, and Butler.

24. Julia Kristeva, "Women's Time," p. 196

25. Julia Kristeva, "My Memory's Hyperbole," trans. Athena Viscusi, *The Female Autograph*, ed. Domna Stanton, spec. issue of *New York Literary Forum* 12–13, 1984: p. 270.

26. Julia Kristeva, "Women's Time," p. 203.

27. Julia Kristeva, "Psychoanalysis and the Polis," trans. Margaret Waller, *Critical Inquiry* 9, 1982: p. 78.

28. Julia Kristeva, "Novel as Polylogue," trans. Thomas Gora, Alice Jardine, Leon S. Roudiez, *Desire in Language:A Semiotic Approach to Literature and Art,*, ed. Leon S. Roudiez (New York: Columbia University Press, 1980), p. 204.

29. Lyotard stresses this turn to the local to create "a politics that would respect both the desire for justice and the desire for the unknown." Jean-François Lyotard, *The Postmodern Condition,* p. 67. Giroux notes that "many feminist theorists welcome the postmodern emphasis on the proliferation of local narratives, the opening up of the world to cultural and ethnic differences, and the positing of difference as a challenge to hegemonic power relations parading as universals." Henry Giroux, "Modernism, Postmodernism, and Feminism," p. 40.

30. As Jameson and others argue, French postmodernists' turn to the local itself has a "local" context, as a reaction against "the centralization of both politics and the university system in France." Fredric Jameson, *The Political Unconscious*, p. 54n.

31. Suzanne Clark and Kathleen Hulley, "An Interview with Julia Kristeva," p. 165.

32. Julia Kristeva, *In the Beginning Was Love: Psychoanalysis and Faith,* trans. Arthur Goldhammer (New York: Columbia University Press, 1987), p. 63

33. In "Julia Kristeva Et Al.; or, Take Three or More," *Feminism and Psychoanalysis,* ed. Richard Feldstein and Judith Roof (Ithaca, N.Y.: Cornell University Press, 1989), pp. 84–104, Paul Smith excoriates Kristeva for what he sees as her bourgeoisification, antifeminism, anti-Marxism, admiration for the U.S., and privileging of literature and psychoanalytic practice as dubious sites for liberation. In *Discerning the Subject,* (Minneapolis: University of Minnesota Press, 1988), Smith is somewhat more positive about Kristeva's political usefulness. Jones critiques particularly Kristeva's recent interest in religion and romantic love, which "have not been alternatives to women's

subordination; they have been the ideologies through which that subordination was lived." Ann Rosalind Jones, "Julia Kristeva on Femininity: The Limits of a Semiotic Politics," *Feminist Review* 18, 1984: p. 70. Yet, Kristeva's recent work is more often about mother-child and even analyst-analysand love than romantic love; and she treats religion as a powerful cultural "discourse for analysis," Julia Kristeva, "My Memory's Hyperbole," p. 272, and faith as a powerful psychic construct, without suggesting that either is "true" or "good."

34. Suzanne Clark and Kathleen Hulley, "An Interview with Julia Kristeva," pp. 153–54.

35. Julia Kristeva, "Stabat Mater," trans. Leon S. Roudiez, *The Kristeva Reader*, p. 185.

36. Julia Kristeva, *Revolution in Poetic Language*, trans. Margaret Waller (New York: Columbia University Press, 1984), pp. 110, 234.

37. Julia Kristeva, "Ethics of Linguistics," *Desire in Language*, p. 23. Elizabeth Grosz suggests that in much recent French theory, "ethics need not imply a moral or normative code, or a series of abstract regulative principles." Elizabeth Grosz, *Sexual Subversions: Three French Feminists* (Sydney: Allen & Unwin, 1989), Glossary, p. xvii.

38. Julia Kristeva, "Stabat Mater," p. 185.

39. Julia Kristeva, "Stabat Mater," p. 182.

40. Elizabeth Grosz, *Sexual Subversions,* Glossary, p. xvii.

41. See esp. Bakhtin's *The Dialogic Imagination: Four Essays by M. M. Bakhtin,* trans. Caryl Emerson and Michael Holquist, ed. Michael Holquist (Austin, Tex: University of Texas Press, 1981). Kristeva introduced Bakhtin's work to a Western audience in her *Séméiotiké* in 1969. For both Bakhtin and Kristeva, linguistic and literary practices both reflect and shape social practices.

42. Julia Kristeva, "My Memory's Hyperbole," p. 267.

43. I develop this point in Marilyn Edelstein, "Metaphor, Meta-Narrative, and Mater-Narrative in Kristeva's 'Stabat Mater'," *Body/Text in Julia Kristeva: Women, Religion, and Psychoanalysis,* ed. David Crownfield (Albany, N.Y.: State University of New York Press, 1992). Clark and Hulley also insightfully discuss the influence of Bakhtinian dialogism on Kristeva's concept of subjectivity.

44. Kristeva clearly differentiates between dialogism, which remains relational and refuses transcendence, and Hegelian or Marxist dialectic, which involves struggle and transcendence. Julia Kristeva, "Word, Dialogue, and Novel," *Desire in Language,* pp. 88-89. Dialogic relations do not guarantee equality, but they are based on respect for alterity. For Emmanuel Levinas, too, "the paradigm of an ethical relation is that of a mother's response to the needs or requirements of a child." Elizabeth Grosz, *Sexual Subversions,* p. xvii. Grosz analyzes Levinas's influence on Irigaray's ethics in Chapter 5; Alison Ainley analyzes his influence on Kristeva's. Alison Ainley , "The Ethics of Sexual Difference," *Abjection, Melancholia and Love: The Work of Julia Kristeva,* ed. John Fletcher and Andrew Benjamin (London: Routledge, 1990), pp. 53–62.

45. Julia Kristeva, "A New Type of Intellectual: The Dissident," trans. Seán Hand, *The Kristeva Reader,* p. 297.

46. Julia Kristeva, "Stabat Mater," p. 179.

47. Ibid., p. 182.

48. Marilyn Edelstein, "Metaphor, Meta-Narrative, and Mater-Narrative."

49. Julia Kristeva, "In Praise of Love," trans. Leon S. Roudiez, *Tales of Love* (New York: Columbia University Press, 1987), p. 14.

50. Julia Kristeva, *In the Beginning Was Love,* pp. 3, 55, 26.

51. Stanton critiques the ontotheological risks of the maternal metaphor in Kristeva. Domna Stanton, "Difference on Trial: A Critique of the Maternal Metaphor in Cixous, Irigaray, and Kristeva," *The Poetics of Gender,* ed. Nancy K. Miller (New York: Columbia University Press, 1986). Grosz argues that "Kristeva's resistance to attributing any female identity to maternity becomes ludicrous, in view of her willingness to describe maternity in biological and physiological terms." Elizabeth Grosz, *Sexual Subversions,* pp. 80–81. Fraser argues that "Kristeva leaves us oscillating between a regressive version of gynocentric-maternalist essentialism, on the one hand, and a postfeminist anti-essentialism, on the other. Neither of these is useful for feminist politics." Fraser, "The Uses and Abuses of French Discourse Theories for Feminist Politics," *boundary 2* 17, 1990: p. 100. See also Rose and Butler. I agree with Moi that Kristeva is neither essentialist nor biologist, (Toril Moi, *Sexual/Textual Politics: Feminist Literary Theory* [London: Methuen, 1985], pp. 163–67), although she does come perilously close to being both. Patricia Elliot also persuasively argues that Kristeva, like other feminists, "rejects the identification of women with mothers as well as the idealization and abjection of both," and "warns against the temptation to either glorify feminine alterity or to annihilate it." Patricia Elliot, *From Mastery to Analysis: Theories of Gender in Psychoanalytic Feminism* (Ithaca, N.Y.: Cornell University Press, 1991), pp. 221, 191.

52. Kelly Oliver astutely analyzes Kristeva's subversion of the paternal function in/of Lacan and Freud. Kelly Oliver, "Kristeva's Imaginary Father and the Crisis in the Paternal Function," *Diacritics* 21, 1991: pp. 43–63.

53. Madan Sarup, *An Introductory Guide to Post-structuralism and Postmodernism,* p. 133.

54. Spivak, "The Politics of Interpretations," *Critical Inquiry* 9, 1982: p. 278.

55. Julia Kristeva, "Psychoanalysis and the Polis," p. 78. Cf. Derrida's critique of Lacan as the "purveyor of truth." Jacques Derrida, "Le facteur de la vérité," *The Postcard: From Socrates to Freud and Beyond,* trans. Alan Bass (Chicago: University of Chicago Press, 1987), pp. 411–96.

56. Suzanne Clark and Kathleen Hulley, "An Interview with Julia Kristeva," p. 165.

57. Spivak, "The Politics of Interpretation," p. 271.

58. Julia Kristeva, "Woman Can Never Be Defined," [interview] with "psychoanalysis and politics," trans. Marilyn A. August, *New French Feminisms: An Anthology,* ed. Elaine Marks and Isabelle de Courtivron (New York: Schocken, 1981), p. 141.

59. Michel Foucault, "The Subject and Power," afterword in *Michel Foucault: Beyond Structuralism and Hermeneutics,* ed. Hubert L. Dreyfus and Paul Rabinow (Chicago: University of Chicago Press, 1982), p. 216.

60. Julia Kristeva, "Woman Can Never Be Defined," p. 137.

61. Although I focus here on those who see feminist ethics and politics as incompatible with postmodernism, some theorists have seen links similar to those I'm trying to elucidate. Steven White argues that "difference feminism," particularly the feminist "ethic of care" and of response to the other (theorized primarily by Carol Gilligan and Nel

Noddings), has strong affinities with postmodernism, particularly in valuing rather than merely tolerating difference. I would argue that Kristeva's dialogic ethics bears at least a family resemblance to the feminist ethic of care, although neither White nor almost anyone writing recently on feminist ethics discusses her work. See, for example, Eve Browning Cole and Susan Coltrap-McQuin, eds. *Explorations in Feminist Ethics* (Bloomington, Ind.: Indiana University Press, 1992), in which there is not a single reference to Kristeva but many to Gilligan. The links between French postmodernist or post-structuralist feminist ethics and American feminist ethics deserve further exploration.

62. Linda Hutcheon, *The Politics of Postmodernism,* p. 22.

63. Linda Alcoff, "Cultural Feminism Versus Post-Structuralism: The Identity Crisis in Feminist Theory," *Signs* 13, 1988: p. 307.

64. Eleanor Kuykendall, "Questions for Julia Kristeva's Ethics of Linguistics," *The Thinking Muse: Feminism and Modern French Philosophy,* ed. Jeffner Allen and Iris Marion Young (Bloomington, Ind.: Indiana University Press, 1989), p. 181.

65. Suzanne Clark and Kathleen Hulley, "An Interview with Julia Kristeva," p. 154.

66. Julia Kristeva, "The System and the Speaking Subject," trans. Toril Moi, *The Kristeva Reader,* pp. 29, 30.

67. Suzanne Clark and Kathleen Hulley, "An Interview with Julia Kristeva," p. 175.

68. Toril Moi, *Sexual/Textual Politics,* p. 171.

69. Rita Felski, *Beyond Feminist Aesthetics: Feminist Literature and Social Change* (Cambridge, Mass.: Harvard University Press, 1989), p. 39.

70. Ann Rosalind Jones, "Julia Kristeva on Femininity," p. 60.

71. Julia Kristeva, *In the Beginning Was Love,* p. 6.

72. Toril Moi, *Sexual/Textual Politics,* p. 171.

73. Julia Kristeva, "Women's Time," p. 199.

74. As Moi notes, "the opposition between feminine and masculine does not exist in pre-Oedipality." Toril Moi, *Sexual/Textual Politics,* p. 165. In "Freud and Love: Treatment and Its Discontents," *Tales of Love,* p. 26, Kristeva discusses Freud's theory of the "father in individual prehistory," with whom the subject identifies pre-Oedipally; she suggests that, "because there is no awareness of sexual difference during that period, . . . such a 'father' is the same as 'both parents'." Cf. Kelly Oliver, "Kristeva's Imaginary Father."

75. Hutcheon, *The Politics of Postmodernism,* p. 152.

76. I understand some of her critics' dismay that when Kristeva writes of such agentic, avant-garde transgression, she usually discusses male writers like Joyce or Mallarmé. Yet, a similar view of aesthetic practices as transgressive, oppositional, and potentially transformative is expressed by African-American feminist theorists like Alice Walker and bell hooks (also an advocate of postmodernism; see her "An Aesthetic of Blackness," *Yearning,* pp. 103–13.). Of course, there is a significant difference between celebrating the agency and creativity of those in dominant groups (and in the canon) and those in marginalized or oppressed groups, for whom art and other forms of creativity may serve different purposes.

77. Elizabeth Grosz, *Sexual Subversions,* p. 234.

78. Kristeva links ethics and aesthetics: "Our notion of the ethical as coextensive with textual practice separates us from the 'scientific morality' that would like to form a normative, albeit apparently libertarian, ethics based on knowledge." Julia Kristeva, *Revolution in Poetic Language*, p. 234.

79. Suzanne Clark and Kathleen Hulley, "An Interview with Julia Kristeva," pp. 176, 167, 179.

80. Ibid., p. 167.

81. Julia Kristeva, *Strangers to Ourselves*, trans. Leon S. Roudiez (New York: Columbia University Press, 1991), p. 173.

82. Iris Marion Young shows how even Kristeva's more explicitly psychoanalytic work can have political uses beyond those to which Kristeva herself puts it. Young effectively uses Kristeva's concept of the "abject" (central in *Powers of Horror*) to analyze some people's loathing of or aversion to groups of others—loathing expressed in racism, sexism, homophobia, ageism, xenophobia, ableism—when the subject's own boundaries feel threatened. Iris Marion Young, *Justice and the Politics of Difference* (Princeton: Princeton University Press, 1990), pp. 146–153.

83. Suzanne Clark and Kathleen Hulley, "An Interview with Julia Kristeva," p. 164.

84. Ibid., p. 171.

85. Julia Kristeva, "Women's Time," p. 209. Feminist theorists are divided about whether surpassing or embracing sexual difference is the proper feminist goal. Kristeva suggests in "Stabat Mater" the possibility of "an acknowledgment of what is irreducible, of the irreconcilable interest of both sexes in asserting their differences, in the quest of each one—and of women, after all—for an appropriate fulfillment." Julia Kristeva, "Stabat Mater," p. 184.

86. Suzanne Clark and Kathleen Hulley, "An Interview with Julia Kristeva,", p. 168. Kristeva is often accused of positive essentialism (idealizing women or maternity), negative essentialism (representing women as "other," as "foreign"), or of effacing, if not erasing, both "Woman" and real women as a distinct group with concrete political interests. These have been major problems for much feminist theory, though, and I'd like to suggest that often Kristeva seems to play with a kind of tactical and temporary essentialism.

87. Julia Kristeva, *Strangers to Ourselves*, p. 181.

88. Ibid., p. 182.

89. Kelly Oliver, "Kristeva's Imaginary Father," p. 61. Patricia Elliot makes a similar point, arguing that "a feminist ethics would aim at the dissolution or the demystification of identity, including its own," and would be "based on the refusal of any fixed identity for women," Patricia Elliot, *From Mastery to Analysis*, pp. 222–23; she sees Kristeva's as such a feminist ethics, as I do. But such "demystifications" of gender and identity are also, as I've been arguing, common to postmodern thought.

90. Elizabeth Grosz, *Sexual Subversions*, p. xvii.

13

Trans-Positions of Difference:
Kristeva and Post-structuralism

Tilottama Rajan

Deconstruction, used synonymously with the term post-structuralism, is often seen as denying the existence of anything outside language. This chapter begins with the assumption that the two are not identical: that post-structuralism is a recent version of a larger movement better described as post-organicist and post-phenomenological than as post-structuralist. Questioning the identity of the *logos* and the unitary subject, this larger movement sees the subject as constructed *in* but not necessarily *by* representation. Post-structuralism, by contrast, is a form of deconstruction that has been mediated by the structuralist reduction of the subject to an effect of social or linguistic structure. It goes beyond structuralism to mount a critique of the sign that had already occurred in deconstruction before the rediscovery of Saussure, as a critique of representation or the image undertaken by phenomenology through the vocabulary of presence and absence. But it also continues the *structuralist* tradition in emphasizing the priority of *langue* over *parole*, of language as a system of differences over the individual utterance.

In focusing on the work of Kristeva I shall try to retrieve an alternative tradition within deconstruction, so as to reframe "post-structuralism" and also to reconsider what constitutes theory. It is well known that Kristeva criticizes Saussurean linguistics and its structuralist developments for a formalism at odds with an ethics of linguistics. Her early work focuses on the generation of structures, and thus on a process or materiality anterior to the signifier. Her challenge to the linguistic model, however, is not simply *post*-structuralist, involving as it does a critique of grammatology as complicit with what it challenges. Thus she positions herself with *and* against the theorists of classical post-structuralism: Derrida, Lacan, and implicitly Foucault.[1] Her difference from de Man is more a matter of a turn in our own intellectual history from the dominance of Yale post-structuralism to a theorist whose current impact signals our own desire for a revision of post-structuralism.

This difference/deferral can be focused through the metaphor of the body as an explicit or effaced figure in the texts of Kristeva and her male contemporaries. Her work in semiotics, culminating in her theory of the genotext, is an attempt not just to see the unconscious as structured like a language, but also to read language as a body. This is in no sense a return to a myth of presence, since the body is conceived in terms of differential pulsions that preclude its being the site of any prereflective immediacy. Kristeva's concern with the body rather than language as the site of difference can be traced back to Nietzsche's *Birth of Tragedy* and *Will to Power,* both strong texts within a post-structuralism whose promotion of the linguistic absolute is thus contested by its own past.[2] But it also links her to the phenomenological concern with the subject's being in the world or (dis)embodiment, thus suggesting that what may be unique about her work is its theorizing of a symbiotic space between deconstruction and phenomenology. To link Kristeva to phenomenology may seem puzzling, given her own critical use of the word. But in this respect she simply accepts Derrida's reduction of phenomenology to the idealism of Husserl, and thus identifies it not only with the transcendental ego but also with Saussurean linguistics.[3] It is, however, useful to distinguish between transcendental (Husserlian) and existential phenomenology. The latter studies affective states such as nausea or cognitive processes like perception and signification, not in purely formal terms but as modes of being in the world that involve the interdetermination of subject and object. While phenomenology is thus characterized by a focus on the subject, it does not necessarily entail a theory of the unitary subject. Indeed Sartre's radical studies of perception in the form of the gaze, and his interest in borderline states like nausea and masochism, call the boundaries of this subject into question. Moreover, as Drew Leder has recently shown, even Merleau-Ponty's more traditional studies of embodiment are on the threshold of a radicalization effected by recognizing the visceral body as the site of the subject's absence from herself.[4]

To locate a phenomenological strand in Kristeva's recent work seems logical enough, given her interest in affective states like melancholia and love. This interest goes back to *Powers of Horror,* which analyzes abjection in ways that are phenomenological and anthropological as well as psychoanalytic. Thus the pre-texts for Kristeva's analysis of the abject include not only Bataille and Mary Douglas, but also Sartre's study of the nausea aroused by the viscous as a form of being that is neither subject nor object and that thus threatens the dualisms necessary to maintain the bounded ego.[5] As significantly, Kristeva's later texts are marked by the intermittent use of the first person: an auto-graphing characteristic of phenomenological writing. However, an unthematized phenomenological element can be said to exist even in her early work. For one thing her focus on the *processes* by which structures are engendered is Romantic as well as psychoanalytic and Marxist. As important, her concern with the subject's relation to the signifier is really a concern with the subject's linguistically mediated being-in-the-world. This is not to say that her work can be identified with phenomenology any more than with psychoanalysis or feminism. Rather the term is a way of articulating Kristeva's difference from post-structuralism, and is itself a difference within her work. Her assimilation of phenomenology functions as a theoretical facilitator that allows her to develop a post-phenomenological concern with the subject as distinct from subjectivity, and is thus an ethical rather than a metaphysical move. In other words Kristeva does not use phenomenology as a position from which she can reestablish the category of the subject, but as a trans-position in which the subject returns as the condition of possibility for restoring ethics to linguistics.

Indeed Kristeva's work as a whole is best described as trans-positional, and thus as an extension of her concept of intertextuality[6] to theory itself as an interdisciplinary practice. We shall return later to Kristeva's choice of the discipline of semiotics as an envelope for this project. What she attempts within this framework is a transposition of linguistics into psychoanalysis which she calls semanalysis, and which she further intertextualizes with social practice in a way quite distinct from Lacan. Semanalysis is not simply a reading of psychoanalysis in terms of Jakobsonian and Saussurean linguistics (which reading, as done by Lacan, Kristeva takes for granted). It is also a counter-formalist re-reading of linguistics through psychoanalysis, so as to shift attention from structures to the process of their generation, from the signifier to the semiotic. The further reframing of psychoanalysis by "practice" is one on which she comments in *Polylogue*. Noting that the Freudian unconscious has made it possible to understand more fully the notions of difference, process, and generation in the Hegelian dialectic,[7] Kristeva then diverges from Lacan's sublimation of Hegel into Freud, to pose the question of a more genuine intertextuality between the two: "Is this to say that, through its kinship with Hegel, the Freudian discovery is susceptible to a reversal analogous to the one that materialism effects upon the Hegelian system, that is to say to . . . an opening of so-called psychoanalytic processes towards the field of sociohistorical contradictions?"[8] To the triad of linguistics, psychoanalysis, and social practice, Kristeva adds a fourth inter-discipline: that of literature. Where Lacan simply uses literature (as in the case of Poe's "Purloined Letter") to demonstrate a thesis about the subversion of the subject, Kristeva uses it to effect something that psychoanalysis does not do and which must nonetheless be constantly tempered by the latter. Criticizing implicitly the ideological investments of psychoanalysis as a (male) institution, she comments on "the silence of psychoanalysis on the literary function insofar as it is a subversion of the symbolic and a putting into process of the subject."[9]

i.

One of the more striking features of Kristeva's early work is her habit of alluding to other traditions and theorists: to Artaud, Bataille, Lacan, to Nietzsche, and Hegel. Unlike Derrida, who typifies the discipline of philosophy in assuming the history of ideas to be a history of error, Kristeva reads the approaches she cites for their corrective potential as well as for their inadequacies. Thus she develops a theoretical practice which is in some ways unique, although its elements exist unthematized in other practitioners of theory as a discourse that draws together (to syncretize rather than to intertextualize) various disciplines. This practice is very much that of a subject-in-process. Reframing one theoretical discourse through another, Kristeva makes us aware of each discourse as a trans-position involved in a supplementary interplay with other discourses from which it differs. Likewise the names she cites do not function within a positivist intellectual history in which she locates a theoretical identity for herself as part of a tradition, but rather function as signifiers which indicate what is left unsaid by some other name that is itself the temporary signifier of a difference.

The containing form for this trans-positional activity is "semiotics," a word that figures in the title of Kristeva's first collection *Semeiotike* (1969), as well as in the *Essays in Semiotics* that she coedited in 1971. But semiotics itself is no more than a theoretical facilitator, an empty form that functions in the manner of the pronoun "I" as described by Benveniste, to whose work she has always been sympathetic. The semiotics to which Kristeva refers is thus a shifter that offers her an enunciative position within the syntactic field of theory, from which she can begin to sketch out something which, as she herself says, is radically different from what either Saussure or Peirce had in mind when they first used the term. This trans-position is both inside and outside linguistics, allowing Kristeva to take account of but also to contest the major developments in theory after Saussure. For semiotics, even as defined by Saussure, goes beyond a focus on the signifier to study the life of signs *in society*. Moreover, in Kristeva's phenomenological sub-version of it, it is also the study of the prelinguistic signifiers that form the conditions of possibility for signs, while also challenging the very ideology of the sign as communication between subjects already interpellated into the symbolic order.

It is of symptomatic importance that the word "semiotic" doubles as the name of a discipline (*la sémiotique*) that includes but is not confined to linguistics, and also as the name of the signifying stratum (*le sémiotique*) that subverts the hegemony of the linguistic paradigm. Semiotics, according to Kristeva, has its beginnings in the recognition that signs "are articulated by a syntax of differences."[10] At the same time, its broader range of concerns is in the process not only of challenging the positivism on which semiotics itself was founded, but also of intertextually transforming the study of language itself. Semiotics, in other words, is not simply the colonization of other signifying practices by linguistics, brought about by various forms of structuralism. In transposing linguistics into the study of fields like magic, alchemy, and zoosemiotics, it becomes a site for re-reading the very assumptions of the linguistic ideology. This ideology can take two forms that are reversed mirror images of each other: that of a positivism that confines communication to the realm of the sign as the union of signifier and signified, and that of a post-structuralism focused on the nonsignifying aporia produced by their failure to coincide.

Kristeva's semiotic project emerges in several texts, one of the earliest being *Essays in Semiotics*. The collection is interesting for its interdisciplinarity, including, along with Derrida's "*Sémiologie et grammatologie,*" Thomas Sebeok's article on chemical signs, which studies, as a system potentially present in human communication, how animals imprint themselves on their environment so as to communicate across the boundaries of time and species. This interest in the nonlinguistic signifier is also a concern of Kristeva's *Language: The Unknown,* which looks at how language has been used and theorized both historically and across different fields, to show that the current model of language is only one among many. Briefly, this model has as its basis "the *concept* as the model interpretant of the elements of language," thus excluding systems like dreams from the category "language."[11] Moreover, the dyadic structure of signifier/signified leads to a representational theory of signs, in which the signifier is removed from "that which it [isn't], but which it name[s] and arrange[s]."[12] The concern with the (im)possibility of representation limits language to a narrowly semantic concept of meaning. The distinction between such meaning and a more broadly based concept of signification is crucial to Kristeva's work, culminating in her distinction between the phenotext and the genotext. If meaning belongs to the order of representation, signification can be "traced but not represented."[13] Meaning is "the *static* term for the mental image that results from the psychological *process* designated by the term *signification.* It is generally admitted that linguistics is concerned only with *meaning,* while *signification* is reserved for a vaster science, henceforth called *semiotics*, of which *semantics* is only a particular case."[14]

Kristeva's study of semiotics includes prealphabetic systems of writing oriented toward rhythm, current semiotic practices that function outside the epistemology of the sign, and also the communications systems of animals and birds, which can radically open up what we understand by the term signification. Crucial for our purposes is her discussion of gesture in *"Le geste, pratique ou communication?"* which she suggests as a paradigm for other semiotic practices bearing a subversive relationship to the symbolic order of the sign.[15] "Gesturality" interests her because it is a "language" in the sense that it "transmits a message," but cannot be analyzed in terms of representational models tied to vision or audition.[16] It therefore opens up the possibility of signification without representation. Two aspects of gesturality are important for understanding how semiotics challenges linguistics. To begin with, the gesture is not only a message but also "the *work* which precedes the constitution of the sign," so that it transcends the dyadic structure of the sign as absent from that which it names. This "practical character" of gesturality,[17] however, does not make it an enactment of its meaning, as in the case of the performative, since the gesture does not so much enact meaning as the desire for meaning.[18] Secondly, gesturality is a way for Kristeva to posit a "productivity anterior to the product," and thus to representation.[19] This productivity (later called the semiotic) marks Kristeva as post-phenomenological in her theorizing of a prelinguistic signifier prior to representation.

ii.

Kristeva's critique of linguistics focuses for the most part on Saussurean linguistics and its derivatives. But although the Derridean notions of the gram and the trace challenge the positivism of this model,[20] grammatology, as she makes clear in *Revolution,* remains an attenuation of semiotics. Deconstructing the possibility of representation, the gram remains tied to its *im*possibility in a negative hypostasis of the logocentric reduction of signification to meaning. Kristeva, however, does not simply theorize a *différance* that deconstructs the phenotext and the symbolic order, but also materializes this difference as a genotext that can signify without meaning semantically. Her divergence from Derrida, despite her approving citation of *Speech and Phenomena,* can be seen in the use each makes of Husserl's distinction between indication and expression.

As Derrida summarizes Husserl, expression is equivalent to voice, as the exteriorizing, the immediate *presentation* of a signified. Indication, by contrast, is caught up in the deferrals of *écriture*: it uses one thing as a sign of something else, thus introducing the problem of *representation*. Undoing Husserl's attempt to posit two different kinds of signs, Derrida argues that expression is always already contaminated by indication. In other words, he uses the term "indication" simply to deconstruct the possibility of an ideal meaning associated with the term "expression." While Kristeva takes for granted this deconstruction of expression, what interests her is precisely Husserl's theorizing of two different kinds of signification: an expressive order that communicates meaning, and an order of marks and traces that signifies even though it does not mean.[21] Her interest is in indication as an autonomous category. Correspondingly, she constructs differences, where Derrida takes apart oppositions.

To put it differently, Derrida operates in the mode of critique, unsettling the economy of the sign by reducing it to the movement of the signifier. What is lost in this reduction is the sense of "a *real*, which previously had somehow to be signified."[22] Kristeva's semiotic materialism, as I shall describe it, is concerned with how this *real,* even though it is unsignifiable *in* language, can nevertheless be seen transversally *through* language. Crucial to this project are her well-known distinction between the semiotic and the symbolic, and the related differentiation of the genotext from the phenotext, terms which in *Revolution* take the place of productivity and the sign. Briefly, the symbolic is the order of representation, the entry into language and thus the stage at which propositions are enunciated and positions taken. But because the symbolic is also the order of law and patriarchy, this language is a "social effect of the relation to the other."[23] In the symbolic order, the subject must be re-presented through an image with which she is not identical. The resistance to this order comes from the semiotic, a region "hidden by the arrival of signification"[24] and preceding the division of subject and object in enunciation. Made up of pulsions and drives, the semiotic is associated with the (m)other's body, but conceived in de-idealized and nonpersonal terms.

Although Kristeva's distinction alludes to Lacan, it also rewrites Derrida by deliberately failing to coincide with the latter's opposition between writing and voice. Briefly, each of Kristeva's terms contains elements of each of Derrida's. The symbolic resembles the *logos* as the law of the same. Indeed the *logos* is an agent of the symbolic which is set in place by the binary division of the sentence into subject and predicate. On the other hand, the symbolic also lacks the self-identity of voice, and participates in the structures of writing as an order of representations in which "the subject must separate from and through his image."[25] But as a dispersal of the unified ego into the drives that (de)compose it, the semiotic also resembles *écriture* in being a process in which the imaginary unity of Derridean voice is lost. That it resembles the category of writing despite its nonlinguistic character is marked by the association of the term "semiotic" with the Derridean trace.[26] On the other hand, the semiotic is connected, if not to *logos,* at least to voice, by its association with music and vocal rhythms[27] and by a link with the body which makes it irreducible to the purely linguistic category of writing.

In transecting Derrida's categories, Kristeva draws distinctions not simply between these categories but also within them. Thus she separates the conservative affiliation of voice with the phallogocentric order, from voice as a figure for an interiority, now associated with the confused experience of the body rather than with the clarity of mind or spirit. As significant is the difference she discovers within the term "writing." She associates the tendency of *écriture* to rupture the security of the *logos* with the semiotic's interruption of the symbolic world of law and family. But its inscription of the subject in systems of signification that create a specular and displaced identity is associated with the symbolic. As important, she transgresses Derrida's alignment of the identity/*différance* distinction with a distinction between the material (voice) and the linguistic (writing). For Kristeva it is the linguistic sign that is the source of identity and the material (the body) that is a site of difference.

Kristeva's rewriting of grammatology cuts across the Derridean opposition between phenomenology and post-structuralism, by locating *différance* in a "pre-symbolic immediacy"[28] that precedes the linguistic signifier. While her semiotic materialism allows her to put *différance* back into the experience of a subject-in-process, it also has political ramifications that she makes explicit in *Revolution.* By conflating the revolutionary potential of the semiotic and the conservative thrust of the symbolic within the category of writing, Derrida neutralizes the political effectiveness of *différance.* He allows the energy of the *chora,* which disperses the representations of the symbolic, to be converted into the subject's dispersal within the symbolic. Thus Kristeva, while conceding the importance of grammatology as a radicalization of Hegelian negativity,[29] also dismisses it as essentially flawed. For even as he criticizes Hegel for recuperating the resistance of negativity to the thetic within the teleological movement of the dialectic, Derrida's supposedly nonsynthetic difference falls into a different kind of positivity:

> In the course of this operation, negativity has become positivised and
> drained of its potential for producing breaks. It holds itself back and

appears as a delaying [*retardement*], it defers and thus becomes merely positive and affirmative, it inscribes and institutes through retention:[30]

By renouncing the dialectical, Derrida, in other words, "neutralizes productive negativity."[31] He renders negativity positive by default, retaining if not affirming, and thus losing the possibility of major breaks in a micrological movement of traces that is indifferent to the "'terms,' 'dichotomies,' and 'oppositions'" that Hegelian negativity concentrates, reactivates and generates."[32]

iii.

Kristeva's relationship to Lacan is harder to pin down because she is seldom overtly critical of him. Indeed she is often dismissed as Lacan's dutiful daughter,[33] despite her attempt to reorient the discourse of psychoanalysis around a maternal function that necessarily cannot be conceived outside of a diacritical relation to the paternal function. That Kristeva is quite consciously unable to overcome the anxiety of Freudian and Lacanian influence is due in part to her belief that the subject must always operate within the symbolic. But her reluctance to make a programmatic break with Lacan can also be attributed to her sense that psychoanalysis is already a double discourse: a knotting or re-turning of the grammatological model (with its abstracting of Freudian into linguistic terminology) into the materiality that the latter seems to have left behind. Thus the "psychoanalytic intervention in the field of language" has, at least potentially, the effect of thwarting "the crushing of the signified by the signifier."[34] Moreover, a further reason why Kristeva may not see a paradox in her use of a Lacanian idiom is that Lacanian psychoanalysis cannot be identified only with Lacan himself. Crucial to the use of psychoanalysis as a sub-version of Derridean grammatology,[35] are the concepts of letters, of the imaginary, and of desire. These concepts bring back the affective dimension of language and symbolization. They do so, as we shall see, because of their own constitution on the trace of a phenomenology that remains intertextually present in the ascetic submission of psychology to the discipline of linguistics.

Rather than seeing Kristeva's relationship to Lacan as her interpellation into the Oedipal structure of the critical family, we can see it as an instantiation of her own theories of positioning and intertextuality. Lacan affords her an enunciative position within the symbolic order of theory, from which she can pursue a project that might otherwise be dismissed as romantic, by effecting a transgression of the symbolic that is produced within and *by* that order itself. Lacan signifies, among other things, a correction of the phenomenological tradition that runs from Hegel through Hyppolite and Kojève to Sartre. But Lacanian psychoanalysis is itself an absorption of phenomenology into grammatology and thus a trans-position.[36] Lacan's appropriation of Hegel by way of Hyppolite and Kojève is well known. Less well-known is the genealogy connecting him to Sartre, by way of the concepts of the imaginary, being-for-others, and the gaze or look. Lacanian psychoanalysis thus gives Kristeva a point of insertion into the discourse of theory that we should think of not as a filial identity but as a mobile position. The notion of positioning, as distinct from interpellation, is one that Kristeva implicitly derives from Benveniste as a way of describing the relationship of the subject-in-process to the symbolic order. Like pronouns in language, theoretical names are not so much sources of identity as shifters which provide Kristeva with a place from which she can articulate a simultaneous inscription in and sub-version of the existing theoretical order. We can approach Lacanian psychoanalysis by beginning not with Lacan himself, but with Serge Leclaire's concept of letters. Seemingly in the tradition of Lacan, his *Psychanalyser* is actually an intertextual transformation of "the agency of the letter in the unconscious." According to Leclaire letters are marks imprinted in the child's body by the mother who, through her caresses, uses a process of differentiation to designate certain zones as erotogenic. Thereafter these affective sites become signifiers: for example the phallus is a "part of the body . . . *and, at the same time, a letter* which can be called the alpha and omega of the alphabet of desire." Letters, however, "cannot be abstracted from the libidinal movement of the body which produces [them] as mark and mask."[37] As physical sites that are already signifiers, they mark conversely the materiality of symbolic signifiers that function as the body's symptomatic displacement in language:

> It is this elective anchoring of a letter (gramma) in a movement of the body which constitutes the unconscious element, the signifier in the true sense of the word. The signifier is as much body as it is letter, it has a somatic and palpable aspect.[38]

Lacan's notion of the letter, by contrast, involves a radical textualization. Although he describes the signifier as a "material" support,[39] he uses the notion of materiality as the opposite of phenomenality, and not to evoke affectivity or embeddedness in history. Where phenomenality suggests the transparency of the signifier to the signified, materiality suggests the fundamental opacity of self-consciousness. Leclaire agrees with Lacan that the unconscious is a letter rather than a meaning. But his argument is framed by the somewhat different project of showing that Freud is both textual and biological, and interimplicates organicism and structuralism in a diacritical dynamic. Alluding to Lacan's concept of the letter,[40] Leclaire thus reconnects language to the body, in a paradoxical relationship that he describes as "abstract materiality."[41] We can note further that when Lacan follows the path of the letter as *"la lettre l'être et l'autre"* in his seminar on Poe's *Purloined Letter*,[42] he charts it as the site of the adult subject's alienation in the symbolic. Leclaire also sees the letter as inscribed within the desire of the other. But he is more concerned with its origins in a prethetic experience that operates transversally to the symbolic.

Leclaire's discussion of letters intersects in interesting ways with Kristeva's slightly later concept of the *chora*. The letter according to Leclaire is the unconscious of the sign: an "oscillating pulsation" that is always in danger of being reduced to the fixity of the sign which constitutes the subject as ego.[43] The semiotic letter is first and foremost a transposition of phenomenology into post-structuralism, as distinct from the *Aufhebung* of the one in the other that we find in Lacan. But while letters as libidinally charged signifiers are points of phenomenological contact between what for Lacan are the dichotomous orders of the symbolic and the real (or the world of appearance and the in-itself), they do not have their origin in a body whose presence to itself would make it the ground of a transcendental ego. The letter expresses what Drew Leder describes as the chiasmatic character of the body, as a place where one is neither quite origin nor effect.[44] For one thing, the significance of the letter is tied up with its production by the (m)other.[45] This sense of the body as inscription is implicit in both the terms "letters" and "semiotic," and constitutes a rethinking of Merleau-Pontian embodiment through a transposition of phenomenology into psychoanalysis.

Leclaire's work provides a ground from which we can discuss Kristeva's attempt to make psychoanalytic and social practice continuous. To begin with, where Lacan locates the agency of the letter *within* the symbolic, using it to mark the instability of an order in which the signifier acts separately from its signification, the letter for Leclaire is grammatological but also presymbolic. This notion of a signifying material that operates outside the symbolic is crucial to what Leclaire does not undertake: namely to Kristeva's project of remobilizing as irruption and the heterogeneous what grammatology reduces to the trace and *différance*.[46] Secondly, Leclaire's account of the formation of letters clarifies what seems to be the undecidable status of drives in Kristeva's work. That drives are socially inscribed signifiers is marked by the word "letters," but these signifiers are imprinted in the body in such a way that they acquire a biological force. This paradox may explain an aspect of Kristeva's work that is potentially troubling to North American feminists: namely the fact that she sees attitudes to the mother as culturally learned, but then seems to endow the abjecting of the mother with the primal power of a drive.

So far we have discussed Kristeva's relationship to psychoanalysis as a critical attempt to find a discourse that will allow her to develop a semiotic materialism. It remains to explore her relationship to Lacan, whose work she has criticized for failing "to give status to affect and to the heterogeneity it introduces."[47] In palimpsestically rewriting Lacan's distinction between the imaginary and the symbolic as her own distinction between the semiotic and the symbolic, she displaces and opens up what remains in his work a politically sterile opposition, while also laying herself open to the possible framing of her own project inside his framework within which the imaginary is held captive by the symbolic. Briefly, the relationship between the two orders in Lacan is not so much dialectical as parallel, while Kristeva's terms are an attempt to reactivate the dialectic reduced by the trace-structure of parallelism. That the Lacanian imaginary is not an alternative to but a sublimatory pre-text for the symbolic is apparent if we think of the mirror stage as a narrative of the relationship between the two orders. The child at first identifies with his image in the mirror, only to recognize that it is an image, thereby crossing the threshold from the imaginary into the symbolic. Inasmuch as it is the mother (as socially constructed subject) who holds the child up before the mirror, the child's jubilant image of himself is already an interpellation into the syntax of the family. Where the imaginary differs from the symbolic is in the way the subject grasps the specular representation of his identity: namely as visual and synchronic rather than linguistic and temporal, and thus as immediate rather than mediated. The imaginary and symbolic are ways of relating to representation, involving, in Lacan's own terms, introjection and projection respectively.[48] They differ only in that the symbolic, as Jane Gallop suggests, appears as "a tear in the fabric of the imaginary,"[49] forcing the subject to experience her identity in the mode of alienation rather than identification.

The function of the symbolic is best approached in terms of the way Lacan distributes the elements of difference and identity between the two orders. The imaginary creates a world of illusory identities (or imagos) impermeable to difference. Although the symbolic can become the locus of the subject's interpellation into the status quo, as an order of representations it demystifies the imaginary presence of identity. The resulting sense of the subject as "absent from the signifier" in Kristeva's words[50] gives the symbolic a purely critical function for Lacan. It is not, as in Kristeva, a way for the subject to position herself within an admittedly repressive order; consequently its negativity remains unconnected to a positivity and thus without issue. On one level Lacan's valorization of the symbolic over the imaginary recalls Freud's choice of the reality principle over the pleasure principle in the sequence of normal human development.[51] At the same time we can speculate that Lacan's identification with Freud, or with a Freud reprocessed through Saussure, is from Kristeva's point of view a (mis)recognition that becomes the site of a splitting of Lacan as (author)ity. For insofar as the symbolic is the order of law and patriarchy, its status in the political economy of Lacan's text is different from its status in Freud. It is not embraced as a necessary stage in the conquest of the id by the ego, but is valorized over the imaginary largely by default. Although the imaginary is a form of narcissism, acceptance of the symbolic is a stoicism that leaves unvoiced a certain desire in Lacan's text.

Kristeva's own distinction is an attempt to articulate what she might see as the political unconscious of Lacan's texts by voicing this desire. In so doing she takes up the intertextual traces that form part of the genealogy of the imaginary. For the concept of the imaginary had already played a crucial role in Sartre, who likewise anticipates the Lacanian notion of the symbolic in recognizing that being is always a relationship to the other. As the subject's flight from this representation by and as the other, the Sartrean imaginary constructs a form of being-in-itself in which the power of negation functions as the ground of the subject's freedom.[52] Lacan's version of this opposition renounces Sartre's nostalgia for being, and crucial to this deconstruction is his subversion of opposition by parallelism, a figure that divests the imaginary of its function as an alternative world. But since Sartre himself recognizes that the imaginary is in bad faith, the deconstruction on one level seems superfluous, as though deliberately blind to the tension between desire and argument in Sartre's texts. For Sartre's word, "imaginary" deconstructs as a nothingness the much more positive romantic notion of the "imagination" to which it alludes transversally, functioning simultaneously to block and to project a transformative relationship between the imaginary and the world of being-for-others. Or to put it differently, the Sartrean imaginary assumes a dialectical relationship toward the world it opposes, but only on an affective and not on a cognitive level.

That Lacan himself was at one point sensitive to the constitutive role of the imaginary is evident from the essay on the mirror stage. Nevertheless in aligning the imaginary/symbolic relation with the distinction between identity and difference, in work after "The Mirror Stage," Lacan confines the imaginary to the realm of narcissistic identity, and affiliates resistance to the symbolic with fantasy and escape. In contrast, Kristeva, by replacing the imaginary with the semiotic, legitimizes resistance as revolutionary by affiliating it with difference. Crucial to her revision of Lacan is a de-idealization of the imaginary which reasserts its materiality by way of a connection to the body and to the real rather than to the private and protected space of fantasy. For the semiotic, as is indicated by the word's connection to the trace, cannot be a source of identity. At the same time, as a site of difference it reconceives the Lacanian representation of difference as a process operating purely within the symbolic, where it is drained of both affect and effect. Thus the concept of the semiotic reclaims the project of freedom (de)constructed by the Sartrean imaginary, dropping the term imaginary so as to avoid its association with illusion, while reinscribing the reference to imagination through the fact that the privileged terrain of semiosis is the poetic. Crucial to the rewriting of the imaginary as the semiotic is the replacement of Sartrean negation by negativity.[53] Because the imaginary was a *negation* of the actual world, it was a predicative faculty which posited an alternative world in bad faith, and which generated a binary and undialectical opposition between the construction and demystification of this world. The semiotic as negativity is the *process* of rejecting thetic formulations, without being reducible to a formulation constituted as a rejection of another formulation. That the interaction of the semiotic and the symbolic may still require a further element in order for it to amount to a praxis is a point to which we shall return.

If the semiotic is a re-vision of the imaginary, negativity is similarly a reworking of Lacanian desire: itself the site of a fault in Lacan's linguistic armature. Kristeva's own reluctance to foreground the term "desire" (despite an appropriateness to her work sensed by her English translators) can be seen as a rejection of Lacan (in her sense of the word "rejection").[54] Her most explicit treatment of desire is as part of a sequence of concepts including Heideggerian *cura,* that stand in place of and reduce the radicalism of negativity.[55] Locating desire as a post-phenomenological displacement of negativity into the language of psychoanalysis, she criticizes the Lacanian concept on two grounds. First of all Lacan focuses on desire itself to the exclusion of its absent cause, thus detaching desire from any reference to the real and reducing it to a movement of the signifier. Secondly, because desire cannot be satisfied, it becomes deradicalized as "an always already accomplished subjugation of the subject to lack.[56] Kristeva's difference from Lacan is stated more positively in "*Le sujet en procès,*" where she disaffiliates desire from its Lacanian definition. Here she argues that what is important in desire is not the metonymic nature of an object which exposes it as illusory, but the production of desire itself as a process in which the object is no more than a heuristic fiction, "permitting the articulation of rejection in social practice."[57]

In tracing the history of desire from Hegel to Lacan, Judith Butler likewise sees Lacan as attenuating the concept in two ways. He denies that desire can be materialized through language, even indirectly. He also displaces the agency of desire from the subject to the unconscious,[58] itself conceived as a signifier and not a location. This absorption of desire within the signifier is, however, unsettled by the genotextual desire aroused through Lacan's own use of the signifier. Crucial to his attempt to represent desire as a process without a subject is his blocking of a conceptual syntax in which there would be a subject of the predicate, a subject of desire. At the same time by making "desire" occupy the position of both verb and (pro)noun, so that it seems to have no subject except the activity that it names, Lacan creates what Neil Hertz in another context calls a pathos of uncertain agency.[59] In other words, his language generates a syntactic desire for the subject it withholds and which continues to inhabit his text as a trace that cannot be deleted. This pathos, to which Kristeva's re-reading of Lacan responds, can only be explained historically. For contrary to what she indicates, in a genealogy of desire that jumps from Hegelian desire as the will of an absolute subject[60] to Lacanian desire as the subversion of the subject, desire is not a post-phenomenological concept. Rather it is through the phenomenological re-readings of desire by Alexandre Kojève and more particularly Jean Hyppolite that Lacanian psychoanalysis emerges as a deconstruction of Hegelian idealism: a deconstruction founded on the ascetic acceptance of the latter's failure, and thus on the trace of a desire in which it too is implicated.

Briefly, Hyppolite's commentary on Hegel focuses on desire as the site of the subject's alienation in the perceptual field of the other, and as the expression of consciousness's inability to be the foundation of its own self-certainty.[61] His account of desire is so radically different from Hegelian *Begierde* as to verge on a deconstruction, *except* that the negativity traversing the nonidentical subject remains, as in Hegel, something to be worked on and transformed. As important the concerns with the other and with lack that Lacan derives from both Hyppolite and Sartre, are played out in terms of the problem of (self)consciousness. The result is that perception and intersubjectivity, motifs that are transcoded into the theme of the signifier as we move from phenomenology to post-structuralism, are still approached as modes of being in the world.

Kristeva's choice of "negativity" to replace "desire" is clearly an allusion to Hegel, in whose concern with the *movement* rather than the predication of the Concept she sees the earliest version of semiotic productivity.[62] But it is also an allusion to Hyppolite, who specifically couples the two terms. As such it re-turns Lacanian psychoanalysis to the desire it has effaced. However, her choice of the word "negativity" should be read genotextually, as differing from and deferring Lacan, rather than phenotextually, as positing her identification with Hegel or Hyppolite. As she herself indicates, she uses the term allusively, as a way of linking "the signifying subject . . . to 'objective' struggles in nature and society,"[63] or as a way of disrupting the discourse of psychoanalysis by introducing into it a heterogeneous signifier that causes us to rethink it. She defers the teleological implications that the word has historically acquired by linking it to the concept of expenditure (*dépense*) in Bataille,[64] a thinker who devotes himself partly to deconstructing Hegel's notion of history as a restricted economy. But this link too is not an identity, because Bataille's sense of the heterogeneous energy to be found in various forms of bodily and social waste is too close to implying an unmediated attainment of *jouissance*. We must therefore approach Kristevan negativity intertextually, as a concept tied into and reframed within more than one theoretical network.

One of these networks is necessarily that of Lacanian desire. The most obvious reason to read negativity intertextually through desire is a cautionary one. The Lacanian concept suggests a certain opacity of consciousness to itself that the Hegelian term tends to veil. But in a curious way Lacan also supplements Kristeva, though it is a Lacan re-read through Kristeva herself so as to articulate a recognition that is not finally Lacanian. Where the semiotic as rejection is negative, Lacanian desire is positive, in the sense that it posits an object of desire. In Lacan himself, this movement is drained of any real positivity because the object is part of a series in which it is its function of substitution rather than the cultural specificity of the object that matters. But Kristeva's notion of the genotext, as a zone that is not linguistic but can be seen in language, is a specific attempt to recover the positivity of desire, as against Lacan's sense that desire cannot be materialized and is unreadable. The genotext requires a reader, in ways that Kristeva has not theorized:[65] it calls for a hermeneutic, which could not occur if there were not something posited, albeit not in a thetic way. While the semiotic is theorized as negativity, in other words, its negativity can function in social practice only if connected to the positivity of desire.

We can return now to a point earlier made: namely that the dialectic of the semiotic and the symbolic in Kristeva's early work seems to lack a mediating category necessary for the transposition of psychoanalysis into practice. Recognizing in *Revolution* that pure semiosis verges on psychosis, Kristeva insists that the subject must also function within the symbolic order. But the examples she provides (from Lautréamont and Mallarmé) of literature as "the *Aufhebung* of the semiotic in the symbolic"[66] seem more nearly semiotic than symbolic, and the dichotomizing of poetry as semiotic and narrative as symbolic is the symptomatic site of this inability to mediate between the two orders. On the other hand, when Kristeva deals with the social text, the problem occurs in reverse. Cultural phenomena like mysticism are attempts to posit the semiotic within the symbolic, which result in a cooptation of semiotic energy within social conformity. Recognizing the inescapability of the symbolic, Kristeva at times risks seeming more Lacanian than she means to be.

Briefly stated, the problem arises from the fact that in the earlier work Kristeva deletes the category of the imaginary as part of her revision of Lacan. She thus leaves herself with the symbolic as the only place where the positing of subjectivity can occur. The effect can be a deferring of the semiotic within the symbolic that is not unlike what she herself criticizes in Derrida. But more recently Kristeva has reintroduced the imaginary as a mediating term in the process operating between the semiotic and the symbolic, and as a means of intimating an ethics of positionality that would avoid pure negativity, while also allowing the positing of identity to function in excess of its inevitable recapture by the symbolic. An example is her concept of the imaginary father. As distinct from the paternal role constructed by the symbolic order, the imaginary father is a "conglomeration of the two parents . . . which is nevertheless to be considered as a father—not one severe and Oedipian, but a living and a loving father." The imaginary father is thus a negation of the symbolic father that posits an alternative, but only negatively, in the line of fiction. To construct such a father requires an imaginative act that resists the symbolic order. At the same time the choice of a father rather than a mother responds to the constraints of that very order, but in a strategic rather than capitulatory manner. For the father does not so much provide an identity for desire as a position, which for the present "permits the investing of our drives in the symbolic."[67]

The subject of the imaginary is further pursued in Kristeva's recent essay, "The Adolescent Novel." Departing from the references to narrative in *Revolution* to construct a homology between adolescence and narrative, Kristeva speaks here of the adolescent's "right to the imaginary." She argues that "imaginary activity . . . gives the subject an opportunity to construct a discourse that is not empty, but that he lives as authentic."[68] Adolescence is the one period in symbolic time when a subjectivity-in-process is socially sanctioned. Its condition of possibility is a semiotic negativity that results in the restless rejection of role after role, and in this respect it is the ideal form of both writing and analysis. For this negativity to express itself, however, the adolescent must try on a number of identities. Some of these will simply reproduce stereotypes so as to contain the semiotic within the symbolic, but some will be "genuine inscriptions of unconscious contents that flower in the adolescent pre-conscious."[69] It is clear here that the imaginary is a positive activity where the semiotic is negative, but that its positivity is positional rather than thetic. In other words the imaginary is paradoxically post-Oedipal and pre-Oedipal, linked to the polymorphous perverse. It constitutes a sub-version of the symbolic in two important ways. Although the identities with which the adolescent experiments are *shaped* by the symbolic order, their functioning may nevertheless transgress this order. For instance, the relationship between the subject and a symbolically pre-scribed enunciative position may be transgressive: a female subject may assume a masculine speaking position or vice-versa. Secondly, the relationship of the adolescent to her identity is not (self-)critical but immediate, and this immediacy is ethically, if not epistemologically, legitimate. In this respect Kristeva returns to Lacan's first formulation of the imaginary as an order of imagos. In "The Mirror Stage," Lacan had associated the imaginary with the formation of the ego, but "before its social determination, in a fictional direction."[70] In commenting on the mirror stage in *Revolution*, Kristeva herself had described the imago as the receptacle for a "voice that is projected from the agitated body,"[71] and had thus allied the imaginary with the subject as much as with the system. Picking up on Lacan's unelaborated antithesis between fiction and social determination, the later Kristeva, we can argue, also returns intertextually to the Sartrean imaginary as a magical reinscription of the actual, in which illusion and narcissism are complexly connected to imagination and freedom.

iv.

Kristeva's difference from classical post-structuralism, as we have suggested, is articulated through her concern with the body: a concern that allows her work to resonate in the three different registers of psychoanalysis, social practice, and phenomenology. The body, however, is in no sense a locus of self-presence. Indeed it might be helpful to set Kristeva's work beside Drew Leder's recent attempt to reconceive phenomenology after deconstruction by theorizing an absent body composed partly of visceral processes that we do not see and cannot represent. This body, as that which is neither wholly inside nor outside, is part of the theoretical content of Kristeva's work elaborated in such concepts as the *chora* and the genotext. However, it is more importantly a *signifier* for her difference from a post-structuralism whose use of *"écriture"* to signify *"différance"* is itself figurative.

As a theoretical figure the body suggests the involvement of *différance* in materiality and affect, and poses a counterweight to the abstraction of linguistics and rhetoric. But as significant as its use by Kristeva is its suppression in Foucault's subjection of the body to discourse, and in de Man's attempt to forget the literal resonances of terms like "defacement" and "disfiguration." I use the word "suppression" deliberately, to indicate that while the body is simply absent from structuralist theory, it persists as a ghostly presence in a post-structuralism whose genealogy is marked as much by its effacement of phenomenology as by its derivation from structuralism. Neil Hertz has recently pointed out that de Man's highly abstract writings are punctuated by figures of anatomical dismemberment and mutilation.[72] Moreover, the body surfaces subtextually in such seemingly incorporeal and rhetorical terms as "disfiguration" or the undoing of a figure.

The metamorphoses of the body allow us to conclude by commenting on the intervention made by Kristeva in the field of theory. The notion of ends—whether it be the end of the book, of metaphysics, or of man himself—has come to dominate the rhetoric of theory. Intertwined with an idealism that forgets the material in the linguistic, the rhetoric of the end disturbingly recalls Hegelian pronouncements about the end of history. This end, for Hegel, was to be accomplished through an *Aufhebung* of art in philosophy, and of phenomenology in logic. In repeating the end of art as the end of man, post-structuralism puts theory in the place occupied by philosophy or logic in the Hegelian system. Yet the *Aufhebung* of criticism in theory is also profoundly at odds with the goals of theory, which announces itself as different from, as deferring, philosophy. The body as an explicit or effaced figure in post-structuralist theory thus becomes one locus for what de Man equivocally calls the resistance to theory. The historical psychodynamics governing Anglo-American appropriations of the theoretical Other are the subject of another paper. Nevertheless it is worth noting that insofar as French theory for the past two decades has provided us with a specular window beckoning us into imaginary identification with an array of theoretical positions, we too are implicated in this resistance.

The resistance to the linguistic ideology is an explicit part of Kristeva's agenda. But where the body is a disciplined or effaced presence it becomes the site of an unthematized resistance to a theory whose rhetoric betrays itself as an apocalyptic displacement of Hegelian teleology. The figure of dis-figuration, for instance, configures in its very structure the continued reference of de Manian rhetoric to what it puts under erasure: namely the subject and the material, the phenomenology that Hegel could not surpass in logic. We could not talk of a self-resistance were it not for the pathos that haunts the writing of both de Man and Foucault, and that invites a symptomatic reading of their rhetoric. That pathos is only augmented by the self-critical presence of phenomenology in the past of both thinkers. This

past allows us to situate the abstraction privileged by theory within a phenomenology of cultural forms like that attempted in the early years of this
century by Wilhelm Worringer. Abstraction, according to Worringer, is
linked to a desire for transcendence on the part of a subject who is not
empathically at home in the world.[73] As such it expresses an impulse in theory that is analogous to the Hegelian *Aufhebung,* the forgetting of matter
in spirit. The effaced figure of the body suspends this project within its cultural moment. As an uncanny element in de Man's *corpus,* it is the site of
a certain haunting: a haunting of post-structuralism by phenomenology
and psychology, of abstraction by the figures that mark abstraction itself
as a figure, and of philosophy or spirit by the image and the imaginary. That
haunting, in turn, generates what de Man calls "resistance": the resistance
to itself that makes post-structuralism theory and not philosophy, and the
resistance that now seems to be leading us beyond post-structuralism to a
rediscovery, in the mirror of French theory, of Kristeva as a figure for our
own return to the absent body.

Notes

1. Kristeva tacitly alludes to Foucault in 1974 when she speaks of a "'discourse' which is
   not a mere depository of thin linguistic layers, an archive of structures, or the testimony
   of a withdrawn body." Julia Kristeva, *Revolution in Poetic Language,* trans. Margaret
   Waller (New York: Columbia University Press, 1984), p. 16. By this time Foucault had
   already published "L'Ordre du discours" (1971) as well as "Nietzsche, Genealogy, History" (1971), in which he speaks of a "body totally imprinted by history and the
   process of history's destruction of the body" (*Language, Counter-Memory, Practice:
   Selected Essays and Interviews,* trans. Donald F. Bouchard and Sherry Simon (Ithaca:
   Cornell UP, 1977), p. 148.

2. I discuss this connection in my essay, "Language, Music, and the Body: Nietzsche and
   Deconstruction," in *Intersections: Nineteenth-Century Philosophy and Contemporary
   Theory,* ed. Tilottama Rajan and David Clark (Albany, N.Y.: State University of
   New York Press, forthcoming).

3. Julia Kristeva, *Language: The Unknown: An Initiation Into Linguistics,* trans. Anne M.
   Menke (New York: Columbia University Press, 1989), p. 221. When Kristeva writes about
   a phenomenological tradition other than the Husserlian one she is much more positive,
   as in her discussion of Kierkegaard, whom she nevertheless criticizes for a lack of concern with social processes. *Revolution in Poetic Language,* p. 125. Moreover, while for
   Derrida Husserl might well stand metonymically for Hegel, Kristeva reads the two very
   differently.

4. Drew Leder, *The Absent Body* (Chicago: University of Chicago Press, 1990),
   pp. 62–65.

5. I refer both to *Nausea* and to Sartre's discussion of the viscous in *Being and Nothingness*
   with which Kristeva, like all French intellectuals of her generation, would have been
   familiar. Kristeva refers to *Nausea* and uses the word as a synonym for abjection. Julia

Kristeva, *Powers of Horror: An Essay on Abjection*, trans. Leon Roudiez (New York: Columbia University Press, 1984), p. 146.

6. Julia Kristeva, *Revolution in Poetic Language*, p. 59.

7. Julia Kristeva, *Polylogue* (Paris: Editions du Seuil, 1977), p. 279.

8. Ibid., p. 280.

9. Ibid., p. 70.

10. Julia Kristeva, *Language: The Unknown*, p. 296.

11. Ibid., p. 15.

12. Ibid., p. 326.

13. Ibid., p. 17.

14. Ibid., pp. 37–8.

15. Julia Kristeva, *Semeiotiké: Recherches pour une sémanalyse* (Paris: Editions du Seuil, 1969), p. 99.

16. Ibid., pp. 93, 91.

17. Ibid., p. 93.

18. Ibid., p. 96.

19. Ibid., p. 93.

20. Julia Kristeva, *Semeiotiké*, pp. 37–8.

21. Ibid., pp. 97–8.

22. Julia Kristeva, *Language*, p. 327.

23. Julia Kristeva, *Revolution in Poetic Language*, p. 29.

24. Ibid., p. 40.

25. Ibid., p. 43.

26. Ibid., p. 40.

27. Ibid., p. 26.

28. Ibid., p. 69.

29. Ibid., p. 40.

30. Ibid., p. 141.

31. Ibid., p. 142.

32. Ibid., p. 141.

33. See for instance Elizabeth Grosz, *Jacques Lacan: A Feminist Introduction* (London: Routledge, 1990), p. 150.

34. Julia Kristeva, *Language*, p. 273.

35. Lacan obviously started writing much earlier than Derrida. However the impact of his work was felt at about the same time as Derrida's, and he himself developed in an increasingly (post-)structuralist direction under the emerging hegemony of the linguistic model. Thus it seems appropriate to see the relationship between the two as dialogical rather than chronological.

36. For a brief discussion of the effacement of the word "phenomenology" from Lacan's writing as it grows more (post-)structuralist, see Herbert Spiegelberg, *Phenomenology in Psychology and Psychiatry* (Evanston, Ill.: Northwestern University Press, 1972),

pp. 141–2. It is also worth mentioning Merleau-Ponty's citation of Lacan, as evidence of his own belief that phenomenology and psychoanalysis could be symbiotically related if not merged. See *The Primacy of Perception,* ed. James M. Edie (Evanston, Ill.: Northwestern University Press, 1964), pp. 136–7.

37. Serge Leclaire, *Psychanalyser, Un essai sur l'ordre de l'inconscient et la pratique de la lettre* (Paris: Editions du Seuil, 1968), pp. 163, 94 [translations mine].

38. From "Les éléments en jeu dans une psychanalyse," quoted by Anika Lemaire, *Jacques Lacan,* trans. David Macey (London: Routledge and Kegan Paul, 1979), pp. 144–5.

39. Jacques Lacan, *Ecrits: A Selection,* trans. Alan Sheridan (New York: Norton, 1977), p. 147.

40. Serge Leclaire, *Psychanalyser,* pp. 50, 64.

41. Ibid., p. 121.

42. Jacques Lacan, *Ecrits,* p. 171.

43. Serge Leclaire, *Psychanalyser,* p. 150.

44. Drew Leder, *The Absent Body,* pp. 62–3.

45. Serge Leclaire, *Psychanalyser,* p. 71.

46. Julia Kristeva, *Revolution in Poetic Language,* p.p. 141, 144.

47. Julia Kristeva, "Within the Microcosm of the Talking Cure," trans. Thomas Gora and Margaret Waller, in *Interpreting Lacan,* ed. Joseph H. Smith and William Kerrigan (New Haven: Yale University Press, 1983), p. 34.

48. Jacques Lacan, *The Four Fundamental Concepts of Psychoanalysis,* ed. Jacques-Alain Miller, trans. Alan Sheridan (Harmondsworth: Penguin, 1977), p. 244.

49. Jane Gallop, *Reading Lacan* (Ithaca, N.Y.: Cornell University Press, 1985), p. 60.

50. Julia Kristeva, *Revolution in Poetic Language,* p. 46.

51. Kristeva comments on the symbolic as a repression of the pleasure principle in "Le sujet en procès," in *Polylogue* (Paris: Editions du Seuil, 1977).

52. Jean-Paul Sartre, *The Psychology of Imagination,* trans. Bernard Frechtman (New York: Washington Square, 1966).

53. Kristeva alludes to Sartre in "Le sujet en procès," where she distinguishes negativity from "[le] néant," the latter being part of a static opposition between "l'*Etre* et le *Néant*" which hypostatizes both terms as "pure abstractions." Julia Kristeva, "Le sujet en procès," p. 61.

54. Like the negativity of which it is the principal agent, rejection is not negation and does not proceed from an ego stably centered in the act of (op)position. It is "no more than a *functioning* discernible across the *positions* which absorb and camouflage it." On the other hand rejection is not purely negative, a fact that Kristeva affirms by referring to "*une multiplicité de rejets.*" Julia Kristeva, *Polylogue,* pp. 67, 58.

55. Julia Kristeva, *Revolution in Poetic Language,* pp. 125–32.

56. Ibid., p. 131.

57. Julia Kristeva, *Polylogue,* p. 89.

58. Judith Butler, *Subjects of Desire: Hegelian Reflections in Twentieth-Century France* (New York: Columbia University Press), pp. 186, 193.

59. Neil Hertz, "Lurid Figures," in *Reading de Man Reading,* ed. Lindsay Waters and Wlad Godzich (Minneapolis: University of Minnesota Press, 1989), p. 86.

60. Julia Kristeva, *Revolution in Poetic Language,* pp. 133–9.

61. Jean Hyppolite, *Genesis and Structure of Hegel's Phenomenology of Spirit,* trans. Samuel Cherniak and John Heckman (Evanston, Ill.: Northwestern University Press, 1974), pp. 156–68.

62. Julia Kristeva, *Polylogue,* p. 341.

63. Ibid., p. 58, 64.

64. Ibid., p. 64.

65. On Kristeva and the reader, see my article "Intertextuality and the Subject of Reading/Writing," in Jay Clayton and Eric Rothstein, eds., *Influence and Intertextuality* (Madison, Wis.: University of Wisconsin Press, 1991), pp. 61–74.

66. Julia Kristeva, *Revolution in Poetic Language,* p. 51.

67. Quoted in Elizabeth Grosz, *Jacques Lacan,* p. 159. Her reference for this quotation, in which Kristeva states the difference between the imaginary and symbolic fathers more clearly than in *Tales of Love,* is inaccurate, and I have been unable to find the correct source.

68. Julia Kristeva, "The Adolescent Novel," in *Abjection, Melancholia, and Love: The Work of Julia Kristeva,* ed. John Fletcher and Andrew Benjamin (London: Routledge, 1990), p. 11.

69. Ibid., p. 22.

70. Jacques Lacan, *Ecrits,* p. 2.

71. Julia Kristeva, *Revolution in Poetic Language,* p. 46.

72. Neil Hertz, "Lurid Figures," pp. 82–3.

73. Wilhelm Worringer, *Abstraction and Empathy: A Contribution to the Psychology of Style,* trans. Michael Bullock (Cleveland and New York: Meridian Books, 1967), pp. 4–25.

14

Transgression in Theory: Genius and the Subject of *La Révolution du langage poétique*

Suzanne Guerlac

"The attentive gaze that *Tel Quel* directs at Breton," Foucault wrote in 1963, "is not a retrospective one."[1] In the 1930's, Breton lamented what he called the dilemma of the modern artist: the impossible choice between aesthetic avant-gardism (or formal innovation) on the one hand, and revolutionary commitment on the other.[2] At the same time, as an official posture, Surrealism proclaimed a union between art and revolution in the names of Marx and Freud. "True art," Breton wrote in 1938, "is unable not to be revolutionary."[3] Many, however, were not convinced by Breton's engagement. In his celebrated essay *What Is Literature?* (1947) Sartre challenged Breton's revolutionary commitment and attacked Surrealist literary avant-gardism—poetry—in the name of responsible writing—prose. Surrealism and its practice of automatism, Sartre contended, does not liberate the subject, as Breton had claimed. Instead it disperses and enervates it, reducing it to a state of passivity incompatible with the active stance necessary for revolutionary action. Only in a classless society, Sartre maintained, can the essence of literature be fulfilled; writing "is the subjectivity of society in permanent revolution."[4] Their disagreements notwithstanding, it seems that Sartre's ambitions for prose coincide with what Breton had hoped for from poetry—true poetry.

If by the 1940's both Breton and Sartre had undertaken to resolve the antipathy between art and revolution, their respective efforts had failed in such a way that each came to represent one horn, as it were, of the dilemma. The name Breton has come to stand for aesthetic avant-gardism, while Sartre represents the position of social praxis. This was the inheritance of the next generation, that of *Tel Quel*, which undertook to replace Surrealism's intuitive grasp of a synthesis of the two great theorists of freedom, Marx and Freud, with a more systematic, a more explicitly theoretical articulation. With *Tel Quel,* art and revolution became reconciled—in theory—and theory itself became *engagé.*

The most systematic effort to perform this reconciliation in the context is, of course, Kristeva's *La Révolution du langage poétique.*[5] This work is not merely a study of the revolutionary poetics of Lautréamont and Mallarmé. It also presents a theory of poetic language as itself revolutionary in the broader political, or social, sense. Avant-garde poetic language, Kristeva claims, generates a new instance of the subject—the revolutionary subject—through the operations of *signifiance.* "The signifying process," she writes of this mode of textual productivity, "gives itself as agent, an 'ego,' [*un moi*] that of the revolutionary."[6] Art, for Kristeva, transvalued as avant-garde poetics, is a vehicle for the manifestation of a radical, irrecuperable negativity. This is not the usual Hegelian negativity of consciousness but a non-symbolized, that is a materialist, negativity. Hegel is read through Freud and Bataille. With the negativity of the *rejet,*[7] it is a question of repressed material which does not pass into symbolic or oneiric representation (or distortion) as in dream work, nor receive a merely intellectual acknowledgment, as in denial [*dénégation*]. Instead, it produces something new, a "marking [*marquage*] in the signifying material."[8] Kristeva identifies the negativity of the *rejet* with Freud's death instinct and with Bataille's term "expenditure" [*dépense*]. She characterizes it as a "movement of the material contradictions that generate the semiotic function,"[9] a movement which coincides with the infinite processes of *signifiance.* At the same time, Hegel (and Freud) are read together with Marx:

> The aim of ancient philosophy was to explain the world. Dialectical materialism, on the other hand, wants to transform it. It speaks to a new subject, the only one capable of understanding it. This is not simply a subject of explanation, of cognition and knowledge but an elusive subject [*sujet insaisissable*] because one that *transforms* the real. This subject, which includes the movements of the subject of knowledge, emphasizes *process* [*le procès,* i.e. process and trial] more than identification, *le rejet* more than desire, *heterogeneity* over the signifier, *struggle* more than structure [original emphasis].[10]

It is this question of the status of subject within the theoretical articulation of art and revolution, the status of a "to give oneself an 'ego' [*se donner un 'moi'*]" that I would like to analyze in the text and argument of *La Révolution du langage poétique.* Kristeva takes the phenomenological given of the subjective position of speech as her point of departure. She then undermines the stability of this position, displacing the structure of signification to the operations, or process, of *signifiance*. She presents *signifiance* as a transgression of the symbolic by the semiotic, Oedipal and pre-Oedipal moments, respectively, in a genetic, psychoanalytic, account of the emergence of the subject. Poetic language is offered as an exemplary instance of *signifiance* which occurs as text. The notion of text is expanded to stand for a signifying practice which opens out directly onto the social-historical world. Poetry—or poetic language—is thus transplanted from the bourgeois realm of aesthetics to the revolutionary field of text. Text, in turn, is dislodged from the printed page and displaced to the social-historical world. Transgression could thus be said to operate on three levels in Kristeva's analysis. First it occurs in relation to the individual "subject-in-process/subject-on-trial [*sujet en procès*]," that is in relation to a genetic account of the constitution of the subject. This involves a displacement of the traditional diachronic psychoanalytic account of a passage from pre-Oedipal to Oedipal stages, for here the pre-Oedipal (the semiotic) returns, as it were, to transgress the law of the symbolic. It also occurs at the level of art, to the extent that poetic language—specifically the discoveries of avant-garde poetic language which date from the late nineteenth century—is taken to be paradigmatic of *signifiance* as transgression of the symbolic by the semiotic. As such, poetic language is considered transgressive of discursive modes or operations of language and hence of a certain notion of truth. Finally, through the notion of text which generalizes the art process of *signifiance,* transgression is transposed into the social or political domain as the liberating sociopolitical transgression of revolution. Transgression is thus the very mechanism of *signifiance,* of which both art and revolution are specific modalities.[11] Thanks to the insistence of this mechanism, and to the revolutionary flavor of its rhetoric, we appear to have here a seamless progression from art to revolution.

And yet, as Sartre had reminded his readers of the previous generation, (avant-garde) art and revolution have different requirements, or require a quite different emphasis, when it comes to the question of the subject. This remains true in Kristeva's argument. It is the transgression of the phenomenological subject, the subject of the symbolic, which constitutes the revolutionary force of poetic language for Kristeva. The art subject, in other words, is a pulverized subject, not unlike the subject of surrealist automatism. "It is in the so called 'art' practices" Kristeva writes, "that the semiotic, condition of the symbolic, also reveals itself to be its destroyer."[12] Taken to the limit then, as the author acknowledges, aesthetic avant-gardism would mark a foreclosure of the symbolic, or of the thetic moment which positions the subject. This, of course, means madness.

Political revolution, however, requires a relation to the subject. It requires a subject of action, as Sartre had argued in *What Is Literature?* Citing the celebrated passage from Breton's manifesto of Surrealism:

> Everything leads us to believe that there exists a certain point in the mind as the point of departure where life and death, the real and the imaginary, past and future . . . the high and the low, are no longer perceived as contradictory. . . . One seeks in vain for any other motivation for Surrealism than the hope of determining this point.

Sartre then comments contemptuously:

> Is this not to proclaim his divorce from the working class public? For the proletariat engaged in struggle needs to distinguish the real from the imaginary, life from death at every moment in order to succeed. . . . It is not by chance that Breton cites these oppositions: they all involve categories of action; revolutionary action, in particular, needs them.[13]

In Kristeva's argument an ambivalence toward grammatology is a symptom of the tensions which result from the conflicting demands placed on the subject by avant-garde art, on the one hand, and revolution, on the other. If Kristeva implicitly acknowledges that her theoretical project belongs within the field of grammatology when she pauses over the Greek etymology of her term "semiotic"—trace, gramme, engraved or written sign, etc.—she explicitly recognizes her debt to Derrida's critiques of phenomenology and structuralism: "The functioning of writing [*écriture*], the trace and the gramme, introduced by J. Derrida in his critique of phenomenology and subsequent versions of it in linguistics [*ses succédanés linguistiques*] points to an essential aspect of the semiotic,"[14] she writes. At the same time she charges that "the grammatological deluge of meaning [*la crue grammatologique*] abdicates the subject and is obliged to ignore its functioning as social practice [*s'oblige à ignorer son fonctionnement comme pratique social*]."[15] Kristeva maintains that the term "semiotic," as it functions in her argument, is to be distinguished from Derridean *différance*, to the extent that, "being part of a signifying practice which includes the symbolic instance . . . it *must* be situated in relation to the subject [*doit se situer par rapport au sujet*]" [emphasis added].[16] The register of obligation can be heard as an overtone to the logical necessity which attaches, as we shall see, to one version of the structure of transgression as it pertains to *signifiance*. In a surprising gesture, then, Kristeva repeats the thrust of Sartre's attack against Breton in her critique of Derridean grammatology, and, to this extent, inscribes the register of engagement within her argument.

If the problem is to accommodate the grammatological term "semiotic" to the imperatives of revolution, Kristeva's ingenious strategy is to "revolutionize" *différance*. What she calls "the revolution of *différance*"[17] is characterized in terms of expenditure, ecstasy, and eroticism—terms which belong to the general economy of Bataille and are associated with the operations of transgression. More specifically, however, and in textual terms, to revolutionize *différance* here, means to attach its operations to a subject. But clearly this cannot be the unified subject of the symbolic, the undisturbed thetic subject. Instead, Kristeva poses the very mechanism of the transgression of this unified subject—the *rejet* itself—as agent of the practice [*pratique*] of *signifiance*. This negativity of expenditure becomes "the maintained and reinforced agent of the signifying process."[18] To the extent that it "produces new cultural and social formations which are innovative and . . . subversive,"[19] it is itself cast in the role of revolutionary subject. Thus, the negativity specific to the transgression of the symbolic by the semiotic, of which it is said earlier that it "cannot be located in any ego [*moi*],"[20] that which threatens to foreclose the thetic, nevertheless functions as an "ego," or a subject of agency, here—". . . in the social configuration of capitalism . . . [it] emerges with all its clear-cut force . . . acts through a negativity. . . ."[21] As activating force of the process of *signifiance,* it enables *signifiance* to become a practice, and to become revolutionary.

The status of the *rejet* as agent, even as "'ego'— that of the revolutionary," is maintained and reinforced textually by being written as *actant* in a number of small narrative sequences.[22] "Decentering the subject, the *rejet* sets its pulverization [*pulvérization subjectale*] against the structures of the natural world, collides with them, rejects them and is de-posited by them [*en est dis-posé*],"[23] we read. What is more, ". . . out of the heterogeneity of its practice *and its experience* [*le rejet*] produces new symbolizations. This is *the mechanism of innovation* which . . . characterizes social practice" [emphasis added].[24] As not merely "motor" but "mechanism of innovation," the *rejet* becomes, in effect, the subject of action necessary to the revolutionary project. If grammatology abdicates the subject, to revolutionize grammatology means here to write it in relation to the agency of the *rejet* itself—"the return of the heterogeneous element in the movement of différance . . . provokes the revolution of différance."[25] For the heterogeneous is the *rejet*, which, as *pulsion,* is heterogeneous because it is at the limit of body and psyche. *Différance,* then, is revolutionized by being written in relation to the theoretical fiction of a revolutionary subject which is itself produced by writing the very mechanism of transgression— the *rejet*—into narrative sequence.

If the *rejet* functions as *actant,* the fable being told here is precisely the story of the engendering of this "different subject [*sujet différent*]"—"the signifying process [*procès de la signifiance*] . . . transforming the opaque and impenetrable subject . . . into the subject in process/on trial [*le sujet en procès*],"[26] or, in another formulation, the "transformation of the thetic position: the destruction of the old one and the formation of another."[27] The fable involves the possibility of "a *subject who speaks its being put in process/on trial through action* [*un* sujet parlant sa mise en procès dans l'action]" [original emphasis].[28] It also involves the possibility of "situating oneself beyond 'art' through 'art'."[29] The underlying fiction, we might say, is the reconciliation of the positions of Breton and Sartre, and, to this extent, the fable suggests a story concerning the constitution of theory itself.

In *What Is Literature?* Sartre accuses Breton, or, more precisely, the Surrealist conception of literature as poetry, of skepticism. He understands this in the Hegelian sense of adhering to an irrecuperably negative moment, a nondialectical negativity of the *néant*.[30] Sartre poses his conception of prose in resistance to this aesthetics of skepticism. In *La Revolution du langage poétique*, Kristeva addresses the issue in fundamentally the same terms in her chapter "*Scepticisme et nihilisme selon Hegel et dans le text*," one which makes the transition between the section entitled "Heterogeneity" and the one entitled "Practice." In her discussion of Hegel in this chapter, Kristeva defends her notion of text against the kind of charge that Sartre had made against Breton. But she also acknowledges the limits of avant-gardism here and associates this perspective of radical avant-gardism with formalism— one horn of Breton's dilemma of the modern artist. "To try to coincide with the logic of the mobile and heterogeneous chora," she writes here "is ultimately to foreclose the thetic. . . . The foreclosure of the subjective and representative thetic phase marks the limit of avant-garde experience: it leads to madness."[31] We are about to leap from one horn of the dilemma of the modern artist to the other, as it were—not Hegel corrected by the materialism of Freud, but of Marx. For it is precisely at this point, at the point of this limit, that Kristeva introduces her discussion of practice [*pratique*] with an appeal to Marxism and to its thinking of the subject: "At this point *it is necessary* . . . to reintroduce the way . . . in which Marxism thinks the subject," she declares here. "[O]ne *must* . . . take up again the subject who says 'I' and struggles in a social community. *It is necessary* to hear the discourse of this subject as well as the heterogeneous contradiction he [*sic*] has deferred and which poets have made it their task to explore" [emphasis added].[32]

The turning point in Kristeva's analysis, the turn toward praxis and thus toward the need for some instance of agency—of innovation—is accompanied by an appeal to a certain prose, or at least, to narrative. "The signifying process," Kristeva writes here, "whose heterogeneous contradiction is the moment of fierce struggle, *ought* to be inscribed [devrait *s'inscrire*] according to a historical logic in this representational narrative"—that is to say materialist history—"which itself attests to the historical process underway in revolutionary class struggles."[33] The step to praxis thus reintroduces the question of meaning [*sens*] which was dismissed earlier on[34] but suddenly emerges as a question of "crucial importance"—the survival of the social function of 'art' is at stake, Kristeva adds in an unmistakable (though, we sense, somewhat reluctant) allusion to Sartre.[35]

We seem to have a contradiction here, or at least a certain ambiguity. But it is one Kristeva explicitly places at the heart of *signifiance* as, precisely, the heterogeneous relation of symbolic and semiotic, and of the transgression of the former by the latter. And it is for just this reason that an appeal to narrative makes sense, both on the macro level of the fable of materialist history and on the micro (textual) level of the constitution of the *rejet* as revolutionary hero in small narrative sequences. For, as Kristeva tells us in an earlier chapter, "Four Signifying Practices," the logic of narrative is to remove contradiction.[36] A narrative moment, a moment of non-disjunction, is altogether appropriate, then, for the theoretical project of Kristeva, which, as she acknowledges, concerns the process of *signifiance,* in its very ambiguity. The practice of text involves not simply the negativity of the *rejet,* but a renewal [*relance*] of the *rejet,* which provisionally positions a new thetic moment. "Our conception of the *rejet* will oscillate between these two poles and this ambiguity will present the ambiguity of the process itself, divided and unitary."[37]

An appeal to narrative serves the interests of Kristeva's theoretical project which, as we have already indicated, concerns the status of the subject in an attempt to reconcile art and revolution—or the positions of Sartre and Breton. Whereas the transgressive force of poetic language entails the pulverization of the unified subject through the material (or libidinal) force of the *rejet,* the process of *signifiance* "gives itself an agent, an 'ego'—that of the revolutionary" by narrativizing, and in this specific sense, making a subject of, the *rejet* itself. This grammatical subject of action becomes the heroic revolutionary subject which engenders new social and cultural forms. If, as Kristeva suggests, text has a social function to produce "a different subject, able to establish new social relations and thus inscribing itself in the process of the subversion of capitalism" that subject is itself generated textually here. Art and revolution, apparently incompatible when it comes to the question of the subject, are thus theoretically reconciled here through the textual performance of this "different" subject.

These textual moments of sliding, just for a moment, from theoretical discourse to theoretical narrative, are crucial to the success of Kristeva's theoretical enterprise. But they cannot do the job alone; they cannot resolve the tension between the conflicting demands placed on the instance of the subject. They receive support on the theoretical level from the *philosopheme* transgression, which includes in itself the ambiguity of the theoretical project, which is also to say of text: "the simultaneity of the limit (which is the One) and the . . . crossing [*franchissement*] of that boundary."[38] This quite precisely characterizes the operation of transgression. Indeed, If Kristeva could be said to succeed where Surrealism was said to fail (by Sartre and then again by *Tel Quel,* in their quite different ways) it is largely because of the mechanism of transgression. More precisely, it is thanks to the inheritance of this term as previously written by Bataille. It is this *philosopheme* which operates to absorb the tension between the two modalities of the subject associated with art, on the one hand, and revolution, on the other.

"Transgression" emerges as a critical term through Caillois, Mauss, and Durkheim, that is to say, at the unlikely juncture of an incipient structuralism and the question of the sacred. It is elaborated in relation to the question of the sacred by Bataille in his essay *l'Erotisme* (1957) and emerges as a philosophical or theoretical term when Foucault published an analysis of Bataille's essay in 1963. Reading Bataille from the perspective of Nietzsche and of Heidegger, Foucault meditates the possibilities of what he calls a philosophy of eroticism in anticipation of subsequent developments of post-structuralist thinking. Important essays by Hollier, Sollers and Derrida follow, which progressively elaborate transgression as a crucially important operation for post-structuralist thinking.[39]

Indeed, a language of transgression soon comes to characterize a *dépassement* of structuralism by post-structuralism, which, in turn, signifies an overcoming of Hegel—a "transgression of philosophy" which distinguishes the intellectual avant-gardism of the theoretical project.

"Perhaps one day," Foucault wrote in his essay *"Préface à la transgression,"* published in 1963, "[transgression] will appear as decisive for our culture as the experience of contradiction once was for dialectical thinking." It is in the context of this remark that we are to understand Kristeva's characterization of the transgressive agent, the *rejet,* as a fourth term of the dialectic. Transgression (as Foucault had already diagnosed when he identified it with "the experience of finitude and of the being of the limit") invited a move away from Hegel toward the ontological thinking of Heidegger. At the same time, the formal proximity of transgression to the Hegelian dialectic invited a double movement of correction—via (a materialist) psychoanalysis on the one hand and through Marxism on the other. This, in turn, enabled the kind of attempt at a theoretical articulation of Freud and Marx that we find in Kristeva's *La Révolution du langage poétique*.

When we return to the text of Bataille we find that the transgression of eroticism—or the development of transgression in *L'Erotisme*—manipulates and composes various inherited elaborations of the term in the context of a strategic relation to Hegel, or, more precisely, Kojève. In relation to a strategy with respect to Kojève's Hegel, Bataille specifically combines two versions of transgression which had been previously contrasted by Caillois as a primitive and a modern sacred. One is dialectical in its operations and the other is not.

Referring his readers to *L'homme et le sacré* of Caillois, Bataille describes the mechanism of transgression as the "dual operation" of interdiction/transgression. This operation, he explains, is dialectical in the classically Hegelian sense; interdiction is retained even as it is canceled through its violation in the act of transgression. This version of transgression, then, is dialectical in the form of its operation, that is, in its reciprocity with interdiction, even as it is nondialectical in its effects, content, or economy. Not to have any effect is the rule of the general economy of sovereignty associated with the experience of eroticism, sacrifice, and poetry. To escape instrumentality is to enter (provisionally) into a general-economy of expenditure. Bataille's transgression (as the dual operation interdiction/transgression) thus stands for a nondialectical negativity—one which refuses that transmutation into positivity which is achieved through the dialectical turn—while at the same time it operates dialectically in relation to its essential counterpart, interdiction.

Caillois distinguishes between this primitive sacred which is a three-term relation—interdiction, transgression and the profane—and a modern, monovalent sacred which exists in opposition to the profane. The second version of transgression could be said to involve an attempt to return from the modern to the primitive version of the sacred by a profanation, or transgression, of the monovalent sacred. Sollers subsequently characterizes this apparently nondialectical sacred in terms of "pseudo-transgression," or an "illusion of crossing the limits."[40] Although Sollers disparages the modern version, in *L'Erotisme*, Bataille intertwines the two structures of the sacred in his writing of transgression. This is perhaps because the alternative primitive/modern is not pertinent to the concerns of Bataille for whom eroticism "only takes place . . . beyond the domain of history and of action."[41] It is this notion of negativity specific to the end of history that, in Kristeva, becomes the epic hero of a revolution yet to be accomplished in history.

The two versions of the sacred, interwoven in the text of Bataille, accommodate the requirements of the two levels of the practice of *signifiance* in Kristeva: art and revolution. "Pseudo-transgression" (to borrow Soller's formula) suits the (avant-garde) art subject. On the other hand, the insistence

of the moment of interdiction which belongs to the dual operation inter-
diction/transgression and its dialectical operation, retains the relation to the
subject necessary for the revolutionary moment in the sociopolitical field.
It is thanks to this structure of transgression that Kristeva can claim that,
"being part of the signifying practice which includes the symbolic . . . the
semiotic ought to be situated in relation to the subject . . ."—unlike grammatology which, according to her, abdicates the subject. Bataille's writing
of transgression thus combines two versions of transgression in such a
way that, coming after him, Kristeva can profit from the hesitation produced by the difference between them while appearing to embrace a stable and unified *philosopheme*. Since, in Kristeva's argument, transgression
is the mechanism of *signifiance* and *signifiance*, as we have seen, requires
two different instances of the subject—the pulverized one in the case of
avant-garde art and the productive subject in the case of text as it belongs
to the social-historical domain—her argument can capitalize on the fact that
two different structures are quietly held within the single operator "transgression." Without the special valences of the term transgression, (and
they are not intrinsic to the concept but are rather due to the specific ways
in which this term is written by Bataille) the tension between the two
structures of the subject would threaten to undermine Kristeva's studiously
rigorous, and relentlessly theoretical, articulation of art and revolution.

The structure of transgression also enables the step into theory. It helps
Kristeva generate a subject of theory which overlaps with the theoretical
fiction of the revolutionary subject. In her chapter "Skepticism and Nihilism
in Hegel and in the Text," Kristeva makes a distinction between what she
calls the modern text and its nineteenth-century avant-garde precursors. In
an implicit allusion to Adorno, she claims that the modern text includes
a self-reflexive moment. Unlike art, she maintains, text is not simply a
marking of the *rejet,* or of the material, or the heterogeneous. It also
includes a second moment. It "unfolds the contradiction *and* represents its
formation" [original emphasis].[42] Text, Kristeva continues, "introduces
into the *rejet* a reversal [*retournement*] of the *rejet* itself which constitutes
the signifying relation [*la liaison signifiante*] . . . [it] introduces *discourse*
into the *rejet*" [emphasis added].[43] Here we have a theoretical elaboration
of the moment of meaning [*sens*] alluded to earlier. With an implicit allusion to Adorno's analyses of modernity, Kristeva inflects the moment of
Hegelian self-consciousness in the direction of a psychoanalytic encounter
in which the reader occupies the position of analysand and text plays the
role of analyst.

Kristeva defines text here as "a practice of the *rejet* which includes the
heterogeneous contradiction as its key moment [*moment fort*] and the sig-

nifying thesis [*la thèse signifiante*] as a necessary pre-condition." Thanks to
the latter, she adds, "the text is already on its way to scientific knowledge
of the process that moves it [*l'agite*] and exceeds it."[44] This is to say that
the "heterogeneous condition" of the subject (the semiotic/symbolic heterogeneity) is doubled by two moments of text, its practice, on the one hand,
and the knowledge [*connaissance*] of this practice—critique or theory—on
the other. Thus we arrive at "the subject of science or of theory."[45]

As we recognize, this development parallels the preceding one. The issue
is still the gap between art and the social or revolutionary imperative.
Only now "art" and "theory" substitute for "art" and "revolution," in
parallel with the terms of the dialectical condition of the subject, which is
to say, in parallel with the terms of the process of signifiance and the
mechanism of transgression. "Combining heterogeneous contradiction
whose mechanism is possessed by the text, with revolutionary critique of
the established social order . . . is a most difficult thing to do [*c'est le plus
difficile à faire*],"[46] Kristeva acknowledges in an understated tone. And she
adds "the moment of the semantic and ideological binding [*liaison*] of
drive rejection [*rejet pulsionnel*] . . . *ought* to be a binding [devrait *être une
liaison*] in and through an analytic and revolutionary discourse" [empha-
sis added].[47] The register of obligation returns, all the more insistent in the
weaker tense of the conditional. And here we have the crucial conclusion:
"articulated in this way, heterogeneous contradiction approaches [*cotoie*]
critical discourse." Critical discourse is defined as the "representative
[*réprésentant*] of a social revolutionary practice." It is clear that a moment
of knowledge [*connaissance*]—or theory—has become a necessary moment
in the articulation of art and revolution operated through transgression. For
it constitutes the moment of practice, activating the relation to the subject
by performing the moment of meaning [*sens*]. The revolutionary subject,
constructed, as we have seen, through the *philosopheme* transgression,
overlaps then with the critical subject—the subject of theory.

"I maintain that Surrealism is still in a preliminary phase," Breton wrote
in the Second Manifesto. "The fact is that generally speaking these pre-
liminaries are 'artistic' in nature. However, I foresee that they will come
to an end and that at that point the earthshaking [*boulversantes*] ideas
that Surrealism holds in reserve [*recèle*] will erupt resoundingly . . . and
give themselves free rein."[48] The *Tel Quel* step into theory advances the Surrealist project beyond its preparatory phase, while at the same time, it displaces it in the direction of Sartre. Theory itself is *engagé*—revolutionary.
The intellectual avant-gardism of the 1970s returns to *engagement* by
returning *engagement* to theory where (we seem to have forgotten) it all
began in the ontological considerations of the second chapter of *What Is*

Literature? Theory—specifically, Kristevan *sémanalyse*—will, in turn, be characterized in terms of a transgression of philosophy, or, if this honor is to be reserved for Bataille, at least a transgression of structuralism or structuralist semiotics.

To appreciate the continuities between the transgressive and revolutionary force associated with theory itself and the theory of transgression or revolution in *La Révolution du langage poétique* we need only look back, in a retrospective glance, at the portrayal of the theoretical breakthrough of Kristevan *sémanalyse* in the appendix to Ducrot and Todorov's *Dictionnaire encyclopédique des sciences du langage.*[49] *Sémanalyse,* the authors write, "gives us to understand the production of meaning as by definition *incompatible with representation* [hétérogène à tout représentable]" [original emphasis].[50] Text, we are told, "has always functioned as a field of transgression [*un champ transgressif*] in relation to the system which organizes our perception, our grammar, our metaphysics and even our science."[51] Indeed, this transgressive field is so radical that the shift from structuralist semiotics to post-structuralist *sémanalyse* is characterized as a "Copernican revolution," an epithet conventionally attributed to the revolutionary force of Kantian critical philosophy. As if to reinforce this implicit allusion to Kant, everything prior to the post-structuralist thinking of *sémanalyse* is characterized as "pre-critical."[52] In the *Dictionnaire*'s portrayal of the transgressive force of Kristevan *sémanalyse,* we recognize something like the violence to purpose associated with the Kantian sublime, itself transgressive of the positions of phenomenality (subject and object) and hence transgressive with respect to the entire field of empirical knowledge. It is in relation to this structure that we can appreciate the more far-reaching epistemological (or anti-epistemological) claim that transgression—or a philosophy of eroticism—implies a transgression of philosophy.

The aesthetics of the sublime has always operated at the limit of the aesthetic (in the narrow sense) and ethical or political domains, just as it has been situated at the limit of philosophy or metaphysics. It carries a critical force which has, over time, both enhanced and challenged the space of the narrowly aesthetic. In Kant the experience of the aesthetic sublime serves as a reminder of the subject's moral destination. It reinscribes, albeit negatively and painfully, the autonomous (that is, moral) subject in its difference from the cognitive subject. One could say that it is precisely in the marking of this difference that the domain of freedom, as Kant writes in the introduction to the *Critique of Judgment,* is "meant to make itself felt in the realm of nature." I would argue that the structure of the sublime plays an analogous role for the theorists of *Tel Quel* except that the place of the moral subject is taken by a political, or revolutionary, subject.

Parallel to the operations of the Kantian aesthetic sublime, the transgressive field of text (as of the sublime) pulverizes the phenomenological subject and, at the same time, obliges a relation to the subject. It seems to be precisely this dissonance which constitutes the revolutionary—and the theoretical—subject in the theory of Kristeva.

To the extent that the aesthetic sublime in Kant, like the judgment of taste which concerns beauty, is presented from the vantage point of the beholder, it is Kant's discussion of genius, where we shift to the position of production, which provides the more precise analogy to post-structuralist textual productivity.[53] Kant's analysis of the art of genius reinscribes the dissonant structure of the sublime—only in reverse. It reinscribes it from the direction of the producer. In the art of genius, there is an excess on the level of intuition, as in the sublime. This excess exceeds the concepts of the understanding whose function is to expound such representations discursively.[54] As a faculty of aesthetic ideas, genius involves the productive, not the reproductive, imagination. This imagination operates spontaneously here, not receptively, as in the case of the aesthetic sublime *per se*. And it is through language that the imagination operates productively in its greatest freedom. It is for this reason that Kant first introduces the notion of aesthetic ideas in relation to the figure of the poet.

In spite of the parallels between genius and the sublime, however—the appeal to ideas of reason, the imbalance between the faculties of the imagination and the understanding, boundlessness or infinity, etc.— Kant explicitly holds to the equivalence between genius and taste from which the aesthetic sublime was excluded. For Kant's discussion of genius also functions to reintegrate the marginalized structure of the sublime (relegated to the status of mere appendix because of the problem of the formless object) within the body of the theory of taste. In order to recuperate genius for beauty, however, it is not enough simply to declare that genius involves an "accordance of the imagination with the legality of the understanding." For this accordance, unlike that involved in the judgment of beauty, needs to be enforced from without. Kant relegates the task to taste itself, which is said to "guarantee ... the accordance of the imagination in its freedom with the conformity to law of the understanding. . . ." The production of art does not simply mean substituting genius for taste. Rather it involves duplicating the terms of the judgment of taste such that, in addition to the imagination and the understanding, we have the terms "genius"—that is, the productive imagination—and "taste"—as representative of a receptive, or expounding, understanding. Taste, Kant writes, "unifies" the other three terms.

Genius involves that mixture of beauty and sublimity which Kant concedes is "even more artistic" than beauty alone. It displays an ambivalence with respect to the position of the subject not unlike the one we have analyzed in Kristeva's argument. On the one hand, Kant's account of genius introduces the excessive economy of the sublime. On the other, Kant sends in taste to control the excesses of genius and, to this extent, to fix the production of art to a subject. But it also intervenes to enforce harmonious relations with the faculty of the understanding. This is to enforce a relation to the structure of the empirical world, which is also to say, to force a relation to the (cognitive) subject in general. Likewise, as we have seen, Kristeva needed both to have art disrupt the position of the phenomenal subject through a movement of overwhelming productivity, and to have art (or text) generate a subject of revolution—or at least of revolutionary theory.[55]

The association between the sublime and genius, of course, antedates Kant and goes back at least to Longinus. The notion of productivity of text, in turn, is modeled after the language of avant-garde poets of the previous century. Breton claims to find the origins of automatic writing among such poets, specifically in Lautréamont and Rimbaud. And it is clear from Breton's discussion that, for him, automatism represented a rejection of a certain bourgeois ideology of genius and its correlate, the masterpiece, fast becoming a commodity. (Breton never tires of citing Lautréamont-Ducasse to the effect that "poetry must be made by all, not by one.")

And this brings us back to our point of departure: Breton's notion of true, that is to say, revolutionary art. Here is the extended citation of the passage already given in an abridged form:

> True art, which is not content to play variations on ready-made models but rather insists on expressing the inner need of mankind in its time—true art is unable *not* to be revolutionary, not to aspire to a complete and radical reconstruction of society. This it must do, were it only to deliver intellectual creation from the chains which bind it, and to allow all mankind to raise itself to those heights which only isolated geniuses have achieved in the past. We recognize that only the social revolution can sweep clear the path for a new culture.[56]

Revolutionary art then is (among other things) a displacement of the structure of genius away from a privileged position of subjectivity, even away from the subject altogether, toward the horizon of language. and something like a productivity of text. What is less obvious, however, than the association between text, genius, and the poetics of Lautréamont and Rimbaud in which Breton found the origins of automatism and Kristeva finds the models for *signifiance* is an association with the nonrevolutionary figure *par excellence,* Valéry. For the *"écriture mécanique"* of automatism refers us back, implicitly, to the displacement Valéry performs on the question of genius in his *Cours de poétique* where it is *l'esprit* itself—"force of transformation"—which operates as an unstoppable productivity of, or as, text.

In 1960, in the opening declaration of *Tel Quel,* Sollers positions the review against Sartre, on the side of Breton—or at least of poetry. If not the poetry of the avant garde, at least that of the high modernism epitomized by Valéry. "To speak today of 'literary quality,'" Sollers announces

> or of "literary passion," let it appear to you as it may. The ideologues have ruled over expression long enough. It can now permit itself to go its own way [*leur fausser compagnie*] ... what needs to be said today is that writing is no longer conceivable without a clear idea of its powers ... a determination that will elevate poetry to the highest level of the spirit [*à la plus haute place de l'esprit*]. Anything else will not be literature [*tout le reste ne sera pas littérature*].[57]

By the late 1960's, of course, it is a different story, or so we would assume from declarations such as *"La Révolution ici maintenant."* But is the story so entirely different? As Sollers will write in his preface to the 1980 edition of *Théorie d'Ensemble* (1968), where he speaks of the powers of literature with the same passion as he did in the 1960 declaration: "not literature in the service of theory but *just the contrary*—[mais très exactement le contraire]" [original emphasis].[58]

In 1980, after the demise of *Tel Quel,* the new review *Infini* opens with a retrospective glance by Kristeva, an essay entitled *"Mémoires."* It gives us this account of Kristeva's first encounter with *Tel Quel*:

> Around the end of 1961, I think it was, the Communist student review *Clarté* published a large photo of Philippe Sollers and a text in which he explained, basically, that only socialist revolution could provide a fertile social ground [*terrain social*] for avant-garde writing. This was my first encounter with *Tel Quel.* And the first seduction.[59]

With Sollers in the role of Breton, the image poses the terms of the theoretical project (and of its seductiveness): avant-garde art and revolution. Another memory surfaces a few lines down, an evocation of the milieu of her student days in Paris, which provides a further clue to this seductiveness:

> The *Ecole des Hautes Etudes* providing a counterbalance to the Sorbonne, *Tel Quel* developing in spite of the *NRF* or *Les Temps Modernes* ... the *dilemma of engagement* was reconfigured for us [*remodelé*], displaced. It was transformed into an implication, a complete inclusion within the

intellectual adventure that we lived as practice [emphasis added].[60]

Kristeva's formula, "the dilemma of engagement," condenses the language of Breton—the "dilemma" of the modern artist—and that of Sartre—engagement. It also suggests the direction, if not the meaning, of the remodeling of engagement in the context of *Tel Quel*. Engagement is "remodeled" not only in relation to what Breton had identified in the thirties as the dilemma of the modern artist, but more specifically in the direction of Breton's position *as it was seen by Sartre*—avant-gardism and radical negativity.

For this is precisely the way the question of engagement is reconfigured in *La Révolution du langage poétique*. Indeed, approximately forty years after *What Is Literature?* Kristeva turns engagement inside out. She succeeds in substituting the taboo term "poetry" (precisely the avant-garde poetry at the origin of Surrealist automatic writing) for the Sartrean term "prose" as the instrument of engagement. In other words she rendered revolutionary (again) that which Sartre attacked in the name of revolution: aesthetic (or anti-aesthetic) avant-gardism. What is more, she does so by reworking the same argument, in effect, that Sartre had used against Breton: that of an irrecuperable negativity. Remodeled as a force of innovation, this negativity itself becomes the subject of action, *engagé*, and revolutionary. Engagement is displaced from prose to poetry, and the strategies of that displacement serve the aesthetic avant-gardism Sartre appeared to so violently reject in *What Is Literature?*

The immediate success of *La Révolution du langage poétique* was a function not only of its theoretical merits, nor, even, of the marvelous *disponibilité* of the new philosophical operator "transgression." It was also a function of the insistence of the concerns inherited from the previous generation which prepared the receptiveness to, precisely, a theoretical resolution of the two cultural positions—avant-gardism and engagement—which had come to be represented by the names "Breton" and "Sartre." The authority enjoyed by theory in the last decades owes something to a displacement of powers previously ascribed to literature (or poetry) into the domain of theory, a gesture already inaugurated by Sartre, and to the displacement of the force of the repressed term "engagement" back into the literary domain of text, where, from Breton's point of view (and, perhaps, from Sartre's, on a different reading of Sartre) it had belonged all along.

Notes

1. Michel Foucault, "*Distance, aspect, origine,*" in *Théorie d'ensemble* (Paris: Editions du Seuil, 1968), p. 20.

2. In "*Position politique de l'art aujourd'hui,*" Breton writes: "The situation . . . of writers and innovative artists is dramatic. . . . In fact, they find themselves faced with a dilemma. Either they must give up interpreting the world according to their inner life—her it is their own possibility of enduring that is at stake—of they must give up their participation in the transformation of this world on the level of action, . . . it seems that they have had only the choice between two abdications." André Breton, "*Positions politique de l'art aujourd'hui,*" *Positions Politiques du Surréalisme* (Paris: Pauvert, 1971), pp. 19–20, [my translation].

3. André Breton and Leon Trotsky, "Manifesto: Towards a Free Revolutionary Art," (1938), trans. Dwight MacDonald in *Theories of Modern Art,* ed. Herschell B. Chipp (Berkeley: University of California Press, 1968), p. 484.

4. Jean-Paul Sartre, *Qu'est-ce que la littérature?* (Paris: Gallimard, 1948), p. 163, [my translation].

5. Julia Kristeva, *La Révolution du langage poétique. L'avant-garde à la fin du 19e siècle: Lautréamont et Mallarmé* (Paris: Editions du Seuil, 1974). English translations are taken, with some adaptation from *Revolution in Poetic Language,* trans. Margaret Waller (New York: Columbia University Press, 1984).

6. Julia Kristeva, *Revolution in Poetic Language,* p. 206. The expression, "*procès de la signifiance,*" carries two meanings in French: the process of signification (or signifying) and also the putting on trial, or calling into question, of signification. I will leave the French word untranslated, in most instances, in order to avoid misunderstanding.

7. In Waller's English translation this term is translated as "rejection." Because of the connotations of this word in English, I prefer to leave the French word untranslated here.

8. Julia Kristeva, *Revolution in Poetic Language,* p. 163.

9. Ibid., p. 119.

10. Ibid., pp. 178–9.

11. Allusions to transgression in *La Révolution du langage poétique* are too numerous to inventory here. That one finds the word itself at least eight times, for example, between pages 58–68 is indicative of its pervasiveness. The word "*franchissement*" also refers us to the operation of transgression, as do the metaphors of "*le toit*" or of "*deux versants*" of *signifiance.* The metaphors allude to the analysis of Bataille and transgression presented by Sollers in his essay entitled "*Le Toit.*"

12. Julia Kristeva, *Revolution in Poetic Language,* p. 47.

13. Jean-Paul Sartre, *Qu'est-ce que la littérature?* p. 189.

14. Julia Kristeva, *Revolution in Poetic Language,* p. 40.

15. Ibid., p. 142.

16. Ibid.

17. Ibid., p. 144.

18. Ibid., p. 162.

19. Ibid.

20. Ibid., p. 164.

21. Ibid., p. 177.

22. I am borrowing the term from Todorov, *Qu'est-ce que le structuralisme? 2. Poétique* (Paris: Editions du Seuil, 1968).

23. Julia Kristeva, *Revolution in Poetic Language*, p. 203.

24. Ibid., p. 179.

25. Ibid., p. 144.

26. Ibid., p. 105.

27. Ibid., p. 59.

28. Ibid., p. 210.

29. Ibid., p. 211.

30. In *Qu'est-ce que la littérature?* Sartre writes: "I perceive a very serious contradiction at the origin of Surrealism." Sartre writes, ". . . to speak in Hegelian terms, I would say that this movement had the concept of totality . . . and that in its concrete manifestations it realized something completely different [*il a réalisé tout autre chose dans ses manifestations concrètes*]. The totality of man is necessarily a synthesis, that is to say the organic unity of all its secondary structures . . . Hegel writes of skepticism: "Thought becomes perfect thought annihilating the being of the world in the multiple variety of its determinations and real negativity [*la pensée devient la pensée parfaite anéantissant l'être du monde dans la multiple variété de ses déterminations et la négativité réelle*] . . . Thus surrealist man is an addition, a mixture, but never a synthesis." Sartre, *Qu'est-ce que la littérature?* pp. 298–301.

31. Julia Kristeva, *Revolution in Poetic Language*, p. 182.

32. Ibid., p. 190.

33. Ibid., p. 191.

34. "Modern poetic language . . . attacks not only denotation (the positions of the object) but also meaning [*sens*] (the position of the subject)." Ibid., p. 58.

35. The quote reads as follows: "This means that the question of the second stage of heterogeneous contradiction, namely that of the *interpretant* or *meaning* in which this contradiction must irrupt, is of crucial importance. What is at stake is not just the survival of the social function of 'art' but also, beyond this . . . modern society's preservation of signifying practices that have a sizeable audience. . . ." [original emphasis]. Ibid., p. 190.

36. "In narrative, instinctual dyads [*la dyade pulsionelle*] (. . . affirmation/negation, life drive/death drive) are articulated as a non-disjunction. In other words, the two 'terms' are distinct. differentiated and opposed; but the opposition is later disavowed [*après-coup déniée*] and there is an identification of the two." Ibid., p. 90. Is Breton's "highest point of the spirit" to be achieved then through narrative? Kristeva continues:

"One could say that the matrix [*matrice*] of enunciation structures a subjectal space
... where the signifying process [*procès signifiant*] is ordered [*agencé*], that is, endowed
with meaning." Ibid. Kristeva also says in this chapter that text can absorb, or subsume, various moments or modes of signifying activity: narrative, metalinguistic, etc.

37. Ibid., p. 148.

38. Ibid., p. 159.

39. See Michel Foucault, *"Préface à la Transgression,"* *Critique* 1963; Denis Hollier, *"Le
Dualisme matérialiste de Georges Bataille,"* *Tel Quel* 25, 1966, republished in English
in a shortened version in *Yale French Studies* 78, 1990; Philippe Sollers, *"Le Toit.
Essai de lecture systématique,"* *Tel Quel* 29; and Jacques Derrida, *"De l'Economie
restreinte à l'économie générale,"* in *l'Ecriture et la Différence* (Paris: Editions du Seuil,
1967).

40. Philippe Sollers, *"Le Toit,"* p. 27.

41. See Georges Bataille, *"Postulat Initial,"* *Deucalion* 2, 1947 [my translation].

42. Julia Kristeva, *Revolution in Poetic Language,* p. 184.

43. Ibid., p. 187.

44. Ibid.

45. Ibid., p. 188.

46. Ibid., p. 191.

47. Ibid.

48. André Breton, *"Second Manifeste du surréalisme,"* in *Manifestes du Surréalisme,* (Paris:
Gallimard), pp. 126–7.

49. (Paris: Editions du Seuil, 1972).

50. Ducrot and Todorov, *Dictionnaire,* p. 451.

51. Ibid., pp. 443–4.

52. Ibid., p. 449

53. The argument summarized here is developed in greater detail in "The Sublime in
Theory," in *MLN,* December 1990. For a reading of Bataille's *l'Erotisme* see Guerlac,
"'Recognition' by a Woman!" *Yale French Studies* 78, 1990.

54. The sublime, as we know, involves a "demonstration," as negative presentation, of the
"nondemonstrability" of concepts of reason through the imagination which operates
as a receptive faculty of intuition or presentation. Genius is the faculty of the presentation of aesthetic ideas, which are defined in the dialectic of the *Critique of Judgment* as "inexponble representations of the imagination," representations which cannot be reduced to concepts of the understanding and therefore seem to move toward
ideas of reason by play of analogy. For further discussion of the sublime see my
Impersonal Sublime: Hugo, Baudelaire, Lautréamont and the Esthetics of the Sublime
(Stanford University Press, 1990) which also contains further references on the sublime in the bibliography.

55. As the *Dictionnaire* put it before the publication of *La Révolution du langage poétique*: "To the estheticizing ideology of the art object as decorative work ... text would
oppose the reinsertion of its signifying practice ... within the articulated whole of the

social practices (the transforming practices) of which it is a part. . . . We can see already why, as soon as it is constituted, this concept of text is found to have an operational value, and not only on the level of 'literary practice' but also on the level of a disruption of the philosophical tradition and equally on the level of a theory of revolution."

56. André Breton and Leon Trotsky, "Manifesto," p. 484.

57. Philippe Sollers, "*Le Toit,*" p. 3.

58. Philippe Sollers, *Théorie d'Ensemble,* preface.

59. Julia Kristeva, "*Mémoires,*" *Infini* 1, 1980: p. 48.

60. Ibid.

Index

Contributors

Judith Butler currently teaches in the Department of Rhetoric at the University of California, Berkeley. She is author of *Gender Trouble: Feminism and the Subversion of Identity* (Routledge, 1990) and co-editor with Joan W. Scott of *Feminists Theorize the Political* (Routledge, 1992). Her book *Bodies that Matter: on the discursive limits of "sex"* is forthcoming from Routledge in 1993.

Tina Chanter is Assistant Professor of Philosophy at Louisiana State University. She is the author of several articles on feminism and recent continental philosophy, and her book *The Ethics of Eros: Irigaray's Re-writing of the Philosophers* is forthcoming from Routledge in 1993.

Marilyn Edelstein is Assistant Professor of English at Santa Clara University, where she also teaches in the Women's Studies Program. She has published articles on contemporary fiction and theory; a previous essay on Kristeva appears in *Body/Text in Julia Kristeva: Religion, Women, and Psychoanalysis* (SUNY, 1992). Her book on the rhetoric of prefaces to novels is forthcoming, and she is working on a book about the "death" and "rebirth" of the author.

Jean Graybeal is Associate Professor and Chair of the department of Religious Studies at California State University, Chico. She is the author of *Language and "the Feminine" in Nietzsche and Heidegger* (Indiana University Press, 1990), and is currently working on a book on religion, language, and the body.

Suzanne Guerlac is Associate Professor of French at Emory University. She is the author of *The Impersonal Sublime: Hugo, Baudelaire, Lautréamont and the Esthetics of the Sublime.*

Alice Jardine is Professor of Romance Languages and Literatures at Harvard University. She is the author of *Gynesis: Configurations of Woman and Modernity*; co-editor of several volumes, the most recent being *Shifting Scenes: Interviews on Women, Writing, and Politics in Post-68 France*; and is currently writing two books: *1951* and *Of Bodies and Technologies: Woman and the Machine.*

Lisa Lowe teaches Comparative Literature at the University of California, San Diego. She is the author of *Critical Terrains: French and British Orientalisms* (Cornell UP, 1991). Her work on gender and decolonization in Asian American and Asian diaspora literatures appears in *Diaspora* and *Yale French Studies.*

Noëlle McAfee is a graduate student in Philosophy at the University of Texas at Austin and the associate editor of the *Kettering Review*. She is writing her dissertation on the topic of citizenship and subjectivity: the political self in the writings of Habermas and Kristeva.

Norma Claire Moruzzi is Assistant Professor of Women's Studies and Political Science at the University of Illinois at Chicago. Her current work deals with the representation of embodied social identities in political theory and practice, including the role of the body in Hannah Arendt's political theory and Western reactions to the politicization of Islamic women's veiling.

Tilottama Rajan has taught at Queen's University and the University of Wisconsin, and is currently Professor of English at the University of Western Ontario, where she also teaches in the Centre for Theory and Criticism. She is the author of *Dark Interpreter: The Discourse of Romanticism* (Cornell UP, 1980), *The Supplement of Reading: Figures of Understanding in Romantic Theory and Practice* (Cornell UP, 1990), and editor of a special issue of *Studies in Romanticism* on *Nietzsche and Romanticism* (Spring 1990). She is currently working on a book on *Romantic Narrative*, and a study entitled *Deconstruction Before and After Post-Structuralism* of which the present essay will form a part.

Jacqueline Rose is Professor of English at Queen Mary and Westfield College, University of London. Her publications include *Sexuality in the Field of Vision, The Haunting of Sylvia Plath*, and *Why War? Psychoanalysis, Politics and the Return to Melanie Klein.*

Allison Weir is a Postdoctoral Fellow with the Social Sciences and Humanities Research Council of Canada. She recently completed her doctorate in the Programme in Social and Political Thought at York University in Toronto. Her book on feminist theories of identity is forthcoming from Routledge.

Mary Bittner Wiseman is Professor of Philosophy at Brooklyn College and Professor of Philosophy and Comparative Literature at the Graduate School of the City University of New York. She is the author of *The Ecstases of Roland Barthes* (Routledge, 1989) and is writing a book on contemporary interpretations of representations of the Madonna in Renaissance art.

Ewa Ziarek is Assistant Professor of English at the University of Notre Dame. Her publications include articles on Melville, Kafka, Joyce, Kristeva, and Marianne Hauser. She is currently completing a book manuscript entitled *Rhetoric of Failure: Skepticism, Modernism, Deconstruction*. She was a Lilly Fellow during the 1991–92 academic year.